MW00487533

The Nature of Physical Reality

Also by SUBHASH KAK

The Architecture of Knowledge
The Astronomical Code of the Ṛgveda
The Gods Within
Mind and Self
The Prajñā Sūtra: Aphorisms of Intuition
The Wishing Tree
In Search of the Cradle of Civilization
The Aśvamedha

The Nature of Physical Reality
(Third Edition)

Subhash Kak

Mount Meru Publishing

Copyright © 2016 by Subhash Kak

All rights reserved. No part of this book may be reproduced or transmitted in any form or by any means, electronic or mechanical, including copying, photocopying, scanning, and recording or by any information storage and retrieval system without written permission from the author, except for material already in public domain or for the inclusion of brief quotations for research or review.

Library and Archives Canada Cataloguing in Publication

Kak, Subhash, 1947-, author

The nature of physical reality / Subhash Kak. - Third edition.

Includes bibliographical references and index.
Issued in print and electronic formats.
ISBN 978-1-988207-07-0 (paperback).--ISBN 978-1-988207-08-7 (html)

1. Physics--Philosophy. 2. Paradox. 3. Reality. I. Title.

QC6 K24 2016 530.01 C2016-901986-1

The views expressed in this book belong solely to the author and do not necessarily reflect the views of the publisher. Neither the author nor publisher is liable for any loss or damages resulting from the use of information presented in this book. Neither the author nor publisher makes any representation or warranty with respect to the accuracy or completeness of the information presented in this book.

Published in 2016 by:
Mount Meru publishing
P.O. Box 30026
Cityside Postal Outlet PO
Mississauga, Ontario
Canada L4Z 0B6
Email: mountmerupublishing@gmail.com

ISBN 978-1-988207-07-0

To Naumi

CONTENTS

PREFACE

I am pleased that the third edition of *The Nature of Physical Reality* is being published. The premise of the book that rational models have limited capacity to explain reality has been validated by the developments of the past two decades. Logical paradoxes plague mathematics and physics, and the promise of a unified theory of physics has not been fulfilled. It is still not possible to reconcile quantum theory with gravitation and string theory has no predictive capacity.

Science is unable to explain why life comes with freedom and intentionality when the inanimate world is governed by physical law. But this does not mean that science is not making progress. There is a hidden order in physical reality that transcends the capacity of rational models and slowly science is providing indirect evidence on the nature of this order. This process has the potential to illuminate the mystery of consciousness.

The new edition has an epilogue that brings the story up to date and shows how the hidden order could be ascertained by scientific argument and experimentation.

Subhash Kak
Stillwater, Oklahoma

March 9, 2016

INTRODUCTION

This book was written with two objectives in mind: to present a summary of the current scientific understanding of the physical world, and to show that man's questioning across the ages has had continuity in terms of preoccupation with paradoxes. Science makes it possible for us to see the unity that lies underneath seemingly unrelated phenomena. This unification does not always resolve difficulties related to interpretation and meaning. Each advance in science resolves paradoxes at one level, but only at the cost of new paradoxes that appear at other levels.

The word paradox comes from Latin *paradoxum* or Greek *paradoxos*, literally 'contrary to opinion,' and it may mean a statement that appears self-contradictory. A Sanskrit cognate is *parokṣa* (antonym of *pratyakṣa*, 'clear to the eye') which has the meaning of being apparently contradictory but leading to a deeper understanding of the subject. There are many paradoxes at the levels of the individual self and the cosmos.

The Ṛgveda, perhaps man's earliest extant composition that is dated variously from 3000 to 1500 BC,[1] articulates the problem of paradox and reality. According to it, rational science can describe the material world but not consciousness. The phenomenal world is characterized by duality but at a deeper transcendent level the universe has a unity. The paradoxes of the Ṛgveda concern time, space, agency and language. These paradoxes are to awaken the reader from a sense of certain knowledge so that he can obtain a deeper understanding of reality.

The Upaniṣads, which explain the philosophical problems of the Ṛgveda, claim that there are two kinds of knowledge: the lower, and the higher. The lower knowledge concerns material things whereas the higher knowledge is about the experiencing self.[2] The Upaniṣads deal with the paradox that inert matter transformed into living form becomes capable of self-awareness and of free-will. They suggest that certain contradictions can only be resolved through intuition and not by reason. To point out the limitations of rational knowledge, the Kena Upaniṣad says: "He who thinks he knows it not, knows it. He who thinks he knows it, knows it not. The true knowers think they can never know it, while the ignorant think they know it."

The atomic school of Kaṇāda points out the paradox of divisibility: If matter consists of atoms, each atom must be point-like because otherwise it would be further divisible. The enlargement of point-like atoms to gross matter with size is another paradox.[3]

Zeno, in ancient Greece, argued that space is neither continuous nor discontinuous. If space is continuous, Achilles, the fleetest warrior, can never win a footrace against a tortoise who starts ahead. It will take him time to reduce the distance to half in which duration the tortoise would have moved further ahead and this will go on ad infinitum. If space is discontinuous, an arrow cannot move because it is either at one point or the next and there is nothing between.

The modern resolution of this paradox is that while space is continuous, Achilles overtakes the tortoise because the infinite series representing the time taken by him has a finite sum. But this raises the question: What is infinity? A hundred years ago, Cantor presented a set-theoretic approach to infinity in which points in a small line can be put into a one-to-one correspondence with the points in a longer line or in a solid. Some mathematicians reject the idea of Cantor's infinite sets, and believe that the only mental constructions permitted should be the ones that are intuitively reasonable. Thus the idea of a potential infinity is reasonable, but not that of an object with an infinite number of members as in Cantor's sets.

Aristotle discussed the liar paradox. Is the statement 'I am lying' true or false? If the man is lying, he is speaking the truth, and if he is speaking the truth, he is lying. In the 1930s Gödel showed that for mathematical systems of sufficient complexity there exist propositions that can be neither proved nor disproved. This implies a denial of the law of excluded middle, which is a basic axiom of logic.

The cosmic edge riddle of the ancients was: What happens to the spear when it is hurled across the outer boundary of the universe? This riddle points to a difficulty in viewing the universe as a whole. One modern version of this riddle, when we consider the time boundary or the beginning of the universe, is: Are the laws of nature the same now as they were at the big bang? Another version: What existed before the big bang?

The paradox of consciousness is not addressed by any discipline of science. If natural laws govern the evolution of the universe, then the behavior of human beings should be completely pre-determined. But human beings do make choices. Is the person visualizing the universe a part in an endless loop?

The speculations of sages and philosophers of ancient India, Greece and other civilizations sought to reconcile the predictability of the inanimate world with the apparent freedom of living creatures. The Greeks viewed the universe as an organism created and overseen by an intelligence in which human beings possess freedom. The Indians viewed the living and the non-living worlds to be governed by natural law, but they believed that consciousness could be trained to transcend its normal confines and reach the intelligence that underlies the universe. Contradictory notions of freedom and determinism inform personal narratives. Intuitions of discreteness and continuity, finiteness and infinity, and multiplicity and uniqueness, when taken to their logical conclusions, throw up other difficulties.

Physicists and mathematicians use intuition to obtain and validate results. It is true that the way intuition is applied in the quantitative sciences differs from its use in addressing qualitative issues. In dealing with broad questions of mathematical and physical structures, modern science has reached results that are intuitively dissonant. Advances in life sciences and the search for unification of all phenomena have led to new riddles.

Information is a transactional property that involves two parties. The very idea of these two parties implies a larger context, spatially and temporally, in which these two parties, or some other experimenter, have determined probabilities associated with the communications between them. Since such a context is absent when the cosmos is being considered, the application of the concept of information at the cosmological level is problematic and likely to lead to a variety of paradoxes.

This issue may also be viewed from the perspective of theory of formal systems. Due to the Gödel's Incompleteness Theorem, we know that there exist statements that cannot be proved or disproved within the framework of a sufficiently rich formal system. Stated differently, *if a formal system is complete within itself, then it is inconsistent.* Since a scientific theory must be a formal system, it implies that such a theory will be incomplete, and it will have paradoxical aspects. On the other hand, there could be other simple formal systems (such as those applied to the social world), which are consistent in themselves, but which do not have any predictive power.

While some paradoxes may owe their origin to the limitations of formal systems, others arise out of the consideration of single whole system like the cosmos. The treatment of the paradox is an excellent place to find out about the underlying philosophical position. A formal system is unable to prove what lies beyond its framework and scientific theory provides no more than inferences inherent in the formal system. There is, of course, the complementary issue of relating a theory to physical reality, but what constitutes information itself is open to different interpretations. If the theory has no terms to describe a phenomenon, that phenomenon would simply not exist within it and it would be taken not to exist in descriptions of physical reality.

The underlying philosophical position, which we call cosmology, might be to take laws to be independent of the universe, or to assume that the laws must, in some sense, be reflective of the nature of the universe. The treatment may rest on the amount and nature of information that the frames have, or it may overlook this information altogether.

The study of the physical world is a continuing task. Often, there is temptation to take a new model of explanation and construct a philosophical structure over it. In the words of Philipp Frank: "Obsolete philosophical views in physics are mostly obsolete physical theories in a state of petrification. Aristotle's philosophy of physics is a petrification of a physical theory which covered the experience of Greek and oriental artisans about physical phenomena. Kant's Metaphysical Principles of Natural Science is a petrification of Newton's physics. Eddington's Philosophy of Physical Science is a petrification of Einstein's relativity and Bohr's quantum theory."[4] Many times in the past it appeared that complete understanding of the physical world was round the corner, only for the whole structure to reveal an entirely new meaning. This happened before the introduction of the relativity theory, the rise of quantum mechanics, and recent unification theories. Current models of the large scale structure of the universe and of elementary particles are either tentative generalizations or simple speculations. To propose that a single formal framework can describe the current state of knowledge is premature.

One may view physics in terms of its few sub-fields, each characterized by its own limits and paradoxes. Normally the difficulties of a theory are downplayed by circumscribing its area of applicability. A few principles are taken to be fundamental such as those of relativity, conservation of energy, increase of entropy, action in terms of quanta and so on but the interpretation of these principles has evolved with time. Thus the principle of conservation of energy was redefined when it was found that mass and energy were interconvertible, and it came to absorb the principle of conservation of mass.

There is tension between atomic and intuitionistic views in scientific knowledge. The atomic view is the belief that all knowledge can be reduced to that concerning a set of primitive concepts. This means that mathematics should be reducible to logic, biology to physics, and physics to mathematical relationships between a few fundamental particles. The intuitionistic viewpoint holds that such reductions are impossible, and that our understanding of the universe reflects the nature of our minds. The atomists cite the successes of their program in defense of their approach, while the intuitionists point to the fact that none of the reductions has yet been fully realized and that it appears that none ever will.

The enterprise of physics is in the spirit of 'A question is best answered by another question.' Questioning at one level reveals connections and new questions that are apt at another level. The complete unraveling of the mystery of reality is nowhere in sight -- the fundamental paradoxes of the ancients remain unresolved.

I PARADOX AND REALITY

Paradoxical aspects of scientific knowledge

We comprehend reality by means of conceptual maps. Each aspect of reality has its own map. The descriptions are refined by a search for consistency, a resolution of inner contradictions, and uniformity in the descriptions used for different kinds of phenomena.

The logic of science, like that of any other dialectic, is two-pronged. On the one hand there is a consistent endeavor to reduce phenomena to primitives; on the other hand one seeks ways to describe complex system behavior. While the underlying assumption for this is that the two approaches imply journey from opposite ends to the same point, it is by no means clear that it is so.

Great progress has been made in the understanding of life, the physical world, and logic. It is known how the deoxyribonucleic acid (DNA) in an organism contains instructions for its development. These instructions are coded as a linear arrangement of different chemicals in the DNA somewhat like instructions in a computer program are expressed as a sequence of zeros and ones. The understanding of the physical world has proceeded to a point that we can ask reasonable questions related to the size, the age, and the nature of the evolution of the universe. A great deal is also known about the structure and interaction of matter. Many fundamental properties of systems of logic are known. We know how to build computers and other versatile machines.

But vexing problems remain. Werner Heisenberg said: "Natural science does not simply describe and explain nature; it is part of the interplay between nature and ourselves; it describes nature as exposed to our method of questioning." We do not yet know what the limitations of our questioning are although we know there exist wide gaps in our understanding of the physical world and of biological processes. There are also fundamental shortcomings in the very nature of mathematical reasoning. We use different kinds of models to explain different phenomena. A quick look at the history of science reveals that scientific understanding develops in leaps, and before each such leap it appears that contradictory notions are being used in the same discipline. A reorganization of knowledge after each leap shows how the earlier contradictions could be reconciled but it creates new contradictions.

Two basic assumptions used by scientists to discover order in nature are causality and determinism. Intuitively, these assumptions are reasonable, because if nature were capricious then scientific laws would be evanescent and useless. But these assumptions lead to a dilemma regarding the freedom of man. If man's actions are completely governed by forces around him, he is an automaton and he has no free will. In a perfectly deterministic world there is no way one can intervene and check for cause and effect relationships. A dichotomy exists between the sciences of the self and the physical world. While some scientists do believe that we need to include consciousness as a 'force' to describe physical phenomena completely, nobody knows how this can be done.

Existence of contradictory frameworks in the system of knowledge points to the tentative nature of our knowledge. The fact that human beings seek to obtain this certain knowledge while trying to remain outside its scope to the extent that they retain their freedom of choice suggests that this knowledge will remain tentative. If this choice were real, the process describing its evolution would constitute an important and legitimate area of inquiry and define a study that lies outside the framework of conventional science.

Science is not only a catalog of relationships between observables but also information regarding the scope of these relationships. We not only seek to know conditions under which a relationship holds but also those where it does not hold. Since a variety of these relationships exists, constant revision and modification of the relationships is required to make them consistent with each other.

What is the process which permits one to divine a relationship? If the sun has been observed to rise every morning over a certain period of time, it is extrapolated to become the law: the sun rises every morning. This extrapolation or induction clearly contains a hypothesis regarding the stationarity of the process. The law has validity only on the set where the observations were made as the sun does not rise every morning at the north and the south poles.

A scientific theory or law should be expressed in a form so that not only is its direct statement valid over the universe of discourse but also that its converse is demonstrably false over the same universe. This makes it imperative that it should be possible, potentially, to falsify the theory. If this requirement were not insisted upon there would be no way to evaluate the worth of the theory. However, our theories have not generally been framed so as to check for their falsifiability.

Knowledge is classified as being analytic or synthetic. Statements connecting objects by means of logical relations constitute analytic knowledge and in a formal mathematical system relations are obtained analytically by proving theorems. Relations that are obtained through observation are termed synthetic. Examples of this are: 'The earth revolves round the sun' and 'The speed of light in vacuum is constant.' Such statements can be made only on the basis of empirical judgment. This classification means that synthetic knowledge cannot be obtained by analytic reasoning. If one should consider man's accumulation of knowledge to follow some law, then a discovery of this law would allow one to determine future observations. Furthermore, if a science of consciousness exists, then this science will make the distinction between the two kinds of knowledge disappear.

Not all our understanding of the world is gained through sensory experience. Some information is transmitted through the genes, which explains how for some animals the new-born is quite capable of looking after itself. Babies also have an inborn idea of spatial distance. While this might be due to the unborn offspring in the womb experiencing reality through sense-organs, the very fact that such a comprehension occurs is due to the genes. Offsprings of different species are prepared differently at the moment of birth.

Mathematical reasoning is the basis for our understanding of the physical universe. It is based on logic, which deals with propositions and geometry, both of which have associated difficulties. We see that outside of easily provable, fundamentally trivial, relations amongst propositions, we must consider statements that are expressed most easily in natural language leading to semantic paradoxes since constructions in language deal with objects defined imprecisely or across different levels. Consider, for example, the following well-known paradoxes or antinomies:[2]

1. In a library there are catalogs which list books. Let the catalogs be listed also. There are some catalogs which list themselves and others which do not. Let K be a catalog which lists all the catalogs which 'do not list themselves.' Is K listed in itself?
2. A village barber shaves 'all the people in the village who do not shave themselves.' Does the barber shave himself?

Antinomies of the above kind can be avoided if we exclude from our constructions those sets that contain themselves as members.

Mathematical paradoxes make it clear that problems arise when intuitions from a finite set are applied to a reality associated with infinity. Although a finite set of individuals may be taken to be truthful or liars, the sentences produced by them are potentially infinite in number, and these sentences may be true, false, or meaningless. The sentence of the liar paradox belongs to the third category.

Zeno's arrow paradox shows that use of logical categories leads to the conclusion that motion is impossible. If we were to take the snapshot of an arrow at a point in its flight, the arrow is motionless. To move, the arrow must get from one point to another, and at each point considered individually, the arrow is still. If at every point and at every moment in its flight the arrow is still, then how is it possible for it to move from the bow to its target? Similar reasoning applies to any other case of motion, and, therefore, the assumption that the arrow is stationary at any point in time or space is wrong. It negates the view that space and time can be considered discrete.

Diogenes Laërtius in *Lives and Opinions of Eminent Philosophers* put Zeno's views in context by listing him as one of the Skeptics who believed that complete knowledge could not be obtained:

> Zeno endeavors to put an end to the doctrine of motion by saying: "The object moved does not move either in the place in which it is, or in that in which it is not."

Zeno clarifies his view of the impossibility of reality being many in this summary by Socrates in Plato's *Parmenides*: "If being is many, it must be both like and unlike, and this is impossible, for neither can the like be unlike, nor the unlike like." Elsewhere, he says that the "hypothesis of the being of many, if carried out, appears to be still more ridiculous than the hypothesis of the being of one."

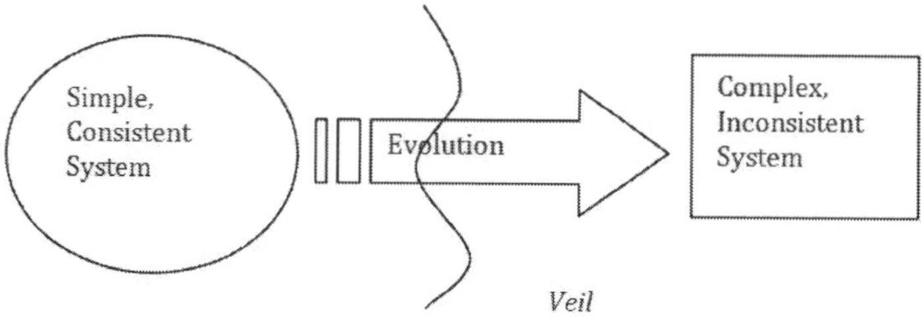

The paradox of estimating the finite basis of the complex system

'Being is one' is the idea that reality must be seen as a unity and not as a collection of parts that are *separate* from each other. Conversely, while analysis may work at some levels of discourse, it will not at other levels.

In early twentieth century mathematicians undertook a program to formalize the method of proof of mathematics with the help of mathematical logic. This required verification of the consistency and, where possible, also the completeness and independence of the formalized system. However, it was soon discovered that in a formal system of sufficient complexity:

1. There exist undecidable problems.
2. The consistency of the system cannot be proved by means of the system.

Figuratively, this can be compared to the impossibility of pulling oneself up by one's own bootstraps. The question of consistency and completeness can, however, be answered if the system's axioms are expanded. Thus formal number theory cannot be shown to be consistent unless its axioms are expanded to include transfinite induction.

The second basic problem in mathematical reasoning concerns the understanding of geometry. For example, there is divided opinion about definition of a line as a sequence of points. Some advanced mathematical structures turn out to be different depending upon whether a line is considered to have a finite or infinite number of points. Dealing with the concept of infinity can lead to other problems as well. A principle that forms the basis of a considerable amount of mathematics is the axiom of choice. According to it, given any collection of sets, whether finite or infinite, one can select one element from each set and form a new set. That this must be true for a finite collection is easy to see but for a collection of sets with infinite number of elements in each it needs an act of faith to believe that elements can be so ordered that the selection of elements can be made repeatedly. While it has not been shown that the axiom of choice produces results that are wrong on physical grounds, its use leads to some puzzling results. One of these is the Banach-Tarski paradox. In one form, this paradox implies that a sphere the size of earth can be compressed into one the size of a small ball by a mere rearrangement of its pieces. With regard to the distinction between reality and model building Einstein wrote in his Sidelights on Relativity: "As far as the propositions of mathematics refer to reality they are not certain, and in so far as they are certain they do not refer to reality."

Definitions in the study of physical phenomena lead to their own difficulties. Consider that an object is defined with respect to its environment so that a definite structure is identifiable with both. In other words, it should be possible to represent an object as an element of a larger system. This leads to the following paradox:

> An object can be described only if it has been defined in relation to its surroundings, which should be well-definable; however, a characterization of the surroundings requires a specification of the system under question.

In practice, to get around this difficulty, it is assumed that successive refinements of the approximate descriptions of the object as well as its surroundings will converge to the exact description. But that is not always satisfactory.

There are linguistic issues also concerning our description of the physical world. These arise when we interpret mathematical symbols and the relations between them that are associated with theory. A given mathematical structure can be interpreted in more than one way. One may view scientific theories as statements about nature in the language of mathematics. As in natural languages like English or Sanskrit, these statements represent symbols, which are primitives of experience, in a linear form. But a linear concatenation of these units of experience is limited by the syntax of the language. Since these units are related to each other across space and time, the linear description will never capture all facets of reality. One may even pose the following riddle: Can a projection of the many dimensional real world on a sequential sensation plane show up regularities that do not actually exist?[3]

The mind-body problem

If one began with the materialist position one can assert that men are machines. This means either the denial of the existence of consciousness or the claim that mental events are epiphenomena and that the material world is causally closed.

Materialism evolved out of early theories of the plenum which led to the continuity description of matter and that of atomism which developed into modern atomic theory and quantum mechanics. Classical materialism assumed that the interaction of two bodies was caused by physical contact where a body or its extension pushed the other body. Newtonian gravitation was the first major revision of this view since it explained interaction as being pull and not push taking place at a distance and not by contact. The theories of electrical and magnetic phenomena of the nineteenth century introduced more complications -- the concept of field and the existence of forces of both the pushing and pulling type. The discovery of electron and other sub-atomic particles showed that there existed no smallest atom, constituent of all matter. Anti-particles showed that no matter was stable, and indeed matter could be converted into light energy and vice versa. The law of conservation of matter had to be given up and replaced by a law of conservation of energy necessitating profound changes in the understanding of space and time.

Viewed from the current materialistic position, man is a complex machine with electrical, chemical and mechanical aspects. The rise of man is a result of the process of evolution through mutation and natural selection. Man's behavior results from inherited traits as modulated by the environment. Man's self-awareness is a consequence of the complexity of his brain and should machines also become equally complex they would possess similar self-awareness. Free will is non-existent. In situations where man is confronted with equally attractive alternatives, his choice is random; in other situations it is determined by biases based on past experience.

There are difficulties associated with the materialistic position. First, it is not clear why the action of deciding on an alternative is accompanied by the subjective feeling of free will. Furthermore, if choices were like random throws of a coin, one's behavior would not be coherent. Second, if the mind is a mere collection of memory imprints in the brain, how does personal identity emerge? This personal identity is a counter-intuitive system that suppresses certain experiences that can only be recollected under hypnosis, if at all. It is also true that if an animal's visual cortex were removed, the animal will be aware of the surroundings without being able to see or formalize the process of awareness. Does this mean that man's awareness of his self predicates his real existence?

Countermodels to materialism begin with the argument that as ordinary matter does not appear to have self-awareness, a machine like man should not have it unless it had an existence of its own. This belief in a mind which is more than an epiphenomenon raises several issues of its own. For instance: What is the seat of the mind in the body? Does the mind outlast the body? Does an overmind, a non-material embodiment of consciousness, pervade the universe of which the individual minds are the temporarily separated fragments? Does the mind enter the body at conception or does it emerge out of the developed body later? Can mind influence matter? Some suggest that the mind exists as a subtle body inside the brain. This represents man as a machine with the mind dwelling within him as pilot. In another view, matter is a mere figment of the mind, but then how to explain the observed regularity and commonality of the physical world. Thus there are several views on the mind-body problem. Some of these are:

1. Materialism: Mind is a record of sensory impressions. Consciousness is a by-product of complex neural events and it first emerged at some state in phylogeny.
2. Panpsychism: Mind is associated with all matter as an inherent attribute. It is reflected as sentience or consciousness in higher animals.
3. Dualism: Both mind and matter have independent existence and consciousness is a reflection of the mind on the body. The material world is causally closed.
4. Monism: The fundamental entity of the universe is consciousness and the physical universe springs from this entity. To understand the universe one needs to understand consciousness.

The mind-body problem is of significance because our understanding of the physical world is ultimately based on observation, and the question arises what is it that observes? Most scientists hold the evolutionist position where the mind is a product of adaptation in response to selection pressures. This does not explain how it is able to obtain insights into number theory, cosmology, genetics, and so on. The logic of this position is like Baron Münchausen pulling himself out of the swamp by his own hair.[4]

An old debate between Prabhākara and Kumārila, two philosophers of the eighth century, describes the possibilities as to the size of mind. According to Prabhākara, mind appears to act instantaneously in combining data from various senses to form an idea. Since no object of any size can move instantaneously, he believed mind was a point-like atom. On the other hand, Kumārila believed that mind was all pervading for it to be able to receive sensations instantaneously.

Recent research on the brain has introduced another complication in our conception of the mind. Clinical studies have shown that the two cerebral hemispheres specialize in different function. This specialization is not an all-or-none phenomenon, but the two hemispheres have different approaches to dealing with different tasks. In over 95 percent of all right-handers, speech is controlled by the left hemisphere; for left-handers about 70 percent have left-hemisphere speech, about 15 percent have right-hemisphere speech, and the remaining 15 percent show bilateral speech control. It may thus be said that in most cases the left hemisphere controls speech. This fact was first noted in 1836 by Marc Dax, a country doctor in France. It is generally believed that a rough characterization of the two hemispheres according to the following categories is possible:

Left hemisphere	***Right hemisphere***
Verbal	Spatio-visual, non-verbal
Sequential, temporal, digital	Simultaneous, spatial, analogical
Logical, analytical	Holistic, synthetic
Rational	Intuitive

Ordinarily, the two hemispheres are connected together with a great number of neural pathways. When these pathways are surgically cut it becomes possible to perform experiments to elicit responses of individual hemispheres. This research on split brains, which started in the 1950s, helped establish the characteristics of the two hemispheres. In an early experiment a cat was trained to do a task with one eye patched, where surgical procedure (that had also cut the optic chiasm) had ensured that information from the open eye flowed only to the corresponding hemisphere. When the patch was switched to the other eye, the cat could not do the task at all. Considerable data has been collected for humans where the split brain surgery was used as a treatment for intractable epilepsy.

It is noteworthy that, in 1910, the yogic philosopher and seer Sri Aurobindo described split brain dichotomy in terms that would be considered accurate even now, hundred years later:[5]

> The intellect is an organ composed of several groups of functions, divisible into two important classes, the functions and faculties of the right hand, the functions and faculties of the left. The faculties of the right hand are comprehensive, creative, and synthetic, the faculties of the left hand critical and analytic ... The left limits itself to ascertained truth, the right grasps that which is still elusive or unascertained. Both are essential to the completeness of the human reason. These important functions of the machine have all to be raised to their highest and finest working-power, if the education of the child is not to be imperfect and one sided.

In fact this insight is a very ancient one. In the Yoga system of Patañjali, one technique of meditation consists of breathing in turn through the alternate nostril (prāṇāyāma), apparently to 'synchronize' the activities in the two hemispheres.

Since the memories of the two hemispheres appear to be distinct for a split-brain individual, some researchers have speculated that this implies that the individual has two minds. In the words of Roger Sperry, a pioneer in this field, "Each hemisphere ... has its own ... private sensations, perceptions, thought, and ideas all of which are cut off from the corresponding experience in the opposite hemisphere. Each left and right hemisphere has its own private chain of memories and learning experience that are inaccessible to recall by the other hemisphere. In many respects each disconnected hemisphere appears to have a separate 'mind of its own.'" Nevertheless, to a casual observer, the behavior of a split-brain patient appears quite ordinary. This may be due to the fact that for such patients connections remain intact between the hemispheres in the area below the cortex. Others claim that the real reason for this is that mind can only be related to linguistic processes, and since the right hemisphere does not have language capability, even split brain patients have a unique mind.

Others believe that the dual mind is the normal situation even in healthy persons and the tension between the two minds, one rational and the other intuitive, leads to man's complex behavior. Within the individual are two selves: one who is in the thick of the flow of events; and the other, who has some distance from the first and is seen as the *witness*.

The classical picture of reality

Everyday life in the ancient world was in communion with nature. Nights were often spent outdoors, so it was natural for the regularities in the motions of the planets and the sun to be noted. The ancient thinker concluded that the inanimate world was predictable and regular, and that living beings had free will and they could intervene in the unfolding of otherwise regular phenomena. Seemingly random events such as earthquakes and epidemics were ascribed to larger or subtle forces.

Perhaps the first grand synthesis of the dichotomous logics of the inanimate and the living worlds was presented in the hymns of the Ṛgveda. The principal idea of these hymns is that reality is paradoxical if analyzed by the categories of time, space, matter, and mind. The Vedic sages argued that since we understand the universe by the mind, deeper understanding is obtained by knowing the nature of consciousness. The Vedic sages asserted that the mind could, through discipline, be trained to transcend its ordinary limitations to apprehend the non-dichotomous reality underlying the everyday reality of our ordinary senses.

According to the Vedic view, reality, which is unitary at the transcendental level, is projected into experience that is characterized by duality. We thus have duality associated with body and consciousness, being and becoming, aggregation and flow, greed and altruism, fate and freedom. The Gods bridge such duality in the field of imagination and also collectively in society: Viṣṇu is the deity of moral law, whereas Śiva is Universal Consciousness. Conversely, the projection into processes of time and change is through the agency of the Goddess. Consciousness (*puruṣa*) and Nature (*prakṛti*) are opposite sides of the same coin.

The other synthesis proposed was that of pure materialism. A school of materialist thought, known as Cārvāka or Lokāyata, attained systematic expression around 600 BC in the aphorisms of a teacher named Bṛhaspati. According to the Cārvākas only the physical world exists. The ultimate elements of matter are earth, fire, air, and water, which combine to produce body and intelligence. The soul is the body transformed by intelligence and when the body dies so does the soul. Knowledge is just a record of perceptions, and any reasoning going beyond sense experience is invalid. Since one can only perceive particulars and not universals, inference, which must include a universal connection, is impossible. The Cārvāka philosophers rejected the concept of causality and introduced in its place the concept of innate nature. The Cārvāka view is quite the same as the mainstream scientific view.

The Vedic view of the world was explained in the Upaniṣads and further elaborated in the Purāṇas. Six systems of philosophy develop[6] these ideas further. Traditionally, they are divided into three groups of complementary pairs: Nyāya and Vaiśeṣika, Sāṅkhya and Yoga, Mīmāṃsā and Vedānta.

Nyāya and Vaiśeṣika

Gotama, the early teacher of the Nyāya, lists four factors involved in direct perception as being the senses (*indriyas*); their objects (*artha*); the contact of the senses and the objects (*sannikarṣa*); and the cognition produced by this contact (*jñāna*). *Manas* (mind) mediates between the self and the senses. When the manas is in contact with one sensory organ, it cannot be so with another. It is therefore atomic in dimension. It is because of the nature of the mind that our experiences are essentially linear, although quick succession of impressions may give the appearance of simultaneity.

A later Nyāya philosopher recognizes four kinds of perception: sense perception, mental perception, self-consciousness, and yogic perception. Self-consciousness is a perception of the self through its states of pleasure and pain. In yogic perception, one is able to comprehend the universe in fullness and harmony.

Vaiśeṣika is attributed to Kaṇāda. According to this system, which constitutes a physical and metaphysical basis for Nyāya, seven categories of experience are defined: substance, quality, action, universality, particularity, relation, and nonexistence. Substance is the most important category, for it is in substance that actions and qualities adhere. The most distinctive feature of the Vaiśeṣika metaphysics is its atomic theory. Each atom possesses size and mass and is distinct from every other atom. Atoms can vibrate in groups and form dyads, triads and so on, until the combinations reach a diameter of one-millionth of an inch, at which state the substances can be identified as earth, or air, or fire, or water. Kaṇāda recognized that the atom had to be point-like, since it could be sub-divided otherwise.

Newton considered space and time to be absolute without explaining what that means. Newton's three laws of motion are: 1. An object remains in the state of rest or motion unless acted upon by a force; 2. Force equals mass times acceleration; 3. To every action there is an equal and opposite reaction. For comparison, we begin with certain propositions of

Kaṇāda that illustrate his system and then present the sūtras that describe physical laws related to motion. Note that Kaṇāda's atoms are in perennial motion and so he distinguishes between internal and outer motions of an object.

Principle 1. कर्म कर्मसाध्यं न विद्यते॥१।१।११॥
karmam karmasādhyam na vidyate (1.1.11).
[Internal] motion does not lead to [outer] motion.

Principle 2. कारणाभावात्कार्याभावः ॥१।२।१॥
kāraṇābhāvātkāryābhāvaḥ (1.2.1)
In the absence of cause there is an absence of effect.

Principle 3. सामान्यं विशेष इति बुद्ध्यपेक्षम् ॥१।२।३॥
sāmānyam viśeṣa iti buddhyapekṣam (1.2.3).
The properties of universal and particular are associated with the mind.

Principle 4. सदिति यतोद्रव्यगुणकर्मसु सा सत्ता ॥१।२।७॥
saditi yatodravyaguṇakarmasu sā sattā (1.2.7).
Existence is [self-defined]. [Likewise] substance, attribute, and motion are sattā (potential).

Principle 5. द्रव्यत्त्वनित्यत्वे वायुना व्याख्याते ॥२।१।२८॥
dravyattvanityatve vāyunā vyākhyāte (2.1.28).
Matter is conserved, as explained for vāyu.

Principle 6. सदकारणवन्नित्यम् ॥४।१।१॥
sadakāraṇavannityam (4.1.1).
What is without cause is eternal (nitya).

The principles have universal applicability. For example, the idea of symmetry is included in the principle of nitya, and Kaṇāda explains the roundness of the atom by this principle. The direct statement of causality in Principle 2 is remarkable. Now I present what may be called Kaṇāda's Laws of Motion.

Law 1. संयोगाभावे गुरुत्वात् पतनम् ॥५।१।७॥
saṃyogābhāve gurutvāt patanam (5.1.7).
In the absence of action, the object falls by gravity.

Law 2a. नोदनविशेषाभावान्नोर्ध्वं न तिर्य्यग्गमनम् ॥५।१।८॥
nodanaviśeṣābhāvānnordhvam na tiryyaggamanam (5.1.8).
In the absence of a force, there is no upward motion, sideward motion or motion in general.

Law 2b. नोदनादाद्यमिषोः कर्म तत्कर्मकारिताच्च संस्कारादुत्तरं तथोत्तरमुत्तरञ्च् ॥५।१।१७॥

nodanādādyamiṣoḥ karma tatkarmakāritācca saṃskārāduttaram tathottaramuttarañca (5.1.17)
The initial motion of an arrow is caused by a force, from that motion is potential (saṃskāra) from which is the motion that follows and the next and so on similarly.

Law 3. कार्य्यविरोधि कर्म ॥१।१।१४॥

kāryyavirodhi karma (1.1.14).
Action is opposed by reaction.

This list above is a somewhat arbitrary arrangement of Kaṇāda's propositions. The first law is effectively equivalent to Newton's first law for due to Principle 2 the object will either continue to be at rest or in state of motion in the absence of action (including gravitation). The second law, in two parts, falls short, although it has something additional regarding potential. What is missing is an explicit definition of mass in relation to force, although mass is otherwise an element of the exposition. Kaṇāda's third law is identical to Newton's third law.

Sāṅkhya and Yoga
According to Sāṅkhya (sixth or seventh century BC), the two fundamental categories of reality are consciousness (puruṣa) and matter (prakṛti). Matter has three attributes (*guṇas*): *sattva* (transparence), *rajas* (activity), and *tamas* (inactivity). Prakṛti is inert when the three guṇas are in a state of equilibrium. When prakṛti comes into contact with puruṣa, the balance of the guṇas is destroyed, and this causes life to be created. In this creation, which proceeds both at the cosmic and the individual levels, the guṇas maintain ever changing ratios. The first to emerge from prakṛti is *mahat*, the cosmic intelligence, and *buddhi*, the intelligence of the individual. This transformation of prakṛti is considered as the actualization of the potential, like pressing a nut into oil.

Out of *mahat*, the next lower category, ego (*ahaṃkāra*), is born; and out of the ego are born the individual mind and various organs of perception and action. When the bond between prakṛti and puruṣa is severed, the former regains its original equilibrium and again becomes inert.

Evolution in Sāṅkhya is an ecological process determined completely by Nature. It differs from modern evolution theory in that it presupposes a universal intelligence. In reality, modern evolution also assigns intelligence to Nature in its drive to select certain forms over others.

The Yoga system is very ancient and its practice seems pictured in the seals of the third millennium BC. One of its early texts is by Patañjali (second century BC). Since we comprehend the universe through our consciousness, in the Yoga system the realization of the ultimate truth is through an understanding of the nature of consciousness.

Mīmāṃsā and Vedānta

Mīmāṃsā, attributed to Jaimini (fourth century BC), is concerned with the interpretation of language. Mīmāṃsā thinkers made important contributions to logic and epistemology. They made the surprisingly modern observation that ascertaining the falsity of a proposition was as important as ascertaining its truth. They also claimed that knowledge could be obtained through direct apprehension.

Vedānta was an attempt to make the aphorisms of the Upaniṣads into a consistent system and is attributed to Bādarāyaṇa (third century BC). Important contributions to this system were made later by Śaṅkara (788-820), who made the dualism of Sāṅkhya look apparent within the framework of monism.

According to Śaṅkara, while constructs of knowledge may be open to doubt, that someone doubts is undoubtable. This is an argument reminiscent of the one used later by Descartes. Knowledge is of two types: empirical knowledge of the senses and transcendent knowledge. There are four states of consciousness: waking, dreaming, deep sleep and *turīya*. In turīya, one realizes that while the world of objects is real, it is not the ultimate reality. Behind the world of empirical reality is the ultimate reality of the Brahman, which is both immanent and transcendent and the cause of all phenomena. The individual self is simply an individuated aspect of Brahman. The world is created by Brahman and in the end becomes again a part of Brahman. The illusion of taking the physical world to be the only objective reality is *māyā*. Conscious mind is an epiphenomenon, because the individual self which is pure consciousness is not conscious.

The Vaiśeṣika system has categories not only for space-time-matter but also for attributes related to the perception of matter. It starts with six categories (*padārthas*) that are nameable and knowable. Nothing beyond these six fundamentals is necessary, because they are sufficient to describe everything in the universe from concrete matter to the abstract atom.

The six categories are: *dravya* (substance), *guṇa* (quality), *karma* (motion), *sāmānya* (universal), *viśeṣa* (particularity), and *samavāya* (inherence). The first three of these have objective existence and the last three are a product of intellectual discrimination. Universals (sāmānya) are recurrent generic properties in substances, qualities, and motions. Particularities (viśeṣa) reside exclusively in the eternal, non-composite substances, that is, in the individual atoms, souls, and minds, and in the unitary substances ether, space, and time. Inherence (samavāya) is the relationship between entities that exist at the same time. It is the binding amongst categories that makes it possible for us to synthesize our experience. In later descriptions of the system a seventh category of 'non-existence' is added.

Of the six categories, the basic one is that of substance and the other five categories are the ones that the mind associates with the substance. Thus observers belong to the system in an integral fashion. If there were no sentient beings in the universe then there would be no need for these categories.

There are nine classes of substances (dravya), some of which are non-atomic, some atomic, and others all-pervasive. The non-atomic ground is provided by the three substances of ether (*ākāśa*), space (*dik*), and time (*kāla*), which are unitary and indestructible; a further four, earth (*pṛthvī*), water (*āpas*), fire (*tejas*), and air (*vāyu*) are atomic composed of indivisible, and indestructible atoms (*aṇu*); self (*ātman*), which is the eighth, is omnipresent and eternal; and, lastly, the ninth, is the mind (*manas*), which is also eternal but of atomic dimensions, that is, infinitely small.

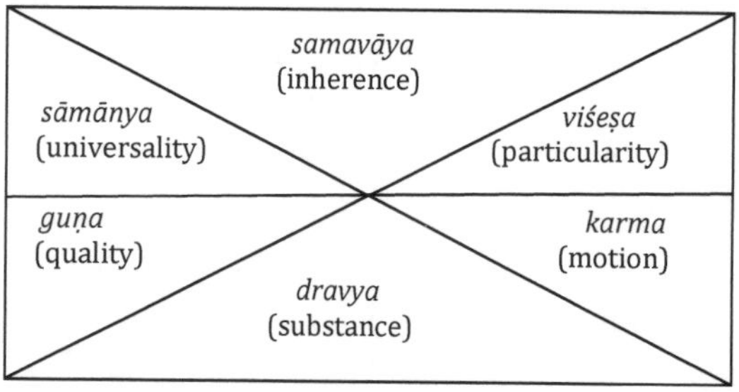

The six categories of Vaiśeṣika

It is postulated that distinguishing characteristics and motion are essential for the classification of matter. Space and time are identified through motion of matter or the sun.

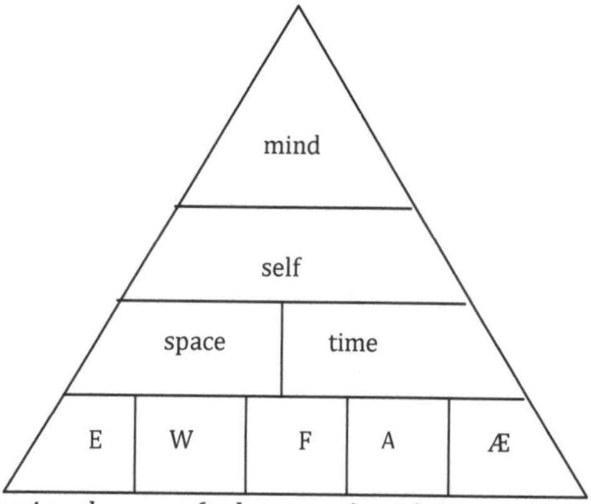

The nine dravyas (substances) with E: earth; W: water; F: fire; A: air; Æ: ether

Of the substances, four (earth, water, fire, and air) are material (that is comprised of atoms) and capable of motion whereas five others (time, space, ether, ātman, and mind) are non-material and, therefore, no motion may be associated with them. It is significant that ātman is listed before mind, suggesting that it is the medium through which mind's apprehensions are received. The atoms of earth, water, fire and air are different and this difference arises out of the different ways the fundamental atom of materiality combines with itself in different arrangements.

The basic atoms of pṛthvī, āpas, tejas, and vāyu will be represented by P, Ap, T, and V, respectively. The sequence of evolution of the elements is given as V→T→Ap→P, although sometimes it also written as T→V→Ap→P. Air is generally mentioned as the medium for the transmission of sound, but a more subtle sound that pervades the universe requires the more abstract vāyu. The ordinary molecules of matter have all the basic atoms present in them. The interactions of the atoms are governed by four different forces: P interacts with all the four, Ap with 3, T with 2, and V with 1.

Scholars of the Vaiśeṣika who wish to reconcile modern physics and the atomic elements consider these to be proton, electron, photon, and neutrino, respectively. Their logic is that since the protons (and related neutrons) provide overwhelming portion of the mass of a substance pṛthvī = proton; when electronic bonds break, the substance becomes a liquid, therefore āpas = electron; tejas (light or fire) is obviously photon; and vāyu is neutrino for it is associated with the decay of the neutron into a proton (of course, this is speculative projection). Kaṇāda insists that only P and Ap have mass; T and V do not. This emphasizes that the atoms are of different size and character. If two of the four do not contribute to the mass of the substance, their nature must be very different. During creation the atoms emerge from ākāśa.

The examination of the various parts of the Vaiśeṣika system reveals that its observables arise through the effect of motion in a consistent manner. As is true of other systems, this system has its own paradoxes. Yet, it offers a comprehensive and scientific view of the universe beginning with gross visible matter all the way up to the subtle invisible mind.

The atom is indivisible because it is a state for which no measurement can be attributed. What cannot be measured cannot be further divided and it cannot be spoken of as having parts. The motion the atom possesses is non-observable and it may be viewed as an abstraction in a conventional sense. Space and time are the two lenses through which matter is observed and they form the matrix of the universe.

The distinction between intrinsic (*karma*) and extrinsic (*kārya*) motions arises from the fact that intrinsic motion is uniform in all directions.

When the universe ceases to be at the end of the cosmic cycle, matter is not annihilated; rather, it reaches a quiescent state where its atoms have no extrinsic motion and so become invisible, which appears very similar to the conception of the state of the giant atom at the beginning of the cycle of creation. The lack of motion represents a cessation of time, because time is a measure of change.

In the epistemology of the Vaiśeṣika system, knowledge is obtained by the agency of ātman or self. The atomic substances exist within the matrix of eternal substances.

Atoms and light

Atoms possess incessant vibratory motion. Heat and light rays consist of very small particles of high velocity. As material particles, their velocity is finite. This is also due to the fact that motion is contingent upon time as one of the dravyas.[10] Particles of heat and light can be endowed with different characteristics and heat and light can be of different kinds. The atoms of light and heat belong to the tejas category. There are four other kinds of atoms with attributes.

There is no difference between the atom of a barley seed and paddy seed, for both these are constructed out of the atoms of earth. Under the impact of heat particles, atoms exhibit new characteristics.

A *bhūta*-atom evolves out of integration from the corresponding *tanmātra*, which is its potential form, indicating a primacy of the abstract over the material. Although atoms are unitary objects their combinations generate various tanmātras. Combinations of rudiment-matter (*bhūtādi*) lead to more specific forms. Atoms vibrate when acted upon by energy.

The atom's potentiality manifests in distinct attributes based on state of conjunction and motion. It is this potentiality that leads to diverse complex atoms with different attributes. These attributes may be viewed as being created by the matrix of space, time and number. Light has a special place in this view as it is both an elementary constituent of matter as well as the medium that shines the inner space of the mind. The atom of light cannot be described fully.

Although the Vaiśeṣika is an atomic theory, it is so only as an idealization and its measurable attributes are in a continuous spectrum as they are generated within the womb of an infinite space-time matrix.

In the Kashmir school of Śaivism, both outer and inner realities (consciousness) are characterized by vibration (*spanda*) and it is this vibration that makes self-referral possible. The ultimate movement takes place not in space and time but inside consciousness. Reality is normally flow and it takes specific form when it is observed. Consciousness guides the evolution of the universe by means of observation.

In summary, then, the six systems of philosophy represent philosophies of logic (Nyāya), physics (Vaiśeṣika), cosmology (Sāṅkhya), psychology (Yoga), language (Mīmāṃsā) and reality (Vedānta)[7] which are different from their Western counterparts[8] in that each one of them has room for the observer and the actor.

In Indian traditions the divisibility and flux of time is considered an apparent phenomenon, the shadow of the permanent and absolute time of Brahman. According to one tradition, time is measured in great cycles (*kalpas*). A kalpa is 12,000 divine years, and a divine year is equal to 360 human years. Each kalpa is divided into four yugas (ages): Kṛta, Tretā, Dvāpara, and Kali. Kṛta Yuga is four times the length of Kali Yuga and Tretā and Dvāpara are three times and twice as long as Kali Yuga, our present age, which lasts for 1200 divine years or 432,000 human years. One thousand kalpas constitute a Brahmā Day, a period of time which begins with the creation of a universe and ends with its dissolution. A Brahmā Day which is a period of activity is followed by a Brahmā Night which is a period of dormancy. Cosmic creation and quiescence follow one another without end. Phenomenal time is thus viewed within a framework of endlessness.[9]

The creation of the world is whimsical like a sport but on being accomplished the evolution of the world proceeds by natural law. The universe comes with a certain mixture and distribution of the guṇas that in itself is the plan for its history. But the creation does not take place at a single moment only. It is a continual process in which consciousness actively guides the evolution through observation.

The Vedic view defines a world governed entirely by well-defined physical and psychological principles. These principles can be discovered by means of systematic observation. Human behavior is ordinarily determined by innate tendencies and the environment. So the world appears material; if one believed in the interaction of mind and matter it appears then as dual. The monistic aspect of reality can be apprehended only through meditation.

Science has progressed by seeking answers to the 'how' of phenomena. At one level the unified world-view is quite in agreement with this approach; at another level it extolls the opposite approach of seeking the causes behind events. Vedism in India helped in the flowering of vigorous science; but the belief in the relative reality of space and time shifted the focus away from a search for invariance principles. Still, great advances in mathematics, linguistics, medicine, physics, and other sciences took place.[10] One of the greatest achievements of this classical age was the science of linguistics with its profound insights in phonetics, etymology and grammar. The earliest grammar that survives is that of Pāṇini (6th century BC), who was already at the end of a long line of grammarians. "Pāṇini is not only the oldest grammarian whose work has come down to us -- he is also the greatest."[11]

The Indian view of consciousness -- that it is a unity and the feeling of sentient beings as being separated from others is a misapprehension -- was endorsed by Schrödinger in his influential book *What is Life*? Indian tradition accepts that consciousness influences nature by the process of observation (*dṛṣṭi* in Sanskrit). This is very similar to the quantum mechanical view of the influence of observation on a physical process by the quantum Zeno effect. But the difference between quantum theory and Indian ideas is that although one speaks of observations in quantum theory there is no place in its ontology for observers. Schrödinger was aware of this limitation and he argued that sense-categories like the tanmātras of the

Sāṅkhya system of creation at the individual or the cosmic level were essential to understand reality.

In traditional art, Śiva (representing individual and universal consciousness) is shown as lifeless next to the vibrant Goddess (who represents Nature or evolving physical reality). Abstract representations of the cosmos show Śiva as a dot (of immateriality) within the (geometric) framework of the material world. Much of Indian mythology is an exposition of Indian epistemology in a coded language.

If the evolution of machines is driven by human intelligence, the case could be made that biological evolution is driven by Nature's intelligence which is an embodiment of consciousness.

One can also assert that biological forms, and by extension machine forms, are latent in the physical law, just as the excited states of the electron orbits are latent in the physics of the hydrogen atom even though these states may not be occupied. Furthermore, ideas can be given the same footing as biological forms or machines although they need appropriate biological structure to be articulated.

The bridging of the worlds of consciousness and matter does not occur at the level of matter or mind. In Indian epistemology, consciousness itself is a transcendent category that goes beyond both matter and mind.

Indian epistemology has some parallels with Western idealism that accepts independent existence of ideas and forms. But it is different from idealism in the sense that the self has access to much more than what the individual obtains through the sense organs. The conception of the self at the individual level (*ātman*) or in its totality (*Brahman*) together with the counter-intuitive notion of equivalence between the two selves makes it possible to see how large scale correlations can exist and how a person can obtain surprising insights through intuition. Naturally, such insights can only be rationalized within the framework of the individual's knowledge. Although ordinarily consciousness and matter are distinct categories, consciousness influences the evolution of matter through observation.

The categories of Indian physics correspond to a cosmology that illuminates the nature of scientific discovery. Consciousness cannot disrupt natural law related to matter but it can guide its evolution by making certain outcomes more likely than others. The universe is closed on itself at the level of consciousness but there are instances of anomalous experience and coincidences at the personal level and such coincidences also occur in the scientific world. Coincidences in Indian scientific texts that support these ideas include the age of the universe, the distance to the sun, and the speed of light. There are also instances of impressive qualitative scientific speculations in the literature.

Indian epistemology could be considered to be falsified if no evidence is found for large correlations in the world but such correlation could be coincidences. One needs carefully devised scientific tests to determine large correlations in the laboratory and in terrestrial and astronomical processes.

=================

At about the same time as the early Indian philosophers, a picture of reality with a somewhat different focus appeared in Ionia, a Greek settlement in Asia Minor, and then spread to the larger Greece. Ionia was on the trade route frequented by traders from several parts of the world, including Mesopotamia and India.

Thales (about 630-546 BC) held that everything was originally water from which earth, air, and living things separated out. Heraclitus claimed that everything must change. He thought fire was the prime element because it was so active and could transform everything. He also introduced the idea of opposites: some things, like flame, move up and others, like earth, move down. The opposites were necessary to each other to define a dynamic world of continuous change.

Pythagoras (582-500 BC) and his followers made the important observation that many phenomena that were qualitatively very different from each other had an identical mathematical structure. They concluded that this structure was the essence of these phenomena. More specifically, they found this essence reflected in numbers and numerical relationships. Their doctrine 'All things are numbers' was an expression of the belief that numerical relationships lay behind all phenomena. The Pythagorean School established the method of proof by deductive reasoning from postulates.

Parmenides (470 BC) was a philosopher of pure reason. He tried to refute the view of Heraclitus that everything changes. If what is, is, and what is not, is not, nothing can ever happen, and change is impossible. The real universe is one and changeless. As our senses show change, we can only conclude that our senses are fallible, and the material world is an illusion. Zeno, a pupil of Parmenides, attacked the School of Pythagoras by his paradoxes which appear to prove logically that time or distance can neither be continuous nor discontinuous. If space is continuous the runner can never reach the goal. If he is half way it will take him time to cross half of the rest and so on ad infinitum. If space is discontinuous the arrow can never move because it is either at one point or the next and there is nothing between.

Plato (427-347 BC) pushed the ideas of Parmenides further. He argued that all forms in the visible world are reflections of their ideal counterparts existing in what he termed the real world. Plato's distinction between the real and the apparent is illustrated by the famous analogy of prisoners in a cave, who are able to look in one direction only because they are bound and who have a fire behind them and a wall in front. On the wall they can see shadows of themselves and of other objects cast by the fire. If the prisoners have seen nothing but the wall all their lives, they regard the shadows as real and have no knowledge of the real objects that have produced them.

By maintaining specific objects to be apparent, Plato was led to the belief that the senses could not yield knowledge. The properties of the ideal objects or universals could be determined only by means of ideas. If knowledge cannot come from the senses, where does it come from? Plato claimed that knowledge was innate and could be obtained by recollecting what was known before birth. This led him to the belief that soul with its knowledge exists before birth and hence to a belief in immortality.

Aristotle (384-322 BC), a pupil of Plato, tried to modify his teacher's theory of ideas so as to make it consistent with the broad outlines of the visible world. He conceived of natural processes in terms of the progression of things toward their ultimate, predestined forms. Cataloging of observed processes to determine the final forms was an important part of his natural philosophy. Aristotle was as a biologist a painstaking observer; as a physicist he gave less importance to experience.

Aristotle's understanding of the evolution of objects to final forms was that it was directed by nature. Thus it is the nature of seed to grow into plant and of egg to turn into chicken. Similarly, a stone falls to the earth because of its nature. Aristotle's ideas of motion were similarly related to fulfillment of potential. Earth and water tended to move downwards whereas air and fire moved upwards. The motion of all planets was circular, their nature being to exist in a continuous and infinite state of motion.

There are many common themes in Indian and Greek philosophies. There is no conclusive evidence that they influenced each other.[12] No doubt similar ideas arose in other civilizations as well, either independently or by mutual interaction. Many early traditions were oral. Records of others were lost in the innumerable destructions of libraries and temples that followed the rise of monotheistic religions. The classical culture of Greece and the Near East declined with the rise of Christianity and Islam. Libraries were destroyed by many early converts on the grounds that these books were redundant if they agreed with their religious books and false if they disagreed. The mature Arab states cultivated Greek and Indian learning on philosophy, mathematics, medicine and astronomy and by that way this learning reached medieval Europe.

Indian learning survived in India but it did not receive appropriate level of patronage since for many centuries many parts of India were ruled by alien rulers. Europeans were introduced to Indian learning through the translations of British scholars which began appearing in the eighteenth century, stirring Western thought. Idealism strangely like Śaṅkara's was conceived by Fichte, and Schopenhauer incorporated Sāṅkhya and Vedānta into his philosophy. More recently, physicists have looked to Indian philosophy to make sense of puzzling aspects of modern science.[13]

A world-image is the embodiment of the experience of reality in a culture. World-images, unlike scientific theories, are hard to falsify. Consider materialism which represents man as a machine. Even if there was behavior that no machine could emulate, the materialist scientist would invoke new, fictitious forces to make this behavior appear machine-like. On the other hand, a believer in astrology will explain all behavior by the positions of the planets and the stars. Cultures contain elements of more than one world-image which is why belief systems have contradictory features.

Although generalizations about any culture are misleading, it can be said that the dominant preoccupation of Western cultures is the external reality related to the physical world and social organization. An emphasis by a society on certain values results in the opposite of these values being accepted in other aspects of life. The opposition occurs at a different level of behavior or perception. Human mind creates patterns so that a color that is muted at one place is accentuated at another. That a dynamic interplay of oppositions creates a tension essential for life is recognized by all traditions. The materialists recognize determinism/free will, the Indians have reality/māyā and Śiva/Śakti, and the Taoists talk of yin/yang. Cultures split up the neutral reality into a mosaic of different hues.

Western cultures did not, until recent times, emphasize a study of the psyche. But there was a long tradition of investigations of the physical world and of social, economic and political institutions.

A world-image structures not only beliefs and behavior but also the manner in which events are perceived. Some elements of the matrix of the Western world-image that were implicitly accepted for a long time although they have been superseded by modern science are: (i) time is uniform and absolute, (ii) space is absolute, (iii) man has a unique and central position in the world, and (iv) man alone has mind. The major Western traditions, viz. Judaism, Christianity, Islam and Marxism, conform to these essentials. In contrast, time and space are considered relative in the Indian world view, and man is not assigned a central position in the universe. Indians believe that animals also have minds and that there are many universes like ours.

The dominant Western world-image evolved through the ages. Its changes were adaptations to the changing economic, political, social and scientific orders. For example, the scientific revolution of the 16th-18th century made scientists alter their belief in a world maintained by God to one that was pre-established and governed by laws of nature. The industrial and post-industrial revolutions strengthened the belief in a materialistic world.

Descartes and Bacon are usually credited with laying the methodological framework for the rise of modern science. Bacon emphasized the empirical approach of arriving at results through experimentation and induction. Descartes divided the universe into two parts: physical and moral. Along with Galileo he recognized extension and movement as the primary physical realities; other aspects of existence, such as colors, tastes, smells were called secondary qualities. Descartes believed that science dealt mainly with the primary realities and to a lesser extent with the secondary ones. He believed further that the domain of passions, will, love, faith was outside the scope of science and lay in fact in the realm of revelation. To him all animals, including man, were in themselves mere machines, but there was a rational spirit dwelling within the human body. Leibniz (1646-1716) strengthened the belief in a physical world governed by scientific laws by propounding the doctrine of preexisting order. Locke (1632-1704), Berkeley (1685-1753) and Hume (1711-1776) stressed the empirical basis of knowledge further while asking questions about its nature. Hume argued that our ideas were a result of sensations. A collection of simple ideas constituted a complex idea. The mind was a collection of sensations and ideas. He also argued that since our perceptions were the result of sensations we have no basis to talk of the physical world having an objective reality. A repeated sensation of an object does not establish that the object exists. Causality is an ordering of ideas that occur frequently. Space and time are the manner and the sequence in which ideas occur. This seemed to suggest that one could not hope to discover laws concerning a permanent, objective physical world. In other words, his philosophy posed the riddle: How can the observation of a connection between events in the past show that such connections would be perceived in the future as well?[14]

Hume's ideas pointed to the difficulty of making any real progress in understanding physical processes. Immanuel Kant (1724-1804) made assumptions that removed some of this difficulty. He postulated that the mind has an innate intuition of space, time, cause and effect, and matter. Actual experiences are perceived in terms of the innate categories. Sense impressions originate in the real world, but this world is unknowable. The world as comprehended is a map constructed of subjective categories supplied by the perceiving mind.

Other mature civilization also had dual traditions of materialism and idealism. We have described only the Indian and the Greek ones because they have survived into our times and because several other traditions borrowed from them. The dominant tradition in India was idealism while in Greece it was materialism.[15] If one stressed the mind, the other stressed the body. Modern science and technology that makes it possible to probe the brain facilitates the study of both mind and body.

The modern view

The rise of the modern view may be traced to the acceptance of two premises: scientific observation should be reproducible, and one can divide the multitude of physical processes into categories that can be studied separately.[16]

Classification and physical description of phenomena is the first step in science. Galileo's view of the enterprise of science is well expressed in the following passage: "True philosophy is written in that great book of nature that lies ever open before our eyes but which no one can read unless he has first learned to understand the language and to know the characters in which it is written. It is written in mathematical language, and the characters are triangles, circles, and other geometric figures."

By their exposition of gravitation, Galileo, Kepler and Newton were able to provide a dynamic description of the world. The Newtonian system marks the beginnings of mechanistic physics in which the same laws govern processes on the earth and in the skies. It considered the universe as a great clockwork running according to well-defined laws and it ascribed independent and real existence to space and time as well as to matter. Space was taken to be at rest and time moved uniformly, at the same rate for all matter. The Newtonian system arose when the most advanced technology of the day was watchmaking and taking the clock as a metaphor for the universe had poetic symmetry.

Heat engines were the great technological advance of the nineteenth century. The mechanistic picture of the world applied to such engines if one used statistical descriptions for assemblies of large numbers of particles. A gas in a cylinder is characterized by pressure and temperature, which are quantities that describe statistically the agitation of the gas molecules. The basic interactions between the molecules are described by Newtonian equations.

The laws of classical mechanics and of electromagnetism involve invariance with respect to time reversal. One may be led to believe, therefore, that the phenomena are reversible. A motion picture of a projectile in motion, of an oscillating spring or pendulum, of two colliding billiard balls, or the moon in its orbit would appear the same if run backward or forward. However, a more careful examination of all these phenomena shows that there is definite time asymmetry in nature. Thus a projectile produces turbulence as it moves through the atmosphere which can be used to determine the direction of its motion. An object accelerating through free space has likewise an asymmetrical field around it which can be used to determine the direction of motion. The study of heat engines demonstrated clearly the irreversibility of phenomena. Reversals of processes, though consistent with energy and momentum conservation, are not observed. A mixture of ice and hot water ultimately becomes tepid water. But tepid water does not spontaneously separate into ice and hot water, although energy conservation will not prohibit half of the molecules from transferring a disproportionate share of their energy to the other half. This irreversibility was summed up in the nineteenth century by the second law of thermodynamics, which in its simplest form states that:

> Heat cannot be transferred spontaneously from a system at a lower temperature to another system at a higher temperature.

Refrigerators and air conditioners transfer heat from cold to warm systems, but they expend energy in the process so that the transfers are not spontaneous. Any process forbidden by the second law of thermodynamics would, if it occurred, be characterized by a spontaneous increase in the order of a system. It was soon found that the second law could also be stated as:

> Any isolated physical system will, if left to itself, proceed toward a state of maximum disorder. If already in a state of maximum disorder a system will remain in that state.

A mechanical interpretation of thermodynamics was proposed by Boltzmann. A particle in itself does not have temperature, heat, and entropy. Boltzmann introduced statistical analogs of these concepts for large collections of particles. He interpreted the second law of thermodynamics to mean that in any isolated system with phases at different temperatures, the system states tend to an equilibrium state of maximum probability, associated with equalization of temperature. This interpretation meant that the law was not immutable but was rather a statistical law.

Boltzmann believed that his theory explained the arrow of time within the framework of Newtonian dynamics. Two important objections were advanced. Loschmidt (1876) argued that since laws of dynamics are symmetric with respect to past and future, the theory should be valid if the velocities of all the objects in the collection were reversed. However, that sends the system back to its initial state which is characterized by low entropy.

Zermelo (1896) objected that according to a theorem of dynamics that had been proved earlier by Poincaré (1890), a dynamical system periodically goes through its initial state. This would imply that, in contradiction to the second law of thermodynamics, molecular processes must be cyclical.

According to one suggestion, a cosmological term needs to be introduced into the equations of motion to express the influence of the expanding universe, which establishes the arrow of time. Nobody knows if this can actually be done. Recently it was suggested that while isolated systems may be becoming more disordered, when considered in entirety most processes of interest are correctly viewed in the framework of open systems. An open system exchanges energy and matter with its environment. A system can have subsystems that are continually fluctuating in character and at times order and structure can arise out of randomness. This does not answer the basic question of asymmetry of time, however.

Eddington had the following to say about the second law of thermodynamics: "From the point of view of philosophy of science the conception associated with entropy must, I think, be ranked as the great contribution of the nineteenth century to scientific thought. It marked a reaction from the view that everything to which science need pay attention is discovered by a microscopic dissection of objects."

By the end of the nineteenth century two contradictory principles had become established in physics and biology. In physics, it was the second law of thermodynamics that stood for the principle of increasing disorder; in biology, Darwin's theory of evolution is a principle of ever-increasing order and organization.

The remarkable success of the mathematical theories of gravitation, mechanics, optics and hydrodynamics in the 17th and 18th centuries made the seeking of the essential mathematical truth that lay behind physical phenomena an attractive goal. The search for mathematical structures to describe different aspects of nature led to the creation of new kinds of algebras and geometries. When shown that differing geometries could fit spatial experience equally well, it was clear that mathematical structures, in themselves, did not express fundamental truths.

In the latter part of the 19th century, mathematicians investigated the logical basis of their theories. Attempts were made to reconstruct mathematics using systematic methods. Soon contradictions were discovered culminating in the results of Gödel that no mathematical system could answer all questions posed within its own framework.

Gottfried Leibniz and George Berkeley criticized Newton's conception of absolute space and motion on the grounds that all relationships are relative. Leibniz claimed that space could not be defined without relation to matter. Berkeley showed in a universe of only two objects, motion about a common axis could never be measured. Mach and Einstein amplified this philosophical position. Mach insisted that a physical theory should deal only with observables and not mental constructs. Furthermore, properties of objects should somehow reflect characteristics of distant matter. Meanwhile it was found that contrary to intuition the speed of light remained unaffected by the speed of its source. Poincaré and Einstein showed that a consistent interpretation of this fact demanded that one should abandon the notions of absolute space and absolute time. According to the theory of special relativity, although two events might be simultaneous when referred to one coordinate system, they would in general fail to be simultaneous when referred to a system moving uniformly with respect to the first. The speed of light in vacuum, c, was taken to be the highest speed of propagation of any influence. It also followed that energy (E) and mass (m) are inter-convertible, a principle summed up by the famous formula $E = mc^2$. The validity of this formula was demonstrated later in the study of nuclear processes and by the development of nuclear energy and weapons.

The general theory of relativity showed a connection between geometry and physics. According to this theory, distances between points in space do not fit the rules of Euclidean geometry in the presence of gravitational fields. This means, for instance, that the sum of the angles in a rectilinear triangle is no longer exactly equal to two right angles. The departure from two right angles is greater the stronger the field of gravitation. Geometry could be either a structural system with arbitrary axioms or a physical theory. In the first case, geometry provides a logical structure to frame experience in; in the second case, the propositions of geometry can be checked by experiment and are as certain or uncertain as statements of any empirical science. In this view of gravitation, matter causes space to become curved. A light ray passing by a massive body is, therefore, bent. Given enough mass, space bends into itself and become closed just as in the one-dimensional case a line can get closed into a circle.

In the standard view, the universe is taken to be finite in size and matter and be closed. It consists of myriads of galaxies that are receding from each other: the further a galaxy, the faster its recession speed. The recession is taken to be a result of the expansion of space, just as points recede on the surface of an inflating balloon.

Once the model of the expansion of the universe is accepted, a backward extrapolation in time leads to a primordial explosion (big bang) of a hyperdense universe. It was suggested in the 1940s, that a relic of the explosion would be a background radiation of a few degrees Kelvin. This radiation was accidently measured in 1965 in a study of electromagnetic noise produced by the galaxy. The radiation was once extremely hot and has now cooled to the current value. The radiation is not completely isotropic which has been taken to mean that the earth has a velocity of about 600 km/sec against the background of an isotropic radiation.

Disturbances in a system can travel in two distinct ways: by the actual motion of particles, and through a wave where particles themselves oscillate around a steady-state position. Although descriptions in terms of particles and waves are mutually exclusive, experiments show that electrons and other particles behave sometimes as waves. The calculus of quantum mechanics gives a procedure to describe such seemingly strange behavior; it defines a framework which is interpreted in many different ways ranging from the statistical to one where the universe splits into several non-interacting copies each moment. The uncertainty relations of quantum mechanics are taken to signify a discrete spacetime, impossibility of precise measurement, and of a principle that allows free will.

When quantum mechanics is combined with relativity, new properties of matter are revealed. Every particle is associated with a field and every field is associated with a class of indistinguishable particles. Furthermore, there exist two fundamental types of particles classified according to their spin angular momentum. Those with half spins (fermions) obey the exclusion principle according to which no two particles can occupy the same state. Particles with integer spins (bosons) are not governed by the exclusion principle.

A general survey of science shows dualism at various levels of conceptualization. We contend with the duality of free will and determinism when we include ourselves as observers and actors in the universe, and there are the dualities of matter and field and wave and particle. Pure matter theories cannot explain attraction; pure field theories lack the capability to include matter. In quantum description, light is not only a wave but also a particle, an electron is sometimes a wave sometimes a particle. What is perceived depends on the situation of the observer.

By the middle of the nineteenth century four forces were thought to be fundamental: gravitation, electricity, magnetism, and the short-range molecular force. The model of atom as the basic form of matter was well established. Close to ninety different types of atoms such as hydrogen, oxygen, iron, zinc were known. Soon it was shown that electricity and magnetism were manifestations of the same basic force which was named electromagnetism. Molecular force, postulated to explain the stability of matter, was later shown to be derived from the electromagnetic force. This force is a result of electromagnetic interaction between positively charged nuclei and negatively charged electrons moving around the nuclei.

Further investigations into nuclear structure showed that many atoms and particles were unstable. For example, the neutron disintegrates eventually into a proton, an electron, and a neutrino. It was realized that two new forces were needed to be added to gravitation and electromagnetism. The short-range strong force is the attraction between nucleons (protons and neutrons) that counters the electric repulsion between the positively charged protons in the nucleus. The disintegration of particles was attributed to another short-range force called the weak force, the name owing to its weakness relative to the electromagnetic and the strong forces.

According to the view held in the 1940s, the stable elementary constituents of all matter were protons, electrons, neutrinos, and their antimatter companions, antiprotons, positrons, and antineutrinos. Matter and antimatter particles annihilate each other releasing radiation energy. The first antimatter particle to be proposed was the positron (antielectron). It was introduced by P.A.M. Dirac in 1931 to overcome certain difficulties in a theory of electrons that he had developed.

In 1934, Yukawa proposed an intermediate particle, later called the meson, to mediate the strong force between protons and neutrons. This proposal was based on the hypothesis that the range of a force is inversely proportional to the mass of the particle that mediates it. The electrical force between two charged particles varies inversely to the square of the separation. The range of the electromagnetic force seems to be infinite, so it stands to reason that the rest mass of the photon should be zero. Since the strong force is short range, Yukawa's meson had a non-zero mass, and he predicted a mass of about 200 to 300 times the mass of the electron. Later, such a particle was discovered in cosmic radiation with a mass equal to 275 times the electron mass.

Yukawa's principle applied to gravity shows that owing to its infinite range gravitons should have zero rest mass. Also, since the weak force has a range even smaller than that of the strong force, it should be mediated by a particle heavier than the meson. In fact current theory indicates that three different particles of the same family mediate this force and these particles are the intermediate vector bosons.

In the 1960s, it was proposed that many properties of strongly interacting particles such as neutrons and protons (also called hadrons) could be better understood if each hadron was taken to be composed of three elementary particles called quarks. If one were to accept electrons and quarks and the neutrinos to be elementary, how is one to visualize them? If they are little spheres of mass, they should be infinitely hard because otherwise one could, in principle, given enough energy, break each one into smaller pieces. But infinite strength must be based on infinite energy, which is impossible. To see this from a different angle, consider collision between two electrons. If they are infinitely hard, then at the moment of the collision each merely reverses its motion without getting flattened as tennis balls do at impact. But an instantaneous reversal of motion implies that the collision has influence on the trailing ends of the electrons in no time. This is forbidden by the relativity principle according to which no influence can travel faster than the speed of light.

If electrons and quarks are pointlike entitles carrying electric charge, this charge would repel itself and energy would therefore be needed to keep it in place. The repulsion force is inversely proportional to square of the separation between the charges. When the radius of the electron is zero, it needs infinite energy to keep the charge in place. Due to the equivalence between energy and mass, this means that the mass of the electron should be infinite. This is contrary to facts: the electron mass is about 9.1×10^{-28} grams.

This means that an elementary particle is much more complex than a small spherical ball or a pointlike object. According to quantum mechanics a particle can also be visualized as a packet of waves. Furthermore, the uncertainty principle allows particles of different energies to be created spontaneously so long as these particles last very briefly. The more the energy of such a particle the shorter is its life span. In vacuum one can visualize such a particle creation in matter-antimatter pairs, so that the particles are being constantly created and destroyed. In the vicinity of a particle such as an electron, one can likewise see a creation of photons (particle-like packets of light) by energy borrowed from the electron. The more energetic the photon the less time it can exist, which implies that it cannot move much distance away from the electron. In fact a photon of such energy, so that it can be observed, may last only 10^{-15} seconds, in which time it can travel barely about 10^{-7} meters. So an electron may be viewed as being surrounded by a swarm of photons of varying energy. There is no limit to the values of energy for the photons, so even in this complex picture the total energy of the electron turns out to be infinite.

It was discovered in the late 1940s that if the infinity for the value of energy in the above model is replaced by the actual measured value it does not mar the predictive power of the theory. Theories where infinities are thus replaced successfully are said to be renormalizable and electrodynamics is renormalizable. This theory of quantum electrodynamics (QED) is one of the most successful in physics and agreement between experiments and theory approaches one part in a billion.

In the 1960s a theory unifying electromagnetism and the weak force was developed. The idea behind the unification is that both these forces arise from a single and more fundamental property of nature and at exceedingly high energies the two forces are indistinguishable. This is seen by assigning the photon and the intermediate vector bosons (W^+, W^-, and Z^0) to a single family of four particles. It is believed that in a primordial state of the universe all the four particles were massless. As the energies decreased, symmetry breaking occurred which by a mechanism called the Higgs mechanism endowed the W and Z particles with mass while leaving the photon massless.

The concept of symmetry breaking was proposed by Werner Heisenberg in his description of ferromagnetic materials. Heisenberg pointed out that the theory describing a ferromagnet has perfect geometric symmetry in that it gives no special distinction to any one direction in space. When the material becomes magnetized, however, the axis of magnetization can be distinguished from all other axes. The theory is symmetrical but the object it describes is not.

The fundamental idea of the Higgs mechanism is to include in the theory an extra field, one having the peculiar property that it does not vanish in the vacuum. The vacuum is generally defined as the state in which all the fields have their lowest possible energy. The energy of the Higgs field is smallest when it has some uniform value greater than zero. The effect of the Higgs field is to provide a frame of reference with respect to which symmetry can be determined. The Higgs field in the unification of the electromagnetic and the weak forces leads to the requirement of another particle called the Higgs boson, which has not been detected. There is also no estimate of the mass of this boson.

The first theory of hadrons assumed three fractionally charged quarks, distinguished by the labels u, d, s, with charges of 2/3, -1/3 and -1/3, respectively. The proton is made up of two u quarks and a d quark (uud), while the neutron is made up of a u quark and two d quarks (udd). Three other kinds of quarks labeled c, b and t have been proposed to explain the existence of other short-lived particles. Leptons and quarks are the only two classes of elementary particles necessary to explain the structure of other particles. After its discovery in 1975, the tau lepton has been added to the lepton family of electron and muon, and there is a neutrino associated with each. Regularities in the elementary particle interactions suggest that quarks and leptons should be grouped into three 'families' or 'generations.' The first of these consists of the u and d quarks, as well as the electron and its neutrino. The second generation is comprised of the c and s quarks and muon and its neutrino. The third generation consists of the b and t quarks and the tau lepton and its neutrino. The particles of the first generation account for all the ordinary matter in the universe. Each quark comes in three colors. The total number of elementary particles therefore consists of quarks in six flavors and three colors, for a total of 18 quarks, plus six leptons. Each of these particles has an antiparticle, which yields a complement of 48 distinct constituents of matter.

A theory of strong interactions directly modeled on quantum electrodynamics was developed in the 1970s. This theory is called quantum chromodynamics (QCD) where chromo refers to forces that act between color charges. The colors are arbitrary labels for mathematical properties that have no relation to ordinary colors or charges. Put another way the strong force among quarks is due to the exchange of massless particles called gluons, analogous to photon exchange in QED. Each quark can come in one of three colors: red, blue, and green. This makes for 8 different colored gluons in contrast to the single colorless photon.

Quantum chromodynamics imbues quarks with the property of asymptotic freedom, which implies that as quarks come closer, the coupling strength weakens and within a hadron the quarks move about like free particles. This also accounts for the confinement of the quarks inside hadrons and the absence of free, isolated quarks.

A beginning has also been made in constructing a theory unifying electromagnetism, the weak force, and the strong force. This theory yields transformations between leptons and quarks of each generation, which means that ultimately none of the elementary particles is stable.

Another approach is to view leptons and quarks to be built up from more elementary particles, which are sometimes called pre-quarks or preons. Several models that account for some characteristics of the observed particles have been proposed.

All unification theories are based on symmetry breaking. It is believed, for instance, that the mechanism of the symmetry breaking between electromagnetism and the weak force becomes apparent at energies of a few hundred billion electron volts. The corresponding figure for symmetry breaking between electromagnetic, the weak and the strong forces is 10^{14} times higher, estimated from the fact that distance and energy are related by the uncertainty principle and the energy needed to probe a given distance is inversely proportional to the distance. The electromagnetic and the weak force become unified at distances of about 10^{-16} centimeter and together with the strong force the unification is at the distance of 10^{-29} centimeter.

In one of the proposals for a unified theory (called SU(5)) 12 new particles are postulated; these mediate transitions between quarks and leptons. The energy required to create such particles (about 10^{16} billion electron volts) is unlikely ever to be generated in a laboratory. Perhaps, there exists no process in the universe where such energies are produced. Cosmologists have conjectured that such particles were produced in an earlier epoch, about 10^{-40} seconds after the big bang, when the size of the universe was comparable to the unification scale. The temperature of the universe was then more than 10^{18} degrees Kelvin and leptons and quarks could freely convert into each other. This proposal further implies that a proton should decay with an average lifetime of 10^{31} years. Experiments to detect both the effects of the generation of such particles at the big bang in the cosmic background radiation as well the decay of the proton has found no evidence in support of these ideas.

Another area of speculation relates to incorporating gravitation in a unified theory. In a theory called supersymmetry it is postulated that each particle of half-integral spin (fermion) has a supersymmetric companion of integral spin (boson) and vice versa. Thus quarks have boson companions and leptons have fermion companions. No such particles have been detected.

The state of our knowledge

Reality has logical, psychological and physical aspects. No observations of the physical world can be made without the experimenter starting with a hypothesis that he wishes to prove or disprove and observations can be interpreted only within a logical framework.

The most astonishing thing about science is that ideas, which are whorls of specific electrical activity in the brain, have been successful in describing so many aspects of the world. Physical theories have progressively become more abstract and mathematical and the work of scientists is now like that of solving a puzzle. Is reality itself mathematical at its essential core?

Although physics has had success in describing the external world, there are theories of physics that are structurally at variance with each other. Given this fact, what is the nature of the physical reality as defined by scientific knowledge? An answer to this question can be found only by determining the limitations of current knowledge.

The success of the models of science is true generally at the level of isolated systems, but even there 'complete' explanations do not always exist. For example, recent theories on unification of the four basic forces suggest particles of one kind transform into another but these theories also show that elementary particles have more fundamental constituents. Are there more quarks and leptons? What is the nature of the field that causes symmetry breaking? How do particles acquire mass? What gravitational effect do vacuum fluctuations have? These and other questions lead to other speculations. For example, at very small (Planckian) lengths the fluctuations in the vacuum become so violent that spacetime has wormholes that appear and disappear continually. In other models, the four-dimensional spacetime of relativity is replaced by higher dimensional spacetime. It is claimed that we are not ordinarily aware of the higher dimensions because they are only a few Planck units wide.

Other theories suggest that the puzzling characteristics of the elementary particles can be revealed by a bootstrap program and, furthermore, properties of the elementary particles somehow reflect characteristics of the universe.

Then there are questions and speculations about the large scale structure of the universe. Is the observed universe only one of many island universes? If the current structure of the universe is attributed to the initial conditions of the primeval atom, what explains the initial conditions? If the universe cycles through alternating phases of expansion and contraction, do the initial conditions in the current expansion reflect the structure of the previous contracting phase? Why does matter exceed antimatter in the universe? Also, are the laws of nature unchanging? Is there a special point in the universe relative to which phenomena appear simpler?

An idea called the anthropic principle is sometimes invoked to explain the initial conditions. According to this idea any other set of conditions would not have led to the development of life and consequently of man. As an example, a smaller universe would not be old enough for the heavy elements essential to life to be synthesized in the interior of stars. If the universe were larger and older, the stars needed to establish the conditions of life would have long since burnt out. In short, the anthropic principle suggests that man's existence is a constraint on the kinds of universes that he can observe.

Each knowledge system comes with a metaphysics that is hard to disprove within the system. While science has undergone great changes in recent decades it remains materialistic in its core. The dominant belief is that both living and non-living matter is describable by the same laws. It is also believed that consciousness results from the great complexity of a goal-seeking system and, therefore, it should be possible to build machines that have an awareness of their selves. Is this belief justified or will future research show that consciousness needs to be addressed very differently from material phenomena?

Our understanding of the world is fundamentally incomplete.[17] Some believe that the next revolution in physics will necessitate a revision of the theories of relativity and quantum mechanics, which are two pillars of our current understanding of the physical world.

II SPACE AND TIME

Space and geometry

There are two distinct views of the universe. First, space exists only by virtue of the objects defining it, and infinite void is meaningless. Second, space exists independent of any material objects and extends endlessly in all directions. These two views have been debated by philosophers for centuries. Coupled with the two possibilities of finite and infinite pasts, one has four models of the universe.

Puzzles that have been posed about these models in the past include: What lies beyond the boundary of the universe? What existed before the universe came into being? Does an infinitely old, infinitely spaced universe evolve? If it does, what is the nature of this evolution?

Ancient cultures, such as the Greek, the Indian, and the Maya also considered the cyclic variant of the infinitely old universe. In particular, the Indians considered the universe to go through phases of creation and destruction rather akin to the modern scientific view of expansion and contraction.

A paradox-free definition of space, time and matter is impossible since they are integral to the definition of the observer himself. Basic definitions involve self-referral. Thus, for example, any observation of space (say distance) is contingent on several assumptions such as the object dimensions remain unchanged from moment to moment, the instruments are unaffected by their environment, not to mention the assumptions made regarding perception by the experimenter. Realization of this fact caused philosophers, even in early times, to assert that space and time are intuitive concepts that cannot be unambiguously defined.

Early civilizations developed techniques to deal with practical problems of space such as estimation of areas and volumes and numerical methods necessary for basic astronomical observations. The Babylonians, the Greeks, the Chinese, and the Indians were aware of the Pythagorean triangle, which is a right-angled triangle. For a triangle ABC with the right-angle at B, $AC^2 = AB^2 + BC^2$. Integers that satisfy such a relationship are called a Pythagorean triple. Pythagorean triples have been found in cuneiform texts from the Babylonian dynasty of Hammurabi (app 1900 BC). The Chinese book of mathematical problems Nine Chapters on the Mathematical Art written during the Han period (200 BC to 220 AD) gives several problems on right-angled triangles that include a procedure to generate Pythagorean triples. In Greece, methods to construct the triples are ascribed to Pythagoras and Plato.

In India, the Śulba Sūtras (800-500 BC), which are manuals to construct altars, state the general rule followed by several examples of

Pythagorean triples. Seidenberg argues that these Sūtras represent a mathematics that goes back at least to 1800 BC.[1]

The earliest statement of the theorem of the square on the diagonal (Pythagoras theorem), together with some examples, is to be found in the geometry text of Baudhāyana (c. 800 BC). In his Śulba Sūtra 1.12 and 1.13, it is stated:

> The areas (of the squares) produced separately by the length and the breadth of a rectangle together equal the area (of the square) produced by the diagonal. This is observed in rectangles having sides 3 and 4, 12 and 5, 15 and 8, 7 and 24, 12 and 35, and 15 and 36.

The Śulba Sūtras provide techniques to draw altars of different shapes and sizes in a convenient manner. The word *śulba* means a cord, rope, or string and the root *śulb* signifies measurement. The cord has marks (*nyañcana* in Sanskrit) that indicate where the intermediate pegs are to be fixed. Thus a cord of 12 units length with *nyañcana* at 3 and 7, can be readily stretched to yield the right-angled triangle (3, 4, 5).

It is significant that of the six examples given by Baudhāyana, five are primitive triples:

3, 4, 5
12, 5, 13
15, 8, 17
7, 24, 25
12, 35, 37

The only non-primitive triple in the list, namely (15,36, 39) seems to have been included because it was widely known to the readers of the Śulba Sūtra as it is fundamental to the design of the Mahāvedī altar of the Vedic ritual. The significance of the (15, 36, 39) triple derives from the fact that the sum of the three numbers is 90 (one-fourth the days in the year) which equals the size of the altar (base = 30, height =36, and top =24). Although the construction of the Mahāvedī altar in the older Śatapatha Brāhmaṇa does not directly mention the use of *nyañcana* of the cord, it is clear how the (15, 36, 39) triple would serve as an excellent check on the altar dimensions traced on the ground.

The astronomical basis of the Vedic altar ritual was concerned with the harmonization of numbers related to the solar and lunar years. This harmonization had a corresponding psychological basis.

According to Proclus, who wrote a commentary on Euclid's Elements and a survey of Greek geometry based on an earlier account written in 300 AD, now extant, "Thales travelled to Egypt and brought geometry to Hellas. He made many discoveries himself, and in many other things he showed his successors the road to the principles."[2] Herodotus had a similar belief: "When the Nile flooded an agricultural tract it became necessary, for the purposes of taxation, to determine how much land had been lost. From this, to my thinking, the Greeks learnt the art of measuring land." [Herodotus, Histories, II 109].

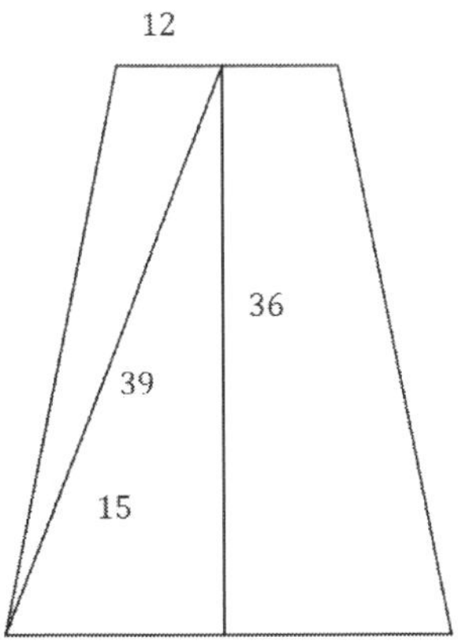

The Mahāvedī altar (base 30, height 36, top 24)

The Śulba Sūtras have different approximations for √2 and π which suggests an understanding of irrational numbers. An irrational number cannot be represented as one integer divided by another, and it requires an infinite number of decimal digits for exact definition. The Śulba Sūtras also dealt with other problems of geometry such as squaring a circle and its inverse of circling a square. The Babylonians also knew approximations to √2. The Greeks found a logical framework in which results of geometry could be proved, as well as established that √2, for example, was irrational.

Consider the proof of the irrationality of √2 that is found in Aristotle's Prior Analytics. Suppose √2 is rational, then √2 = p/q, where by dividing common factors we have ensured that p and q are not both even. Squaring both sides

$$p^2 = 2q^2$$

Since the square of an odd number is odd and that of an even number is even, p alone or p and q both cannot be odd. The case q odd and p even is not possible either because p^2 would be divisible by 4 and $2q^2$ only by 2. By showing that our supposition √2 = p/q is untenable, we have proved that √2 is irrational. The fact that distances in space needed to be represented by quantities other than rational numbers was very disturbing to the Pythagoreans who believed that all things can be reduced to whole numbers.

The dilemma that the Pythagoreans faced was simply due to the implicit assumption that space was a continuum. If space were discrete then one could not always draw straight lines between two points. Nor could points be defined at all places in space. A discrete space assumption would avoid irrational numbers, but it would make most constructions of elementary geometry invalid. The notion of discrete space creates other problems such as what is length of a diagonal in a square? Does the grid of discrete space define an absolute direction in space? The continuum model of space is the pragmatic position since it allows straightforward constructions in geometry. Such a position is also consistent with terrestrial observations.

Euclid expressed geometry in an axiomatic form. In his Elements he systematized geometry by developing a formal system based on axioms. One of the axioms, called the parallel-axiom, asserts that one can draw only one parallel to a given straight line through a given point. This axiom has the character of an observed fact rather than being self-evident, and therefore various efforts were made to derive it from others. His geometry actually implied a space of infinite extent where the shortest distance between two points was given by a straight line. This is equivalent to the sum of angles of a triangle being always 180 degrees. When the earth is taken to be flat with the sky like a dome on it, Euclidean geometry correctly describes the shortest distance between two points being a straight line. But there are difficulties with the notion of the infinite expanse of space. The parallel postulate was examined to determine the nature of its relationship with the other postulates.

Girolamo Saccheri (1667-1733) thought the best way to investigate the significance of the parallel-axiom was to assume that it was false and see its consequences. His treatise derived much of the non-Euclidean geometry, showing that there are three types of geometry based on whether the sum of the angles of a triangle is greater than, equal to, or less than 180 degrees. He took the straight line to have infinite length, which ruled out the first type. In the third type, two straight lines can approach each other indefinitely without ever intersecting, which he believed was unreasonable, causing him to reject this as well.

In the model of infinite space, which was widely accepted during the middle ages, the system of Euclidean geometry appeared perfectly natural. There was resistance in the mathematical circles when Bolyai and Lobachevskii presented approaches to geometry without Euclid's parallel postulate. These approaches were put in perspective by the works of Riemann and Beltrami in the 1860s. According to Riemann, space at each point could be associated with a different value of curvature. Only when curvature is everywhere zero do we get Euclidean geometry. If curvature is non-zero, objects do not move in straight lines. When curvature is zero or constant we can move objects in the space without changing their shapes; otherwise distortions would occur. Riemann also distinguished between the unbounded and the infinite. An example of a curve that is finite but unbounded is the circle. A space may be unbounded but finite and if it has constant positive curvature it has finite radius.

Astronomy and measurement of time

Archaeoastronomical sites are a testament to the ancient man's desire to understand the universe. These sites concern the sun's orbit in terms of its thresholds marking the seasons. Structures were aligned with equinox and solstice days and moon and planet positions in different seasons were marked.

The temple served as the place where time-bound ritual was conducted and keeping time was one of its functions. The English word *temple* is derived from the Latin *templum,* which is sacred space, facing west, that was marked out by the augurs. The east-west orientation of the axis of the temple, which is strictly true only on the two equinoxes, is a testament to the understanding of the annual circuit of the sun.

In India, the temple is associated with the east-west axis and we can trace its origins to priests who maintained different day counts with respect to the solstices and the equinoxes. In the historical period, astronomical observatories were part of temple complexes where the king was consecrated. Such consecration served to confirm the king as foremost devotee of the chosen deity, who was taken to be the embodiment of time and the universe. For example, Udayagiri is an astronomical site connected with the Classical age of the Gupta dynasty (320-500 AD), which is located a few kilometers from Vidisha in Central India. The imperial Guptas enlarged the site, an ancient hilly observatory going back at least to the second century BC at which observations were facilitated by the geographical features of the hill, into a sacred landscape to draw royal authority.

Indian astronomy is characterized by the concept of ages of successive larger durations, which is an example of the pervasive idea of recursion, or repetition of patterns across space, scale and time. An example of this is the division of the ecliptic into 27 star segments (*nakṣatras*), with which the moon is conjoined in its monthly circuit, each of which is further sub-divided into 27 sub-segments (*upa-nakṣatras*), and the successive divisions of the day into smaller measures of 30 units. The idea of recursion underlies the concept of the sacred landscape and it is embodied in art, providing an archaeoastronomical window on sacred and monumental architecture. It appears that this was an old idea because intricate spiral patterns, indicating recursion, are also found in the paintings of the Mesolithic period.

According to the Vāstu Śāstra, the structure of the building mirrors the emergence of cosmic order out of primordial chaos through the act of measurement. The universe is symbolically mapped into a square that emphasizes the four cardinal directions. It is represented by the square vāstu-mandala, which in its various forms is the basic plan for the house and the city. There exist further elaborations of this plan, some of which are rectangular.

It is significant that yantric buildings in the form of mandalas have been discovered in North Afghanistan that belong to a period corresponding to the late stage of the Harappan tradition, which provides architectural evidence in support of the idea of recursion at that time. Although these buildings are a part of the Bactria-Margiana Archaeological Complex (BMAC), their affinity with ideas that are also present in the Harappan system shows that these ideas were widely spread.

India's archaeological record in the northwest has unbroken continuity going back to about 7500 BC at Mehrgarh, and it has a rock art tradition, next only to that of Australia and Africa in abundance, that is much older. Some rock art has been assigned to the Upper Paleolithic period. There is surprising uniformity, both in style and content, in the rock art paintings of the Mesolithic period (10,000 – 2500 BC).

The archaeological phases of the Indus (or Sindhu-Sarasvati) tradition are divided into four eras: *early food-producing era* (c. 6500- 5000 BC), *regionalization era* (5000 – 2600 BC), *integration era* (2600 – 1900 BC), and *localization era* (1900 – 1300 BC). The early food-producing era lacked elaborate ceramic technology. The regionalization era was characterized by styles in ceramics, lapidary arts, glazed faience and seal making that varied across regions. In the integration era, there is significant homogeneity in material culture over a large geographical area and the use of the so-called Indus script, which is not yet deciphered. In the localization era, patterns of the integration era are blended with regional ceramic styles, indicating decentralization and restructuring of the interaction networks. The localization era of the Sindhu-Sarasvati tradition is the regionalization era of the Ganga-Yamuna tradition which transforms into the integration era of the Magadha and the Mauryan dynasties. There is also continuity in the system of weights and lengths between the Harappan period and the later historic period.[3]

The cultural mosaic in the third millennium BC is characterized by the integration phase of the Harappan civilization of Northwest India, copper and copper/bronze age cultures or Central and North India, and Neolithic cultures of South and East India. Five large cities of the integration phase are Mohenjo-Daro, Harappa, Ganweriwala, Rakhigarhi, and Dholavira. Other important sites of this period are Kalibangan, Rehman Dheri, Nausharo, Kot Diji, and Lothal.

A majority of the towns and settlements of the Harappan period were in the Sarasvati valley region. Hydrological changes, extended period of drought, and the drying up of the Sarasvati River due to its major tributaries being captured by the Sindh and Ganga Rivers after an earthquake in 1900 BC led to the abandonment of large areas of the Sarasvati valley. The Harappan phase went through various stages of decline during the second millennium BC. A second urbanization began in the Ganga and Yamuna valleys around 900 BC. The earliest surviving records of this culture are in Brahmi script. This second urbanization is generally seen at the end of the Painted Gray Ware (PGW) phase (1200- 800 BC) and with the use of the Northern Black Polished Ware (NBP) pottery. Late Harappan was partially contemporary with the PGW phase. In other words, a continuous series of cultural developments link the two early urbanizations of India.

The setting for the hymns of the Ṛgveda is the area of Sapta Saindhava, the region of north India bounded by the Sindh and the Ganga rivers although regions around this heartland are also mentioned. The Ṛgveda describes the Sarasvati River to be the greatest of the rivers and going from the mountains to the sea. The archaeological record, suggesting that this river had turned dry by1900 BC, indicates that the Ṛgveda is prior to this epoch. Early Vedic literature has astronomical references related to the shifting astronomical frame that indicate epochs of the fourth and third millennium BC which is consistent with the hydrological evidence. The nakṣatra lists are found in the Vedas, either directly or listed under their presiding deities, and one may conclude that their names have not changed. Vedic astronomy used a luni-solar year in which an intercalary month was employed as adjustment with solar year.

The shifting of seasons through the year and the shifting of the northern axis allow us to date several statements in the Vedic books. Thus the Śatapatha Brāhmaṇa (2.1.2.3) has a statement that points to an earlier epoch where it is stated that the Kṛttikā (Pleiades) never swerve from the east which corresponds to 2950 BC. The Maitrāyaṇīya Brāhmaṇa Upaniṣad (6.14) mentions the winter solstice being at the mid-point of the Śraviṣṭhā segment and the summer solstice at the beginning of Maghā, indicating 1660 BC. The Vedāṅga Jyotiṣa says that the winter solstice was at the beginning of Śraviṣṭhā and the summer solstice at the mid-point of Āśleṣā, which corresponds to about 1300 BC.

The nakshatras in the Vedāṅga Jyotiṣa are defined to be 27 equal parts of the ecliptic. The nakṣatra list of the late Vedic period begin with Kṛttikā (Pleiades) whereas that of the astronomy texts after 200 AD begin with Aśvini (α and β Arietis), indicating a transition through two nakshatras, or a time span of about 2,000 years.

The foundation of Vedic cosmology is the notion of *bandhu* (homologies or binding between the outer and the inner). In the Āyurveda, the medical system associated with the Vedas, 360 days of the year are taken to be mapped to 360 bones of the developing fetus that later fuse into the 206 bones of the person. It was estimated correctly that the sun and the moon were approximately 108 times their respective diameters from the earth (perhaps from the discovery that the angular size of a pole removed 108 times its height is the same as that of the sun and the moon), and this number was used in sacred architecture. The distance to the sanctum sanctorum of the temple from the gate and the perimeter of the temple were 54 and 180 units, which are one-half each of 108 and 360. Homologies at many levels are at the basis of the idea of *recursion,* or repetition in scale and time. The astronomical basis of the Vedic ritual was the reconciliation of the lunar and solar years.

Texts of the Vedic and succeeding periods provide us crucial understanding of the astronomy and the archaeoastronomy of the historical period throughout India. The medieval period was characterized by pilgrimage centers that created sacred space mirroring conceptions of the cosmos. Sacred temple architecture served religious and political ends.

The instruments that were used in Indian astronomy include the water clock (ghaṭī yantra), gnomon (śaṅku), cross-staff (yaṣṭi yantra), armillary sphere (gola yantra), board for sun's altitude (phalaka yantra), sundial (kapāla yantra), and astrolabe.

Ancient cities and sacred geometry

The plan of the city of any ancient civilization reveals much information about the underlying cosmology. If the temple is a representation of the cosmos, so is the sacred city. It is believed that the cardinal orientations of the pyramids were done according to the positions of two stars in the Plough and the Big Dipper, which was known to Egyptians as the thigh. A vertical alignment between these two stars ascertained the north direction.

The Incan Empire was arranged according to their cosmology. The capital, Cusco, was connected to the regions by means of conceptually straight lines radiating out from it. The Indian city reflected either the dichotomy between the sacred and the non-sacred or the trichotomy of the three regions of the earth, the atmosphere, and the sky, which is fundamental to Vedic thought.

The city of Mohenjo-Daro (2500 BC), like most other Harappan cities (with the exception of Dholavira as far as we know at this time) was divided into two parts: the acropolis and the lower city. The Mohenjo-Daro acropolis, a cultural and administrative centre, had as its foundation a 12 meter high platform of 400 m × 200 m. The lower city had streets oriented according to the cardinal directions and provided with a network of covered drains. Its houses had bathrooms. The city's wells were so well constructed with tapering bricks that they have not collapsed in 5000 years. The Great Bath (12 m × 7 m) was built using finely fitted bricks laid on with gypsum plaster and made watertight with bitumen. A high corbelled outlet allowed it to be emptied easily. Massive walls protected the city against flood water.

The absence of monumental buildings such as palaces and temples makes the Harappan city strikingly different from its counterparts of Mesopotamia and Egypt, suggesting that the polity of the Harappan state was decentralized and based on a balance between the political, the mercantile, and the religious elites. The presence of civic amenities such as wells and drains attests to considerable social equality. The power of the mercantile guilds is clear in the standardization of weights of carefully cut and polished chert cubes that form a combined binary and decimal system.

Mohenjo-Daro and other sites show slight divergence of 1° to 2° clockwise of the axes from the cardinal directions. It is thought that this might be due to the orientation of Aldebaran (*Rohiṇī* in Sanskrit) and the Pleiades (*Kṛtikkā* in Sanskrit) that rose in the east during 3000 BC to 2000

BC at the spring equinox; the word 'rohiṇī' literally means rising. The slight difference in the orientations amongst the buildings in Mohenjo-Daro indicates different construction periods using the same traditional sighting points that had shifted in this interval.

Mohenjo-Daro's astronomy used both the motions of the moon and the sun. This is attested by the use of great calendar stones, in the shape of ring, which served to mark the beginning and end of the solar year.

Dholavira is on an island just north of the large island of Kutch in Gujarat.[4] Its strategic importance lay in its control of shipping between Gujarat and the delta of the Sindh and Sarasvati rivers. The layout of Dholavira is unique in that it comprises of three 'towns,' which is in accord with Vedic ideas, and the feature of recursion at different scales. Specifically, the design is characterized by the nesting proportion of 9:4 across the lower and the middle towns and the castle. The proportions of 5/4, 7/6, and 5/4 for the lower town, the middle town, and the castle may reflect the measures related to the royal city, the commander's quarter, and the king's quarter, respectively, which was true of Classical India.

A Dholavira length, D, was determined by finding the largest measure which leads to integer dimensions for the various parts of the city. This measure turns out be the same as the Arthaśāstra (300 BC) measure of dhanus (arrow) that equals 108 aṅgulas (fingers). This scale is confirmed by a terracotta scale from Kalibangan and the ivory scale found in Lothal.

The analysis of the unit of length at Dholavira is in accord with the unit from the historical period. The unit that best fits the Dholavira dimensions is 190.4 cm, which when divided by 108 gives the Dholavira aṅgula of 1.763 cm. The subunit of aṅgula is confirmed when one considers that the bricks in Harappa follow ratios of 1:2:4 with the dominating size being 7 × 14 × 28 cm. These dimensions can be elegantly expressed as 4 × 8 × 16 aṅgulas, with the unit of aṅgula taken as 1.763 cm. It is significant that the ivory scale at Lothal has 27 graduations in 46 mm, or each graduation is 1.76 mm.

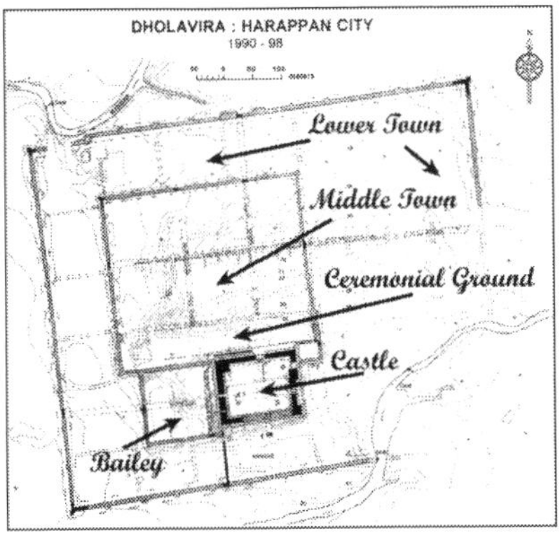

Map of Dholavira

With the new Dholavira unit of D, the dimensions of Mohenjo-Daro's acropolis turn out to be 210 × 105 D; Kalibangan's acropolis turn out to be 126 × 63 D. The dimensions of the lower town of Dholavira are 405 × 324 D; the width of the middle town is 180 D; and the inner dimensions of the castle are 60 × 48 D. The sum of the width and length of the lower town comes to 729 which is astronomically significant since it is 27 × 27, and the width 324 equals the nakṣatra year 27 × 12.

Continuity has been found between the grid and modular measures in the town planning of Harappa and historical India, including that of Kathmandu Valley. The measure of 19.2 meters is the unit in quarter-blocks of Kathmandu; this is nearly the same as the unit characteristic of the dimensions of Dholavira. It shows that the traditional architects and town planners have continued the use of the same units over this long time span.

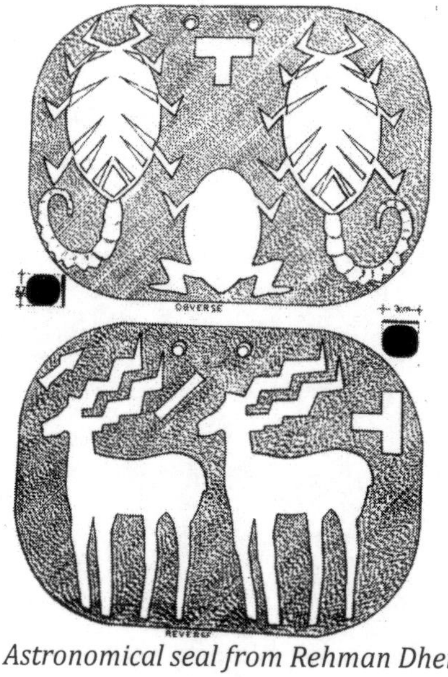

Astronomical seal from Rehman Dheri

A 3rd millennium seal from Rehman Dheri, showing a pair of scorpions on one side and two antelopes on the other, suggests knowledge of Vedic themes. This seal most likely represents the opposition of the Orion (Mṛgaśiras, or antelope head) and the Scorpio (Rohiṇī of the southern hemisphere which is 14 nakshatras from the Rohiṇī of the northern hemisphere) nakshatras. The arrow near the head of one of the antelopes could represent the decapitation of Orion. It is generally accepted that the myth of Prajāpati being killed by Rudra represents the shifting of the beginning of the year away from Orion and it places the astronomical event in the fourth millennium BC.

Neolithic and megalithic sites

Very old Neolithic megaliths with astronomical significance have been discovered in southern Egypt in Nabta Playa and dated to about 2800 BC. In Europe, the oldest megalithic site of astronomical significance is the Passage Grave in Newgrange Ireland with a date of about 3100 BC. For a few days around the winter solstice light, through a hollow box above the main doorway, shines along the central passageway into the heart of the tomb. Stonehenge (3000-1500 BC) in southern England is a spectacular archaeological site. It consists of massive circle of standing stones capped by lintels and in the outer circle the stones are 14 feet high. It is characterized by several alignments of which the most famous is the midsummer alignment in which the sun rises over the Heel Stone.

Interesting sites of archaeoastronomical interest include the Neolithic site of Burzahom from Kashmir in North India, and megalithic sites from Brahmagiri and Hanamsagar from Karnataka in South India.

The Neolithic site of Burzahom is located about 10 km northeast of Srinagar in the Kashmir Valley on a terrace of Late Pleistocene-Holocene deposits. Dated to around 3000 - 1500 BC, its deep pit dwellings are associated with ground stone axes, bone tools, and gray burnished pottery. A stone slab of 48 cm × 27 cm, obtained from a phase dated to 2125 BC shows two bright objects in the sky with a hunting scene in the foreground. These have been assumed to be a depiction of a double star system.

The megalithic stone circles of Brahmagiri in the Chitradurga district of Karnataka in South India, which are dated to 900 BC, show astronomical orientations. It has been suggested that site lines from the center of a circle to an outer tangent of another circle point to the directions of the sunrise and full moon rise at the time of the solar and lunar solstices and equinox.

Hanamsagar is a megalithic site with stone alignments pointing to cardinal directions. It is located on a flat area between hills about 6 km north of the Krishna river at latitude 16° 19′ 18″ and longitude 76° 27′ 10″. The stones, which are smooth granite, are arranged in a square of side that is about 600 meters with 50 rows and 50 column (for a total of 2,500 stones), with a separation between stones of about 12 m. The stones are between 1 to 2.5 m in height with a maximum diameter of 2 to 3 m and there is a squarish central structure. The lines are oriented in cardinal directions.

It appears that the directions of summer and winter solstice can be fixed in relation to the outer and the inner squares. It could have been used for several other kind of astronomical observations such as use of shadows to tell the time of the day, the prediction of months, seasons and passage of the year.

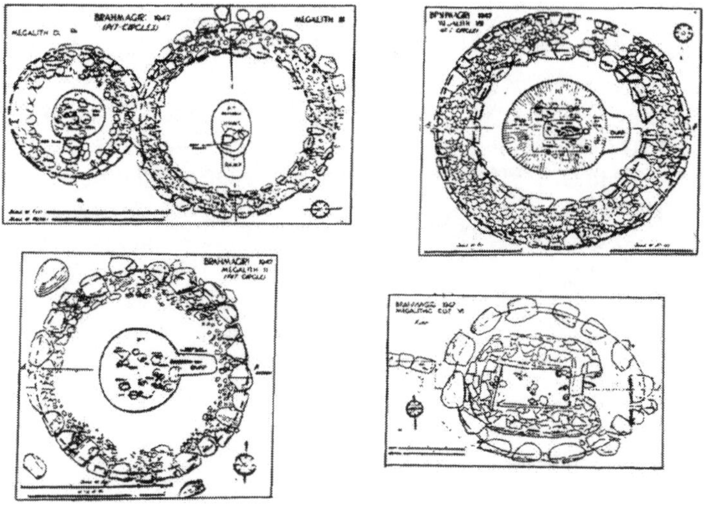

Megalithic stone circles of Brahmagiri

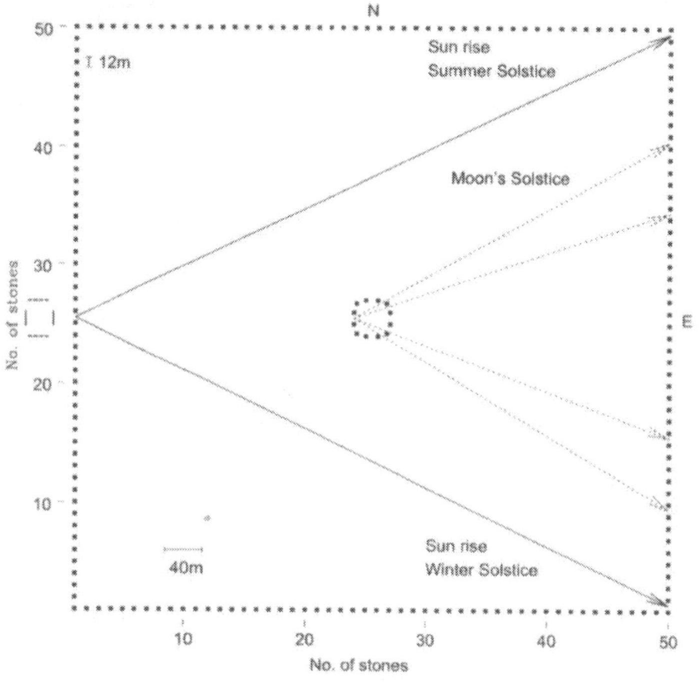

Alignments at Hanamsagar

The plan of the temple

The sacred ground for Vedic ritual is the precursor to the temple. The Vedic observances were connected with the circuits of the sun and the moon. The altar ritual was associated with the east-west axis and we can trace its origins to priests who maintained different day counts with respect to the solstices and the equinoxes. Specific days were marked with ritual observances that were done at different times of the day.

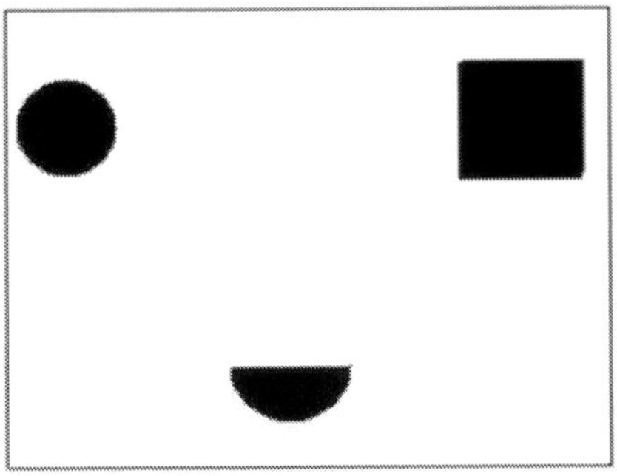

The three altars of the Vedic house: circular (earth, body), half-moon (atmosphere, prāna), square (sky, consciousness)

In the ritual at home, the householder employed three altars that are circular (earth), half-moon (atmosphere), and square (sky), which are like the head, the heart, and the body of the Cosmic Man. In the Agnicayana, the great ritual of the Vedic times that forms a major portion of the narrative of the Yajurveda, the atmosphere and the sky altars are built afresh in a great ceremony to the east. This ritual is based upon the Vedic division of the universe into three parts of earth, atmosphere, and sky that are assigned numbers 21, 78, and 261, respectively. The numerical mapping is maintained by placement of 21 pebbles around the earth altar, sets of 13 pebbles around each of 6 intermediate ($13 \times 6 = 78$) altars, and 261 pebbles around the great new sky altar called the Uttara-vedi, which is built in the shape of a falcon. These numbers add up to 360, which is symbolic representation of the year. The proportions related to these three numbers, and others related to the motions of the planets, and angles related to the sightings of specific stars are reflected in the plans of the temples of the historical period.

The Agnicayana altar is the prototype of the temple and of the tradition of architecture (*vāstu*). The altar is first built of 1,000 bricks in five layers (that symbolically represent the five divisions of the year, the five physical elements, as well as five senses) to specific designs. The altar is constructed in a sequence of 95 years, whose details are matched to the reconciliation of the lunar and solar years by means of intercalary months.

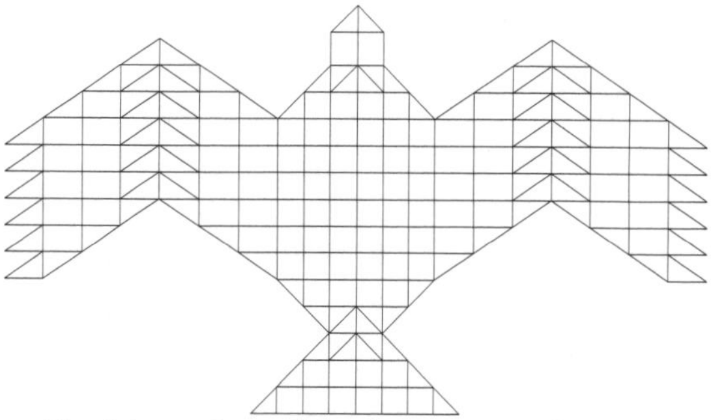

The falcon altar of the Agnicayana altar

In the ritual ground related to the ceremony, the Uttara-vedi is 54 units from the entrance in the west and the perimeter of the ritual ground is 180 units. These proportions characterize many later temples.

Invariance Laws

The archaeoastronomical sites that are a record of man's determination of the regularities in natural phenomena were the first steps in the discovery of the laws of nature. The universe was first conceived to be a hollow sphere. The motions of the planets and the stars were understood.

The understanding of space and time evolved as the focus changed from what is changing to laws on what remains unchanged or invariant. While such laws[5] skirt the question of what space and time are, they make it possible to discover their symmetries. In turn, symmetries can be related to conservation laws.

The first step required for understanding is to accept the proposition that laws of nature determine the domain of regularities of the world and observed irregularities are due to irregular initial conditions. Initial conditions can be related to still earlier initial conditions, which lead to the cosmological problem of the creation of the universe. There is also the problem of the evolution of the world.

The second step to our understanding is the fact that given a set of initial conditions we get the same result, no matter where and when the process is studied. In other words absolute time and space do not form a part of the initial conditions. Put still differently, the laws of nature are invariant with respect to the displacement in space and time.

A superficial observation of natural phenomena, which corresponds to an intuitive or commonsensical understanding, suggests that all bodies persist in their state of rest unless acted upon by an external force, and the laws of nature apply equally irrespective of the absolute magnitude of objects (the principle of similitude). Both these principles held sway in physics over long intervals of time.

A closer examination of physical processes reveals that both of the above hypotheses are not completely correct. In fact careful observation shows that physical laws are invariant not only with respect to the absolute position and time as also to the object's orientation and its state of motion, as long as this remains uniform, free of rotation, and on a straight line. In fact representation of the object in a stationary and a moving frame allow two complementary descriptions. Various kinds of upper and lower limits in physics (such as the speed of light, quantum of action) disprove the principle of similitude. This shows that the laws of invariance are obtained by empirical observations and do not follow from any a priori logic.

Invariance laws are often determined by examining the symmetries apparent in nature. The most familiar symmetries are spatial or geometric. Thus if a square were to be rotated through 90 degrees it leaves the figure unchanged. In other words a square is invariant with respect to 90 degree rotations and a circle has continuous symmetry because rotation by any angle leaves it unchanged. An example of non-geometric symmetry is the charge symmetry of electro-magnetism. For a system of charged particles the forces remain unchanged if all the charges are reversed.

It was Emmy Noether who in her work between 1910 and 1920 discovered the link between symmetry properties of physical objects and conservation laws. She found that if one requires the action of any field to be unchanged under a continuous symmetry operation, then there exists a field quantity, characteristic of that operation, which is conserved. A continuous operation is one which can be obtained by a continuous succession of small steps from the identity operation. Examples of continuous operations are translations in time, translations in space, and rotations in space. Noether's result enables one to see the law of conservation of energy as a consequence of symmetry with respect to translations in time. In a similar manner, symmetry with respect to the three spatial translations can be interpreted as the laws of conservation of the three components of momentum, and invariance under spatial rotations can be looked upon as the law of conservation of angular momentum.

Relativity of space and time

Āryabhaṭa (born 476) was the first person to speak of relativity of space and time. He took the earth to be spinning on its axis and he gave the periods of the planets with respect to the sun. His figure for the sidereal rotation of the earth was extremely accurate. He made important innovations in planetary computations by using simplifying hypotheses, and he presented a method of finding the celestial latitudes of the planets.

Galileo is generally credited with the relativity principle defined as the impossibility of using "any mechanical experiment to determine absolute uniform velocity." Although there is no explicit mention of this impossibility principle in Āryabhaṭa's work, most elements that contribute to this principle are stated. In particular, there is explicit mention of relativity of space, and there is also mention of relativity as in the [uniform] motion of the boat, as well the [regular non-uniform] motion of the stars. In his book, Āryabhaṭīya, it is claimed:[6]

> Similar to a person in a boat moving forward who sees the stationary objects on the bank of the river as moving backwards, the stationary stars at Lanka (equator) are viewed as moving westwards .
>
> An illusion is created similarly that the entire structure of asterisms together with the planets is moving exactly towards the west of Lanka, being constantly driven by the provector wind, to cause their rising and setting.
>
> Heavens and the Meru mountain are at the center of the land (i.e., at the North Pole); Naraka and the Badavamukha are at the center of the water (i.e., at the South Pole). The gods (residing at the Meru Mountain) and the demons (residing at the Badavamukha) consider *themselves positively and permanently below each other.*
>
> Divide the distance between the two bodies moving in the opposite directions by the sum of their speeds, and the distance between the two bodies moving in the same direction by the difference of their speeds; the two quotients will give the time elapsed since the two bodies met or to elapse before they will meet.

Āryabhaṭa states that observers on earth do not experience their own rotational motion, observers away from the earth will detect a westward motion. Implicitly, the laws of motion remain the same for moving objects on earth. This amounts to the position that regular motion can be detected only by observing the system from another reference frame, a view that is virtually identical to Galilean relativity.

Newton wrote in Principia: "The relative motions of two bodies in a given space are identical whether this space is at rest or whether it moves uniformly in a straight line without circular motion." He affirmed a principle of relativity of motion although he also postulated the existence of an absolute space. This was partly owing to his preoccupation with circular motion which he tried to show to be absolute by his famous experiment on the curvature of the water surface in a rotating pail. He ended up asserting that "absolute space was defined by its own nature, without relation to anything external, remaining always similar and immovable." In a similar vein he defined the concept of "absolute, true and mathematical time" which "of itself and from its own nature, flows equally without relation to anything external, and by another name is called duration."

In absolute time one can talk of absolute simultaneity of events and of absolute rest and absolute motion. As a logical extension of these ideas, Newton claimed that the center of the system of the world was at rest. But an identification of the center of the world or of the state of absolute rest defines directional characteristics of space and time that could be valid only if the laws of nature were non-uniform. During Newton's time his views were challenged by Huygens and Leibnitz who did not believe in absolute space. But the debate did not separate the problem of relativity into that of circular and rectilinear motions.

Descartes' (1644) mechanistic conception of the universe raised the problem of the nature of the interplanetary space that was permeated by ether. The wave theory of light of Hooke (1667) and Huygens (1678) made ether imperative. Since it had been demonstrated earlier that light could travel through vacuum, it was clear that ether permeated matter and vacuum as well.

In a lecture given in 1905, Minkowski argued, "No one has yet observed a place except at a time, nor yet a time except at a place." Therefore, an object should be defined by means of a curve in a four-dimensional continuum spanned by three spatial dimensions and one time dimension.

Light and its speed

The nature of light was debated between the proponents of the wave-theory and that of the corpuscular theory. By the early nineteenth century the wave theory was quite firmly established. Young proposed the general law of interference of light to explain reflection, refraction and diffraction. He also explained stellar aberration, an apparent elliptical motion of the stars associated with the earth's motion around the sun, by using wave theory. He suggested that if the ether surrounding the earth is at rest and unaffected by the earth's motions, then light waves will not be affected by the motion of the telescope and the image of the star will be displaced by a distance equal to that which the earth travels while the light is traveling through the telescope, in agreement with what is actually observed. Meanwhile by experiments on polarization it had been established that light vibrations were transverse.

The speed of light was measured by Rømer (1675) on the basis of the delays observed in the eclipses of the satellites of Jupiter. Experiments were performed (1810) to determine whether this speed was dependent on the speed of the source. The negative result of this experiment could not be explained by Young's hypothesis. Fresnel was, therefore, compelled to put forward a new hypothesis of the partial dragging of the ether by bodies with an index of refraction larger than that of vacuum.

Faraday (1831) had about this time initiated the study of propagation of electric and magnetic forces. Maxwell by 1862 completed a mechanical theory of the propagation of the electrical and magnetic fields through a medium taken as an elastic solid. There was a tendency to consider this elastic solid to be the same as the ether. By 1864 Maxwell presented another version of his theory that did not invoke the solid medium.

Michelson and Morley (1887) performed an experiment to measure the speed of the earth through ether. The basic idea of the experiment was to compare the times (or velocities) along two paths at right angles, one of which may be thought of as aligned with the earth's motion. The velocity along the perpendicular direction should not be affected by the motion and the comparison should make possible a determination of v, the ether velocity. The comparison of the two times was made by letting the two light rays interfere. The result of this experiment was negative.

To explain the null result regarding ether speed, Fitzgerald, Lorentz, Larmor and Poincaré suggested that bodies in motion through ether underwent a contraction in the motion's direction by a factor $\sqrt{(1 - v^2/c^2)}$, where c is the speed of light. Furthermore, to keep the equations of motion unaltered in form while going from the frame of reference S of the ether to the terrestrial frame S', the following transformation for the time was postulated

$$t' = (t - vx/c^2) / \sqrt{(1 - v^2/c^2)}$$

where t is the time in S, t' in S' and the relative motion is along the x axis.

Lorentz believed that the ether was at rest in absolute space and contraction of time and space were introduced as postulates to account for electrodynamic events being perceived similarly by two observers in uniform motion with respect to each other. Poincaré and Einstein in 1905 showed that Lorentz transformations followed from the relativity principle. According to this principle all observers subject to no forces (inertial observers) were equivalent, and that the speed of light was constant for all inertial observers. This principle was independently formulated earlier by Poincaré[7] in 1904.

The relativity principle embodies the fact that attempts to find the influence of the motion of the earth on mechanical, electromagnetic, and optical phenomena have been fruitless. It implies that one cannot associate an objective value of size, velocity or passage of time with any object. A classification of objects may be done on the basis of uniform velocities or accelerated motions and not on the basis of absolute rest.

The concept of absolute simultaneity becomes invalid. To see this consider a square ABCD whose diagonals intersect at E. If light flashes occur simultaneously at the nodes A, B, C, and D this fact would be recorded so by an observer at E. Consider, now another observer who is moving at a high velocity along the diagonal AC. With respect to this observer the flashes at A and C would have occurred prior to those at B and D simply because relative to it the length AC is smaller than BD. As another example, consider a spaceship in which an astronaut arranges for two pulses of light to be sent out at the same time, from the center of the spaceship to its ends. He would see the pulses strike the opposite ends of the spacecraft simultaneously.

However, with respect to an observer on the earth, if the spacecraft is moving away with a large speed the pulse to the rear end would reach sooner than to the front end. This is because the light pulses travel with constant speed with respect to the earthbound observer as well, and subsequent to the flashing of the pulses from the center, the rear end approaches, and the front end retreats from its pulse. In fact one cannot, in general, synchronize clocks because one does not know what correction should be made for the distance travelled by light flashes if these are used for synchronization purpose. On the other hand, if one took a collection of clocks and physically transported it to other stations, there would be no way one could determine the effect of transportation on the rate of the clocks.

It should be clear that Newton, by accepting instantaneous action at a distance in his theory of gravitation, had to consider time as absolute; if we formally put $c = \infty$ in the time and length contraction formulas, we obtain $t' = t$. Instantaneous transmission of signals would allow us to synchronize clocks in all inertial systems independently of their relative velocities. In Newtonian mechanics, gravitational forces play the part of such instantaneous signals.

The relativity of time does not imply a rejection of the objectivity of its measurement in any given system of reference. For each system of reference, its own time is completely objective. This is similar to the relativity of time datum in different time zones on the earth. In fact why it is hard for flat-earthers to accept the sphericity of the earth is the belief in an absolute direction of space, which implies that a man walking on the opposite side of the globe would simply fall off.

The preceding ideas imply a structure relating space and time is inferred from the fact that the Lorentz transformation leaves the following quantity unaltered:

$$c^2t^2 - \ell^2 = c^2t'^2 - \ell'^2 = s^2$$

where $\ell^2 = x^2 + y^2 + z^2$.

We can now speak of spacetime as having three space coordinates with time (*ict*) as the fourth coordinate. The quantity (*is*), which is the interval between two events, is thus a generalization of the notion of distance:

$$-s^2 = x^2 + y^2 + z^2 - c^2t^2.$$

Let the spatial distance between the points at which two events occurred be taken along the abscissa, and the interval of time between them, along the ordinate axis. To begin with, if $ct > \ell$, $s^2 = c^2t^2 - \ell^2$.

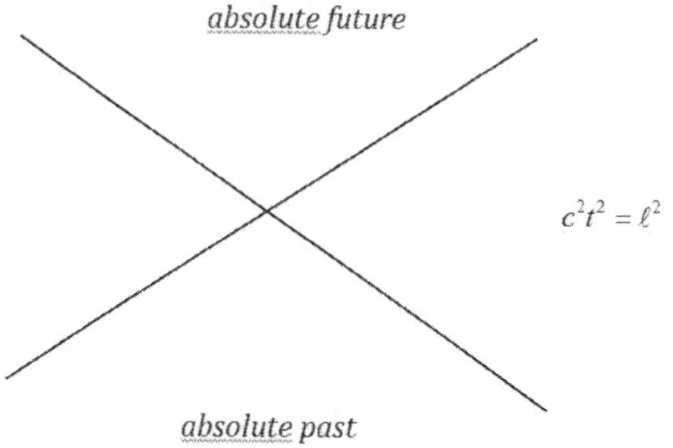

We consider values of *ct* and ℓ corresponding to two definite events measured in different inertial systems. No matter what are the values of individual measurements of ct and ℓ, the time interval *s* between the events is the same. It follows that the locus of the points, for all possible spatial distances ℓ and time intervals *ct*, is an equilateral hyperbola $s^2 = c^2t^2 - \ell^2$. Two branches of the hyperbola are possible: one lies in the past relative to the event that occurred at *t=0, x=0,* while the other is completely in the future. It is easy to see that such a relationship inevitably results if the events are causally related.

Examining the figure one can check that absolute nature of the simultaneity of two events has no meaning. Two events that appear simultaneous in a certain frame of reference may not appear so in another frame. In general, concepts have no meaning unless one defines the necessary measurements which give meaning to these statements. This approach to the definition of concepts in terms of precise measurement procedures has had a great deal of influence on the development of modern science.

The application of the transformation relations of the relativity theory to expressions of energy yields the equation $E = mc^2$, which connects the mass of an object to its energy. It has been confirmed in both laboratory scale and large scale nuclear reactions providing experimental support for the underlying theory.[8]

Amongst evidence supporting time dilation is the apparent increase in lifetime of muons which are elementary particles that are produced at heights of about 10 kilometers by cosmic ray showers. The lifetime of a muon with respect to an observer moving with the particle is about 2 microseconds. During this lifetime a muon can penetrate barely a mile of the atmosphere. The time dilatation factor for the muon at its speed of about .995*c* is of the order of 10, which explains how these particles penetrate 10 kilometers of the atmosphere with relative ease to arrive on the surface of the earth.

Specially designed clocks were flown in 1971 on jet planes, traveling at about 600 miles per hour, on two trips circumnavigating the earth, one eastward and the other westward. The theory predicts a difference between the times on these clocks with the time of an earthbound clock. The observed values of time were in good agreement with the predicted values. Experiments with electrons in magnetic fields also confirm the time dilation effect. The most accurate verification of time dilation was made on an experimental setup using lasers.[9]

Time dilation opens up the possibility of travel to the distant reaches of the universe, if only in theory. By traveling at a speed that is within one hundred miles per hour of the speed of light, an astronaut can journey to the nearest star in less than one day (by his clock), even through the same journey measured from the earth takes over four years. At a speed of only one mile per hour less than the speed of light, the time dilation is so large, that the astronaut can circumnavigate the entire galaxy in a few years and return to the earth to find himself in 400,000 AD! However, such time travel belongs to the realm of science fiction because the energy required to speed up the spacecraft to high enough values is so large so as to be unattainable.

Paradoxes of relativity

Many paradoxes related to special relativity are known.[10] We will describe a few representative ones.

The Trapdoor Paradox

A rigid measuring rod of length 2L is accelerated to a velocity close to that of light and made to enter a box of width L through a trapdoor. Relative to the box the rod is very short and therefore there is enough time to shut the trapdoor. Relative to the rod the box is too small for the trapdoor to shut. What happens?

The Railway Paradox

A train approaches the gap in the lengths of the railway track at a speed near that of light. Relative to the train the gap is infinitesimal in width and the ride should be virtually bump free. Relative to the track the train is shorter than the width of the gap and so it should fall in because of gravity. Does the train fall in?

The Twin Paradox

Alice and Bob are twins. Alice stays at home and Bob travels in a spacecraft at a speed close to that of light and eventually returns to Earth. Alice has meanwhile aged 60 years. She expects Bob to have aged only 4 years during this period owing to time dilation. Relative to Bob Alice has been moving at high speeds, and therefore on his return she should have aged only 4 years. Can the question of the actual aging of Alice and Bob be resolved?

Several arguments are proposed to resolve these paradoxes. For the first two it is claimed that there is no paradox because with respect to both the viewpoints the situation is ultimately the same. In the trapdoor paradox there is not enough time to spring the trap and therefore the rod will bounce out. In the railway paradox, the train would be carried over the gap by its momentum.

The twin paradox was first described by Langevin in 1911 and it is also called the clock paradox. A large number of papers were written on this paradox with many explanations some of which contradict each other. According to Einstein, Bob would be the younger person on the return from his journey and "if we placed a living organism in a box ... one could arrange that the organism, after any arbitrary lengthy flight, could be returned to Its original spot in a scarcely altered condition, while corresponding organisms which had remained in their original positions had already long since given way to new generations. For the moving organism the lengthy time of the journey was a mere instant, provided the motion took place at approximately the speed of light."

The slowing down of the aging process of Bob is taken to be the result of time dilation. This argument is criticized on the grounds that since the situation is essentially symmetrical there can be no absolute time dilation effect. In my view the motions of the two twins must be considered relative to the rest of the universe.[11]

In other paradoxes the difficulty is due to the consideration of a setting which is physically impossible. Thus absolutely rigid objects do not exist in addition to being incompatible with the special theory of relativity. Thought experiments dealing with rigid objects lead to paradoxes. When non-uniform motions are involved one requires a deeper study of space and time. To illustrate this consider a long blade moving at a constant angular velocity. If the blade is long enough and the angular velocity is sufficiently large, the tip of the blade should move at speeds faster than light. Since that is forbidden by the relativity principle, acceleration of the tip to such high speeds is not possible.

The contradictoriness related to the paradox may be due to the fact that the statement is interpreted in different ways by different readers. In the twin paradox, a 'resolution' may ignore the fact that the earth itself is not in uniform motion, and that it is moving around the sun, which, in turn, is moving in the galaxy, and so on, and that there is a further accelerating expansion of the universe. Or, a 'resolution' might privilege one frame against another, by assuming knowledge beyond what is in the statement of the paradox.

Here's a variant to the Twin Paradox: One of the two twins goes off in the direction opposite to the earth's rotation around the sun in a spaceship, and starts lagging it further and further. To do so, it must accelerate and then at some point decelerate to establish its orbit. The earth, since it is going faster, eventually catches up with the spaceship. When the twins meet and compare their clocks, the clock of which twin loses time? According to the earthbound twin, it is the twin in the spaceship whose clock would register less time since it was the one that went through acceleration and deceleration. But with respect to the Sun, the twin in the spaceship had lesser speed, and it should have lost less time than the twin who remained on the Earth.

The Triplet Paradox

Let's say the earth has a hole that goes right through it. Two of the triplets fall right through it and oscillate at high speed through this cylindrical hole. If this continues for a long time, they would be 'younger' to their third brother on the ground. Now how about if they fall from opposite ends? They are moving with respect to each other, so how much does each one of them age compared to the triplet on the ground?

Non-uniform motion

Consider two frames: A is stationary and B is in non-uniform motion. The motion of B is not only being viewed in relation to A, but the rest of an isotropic universe. The motion of B begins at time 0 and it continues until time *W*.

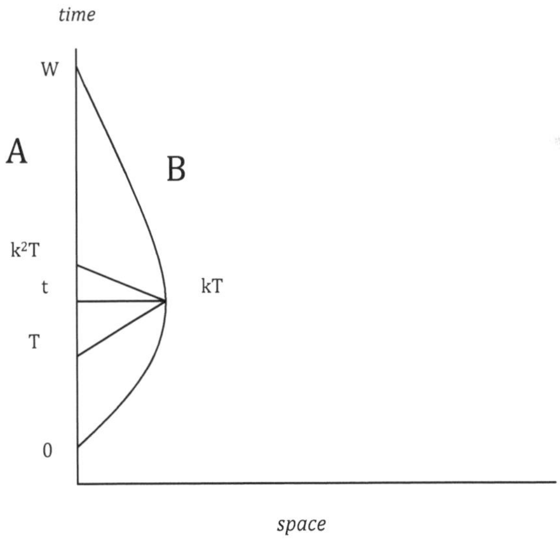

The functional relationship describing the distance of B with respect to A is $x = f(t)$ and, naturally, $f(0) = f(W) = 0$. We now consider the specific example

$$x = a\,Wt - a\,t^2$$

Due to the non-uniform motion of B, the velocity of B changes and it is equal to $v(t) = \frac{dx}{dt} = aW - 2at$. If A signals B at its own time T, it is received by B at its own time kT, where k represents the measure of time dilation, and it is received back by A at the time k^2T.

The velocity of light c for frame A is

$$c = \frac{2x}{(k^2 - 1)T}$$

$$v = \frac{x}{t} = \frac{f(t)}{t}$$

A straightforward calculation shows that

$$\frac{v}{c} = \frac{k^2 - 1}{k^2 + 1} \qquad k = \sqrt{\frac{c + v}{c - v}}$$

This can also be written as the ratio of the two clock times t_1 and t_2, $d = t_1/t_2$:

$$d = \frac{1}{\sqrt{1 - \frac{v^2}{c^2}}}$$

The significant thing is that this does not require the assumption of uniform motion but the ratio of the two time clocks will continue to change as the velocity of B changes.

One may also write

$$\int_0^W \frac{t_1^2 - t_2^2}{t_1^2} dt = \frac{a^2 W^3}{3c^2}$$

This tells us that the cumulative per unit difference in squares of the times on the two clocks is proportional to cube of the time at which the two frames meet.

III MATTER AND MOTION

Gravitational attraction

Time, space and matter are three entities that must be defined in relation to each other. Matter interactions are mediated through several kinds of forces, of which gravitation was historically the first to be carefully examined. Gravitation is different from other forces in so much that it can be expressed as a property of space-time. All particles react to the gravitational field, and in fact they react in the same manner, independent of their mass or composition. Near the earth's surface this is exemplified by Galileo's law that acceleration due to gravity is independent of mass. Contrast this with the electromagnetic force where the resulting accelerations depend on the nature of the charged particles.

The fact that objects on the surface of the earth react almost equally to its gravitational field owes to the property that this field is effectively uniform at any height for a flat terrain. For a planet revolving round the sun, its regions nearest and farthest from the sun experience different forces, resulting in solar tides. The universal observable of gravitation is the relative acceleration of neighboring particles.

The study of the motions of the sun and the planets against the background of the fixed stars led to the science of astronomy. These motions are quite predictable among the stars, the sun completing its circuit once a year and the moon about once a month. The motion of the planets, viewed from the earth is complicated by the earth's own motion, and the planets appear to move forward sometimes and backward at other times. Aristarchus in the third century BC proposed a heliocentric model where the planets move in simple circles around the sun. Since the actual orbits deviate from circularity, a prediction using the Aristarchus model could be considerably in error. In the second century, Ptolemy presented a method of predicting planetary motions to within a maximum of about one percent. In this method, the apparent complexity of the motions was accounted for by assuming that the planets moved in epicycles in their orbits around the earth. The followers of Ptolemy believed that this method represented the actual reality, and soon the geocentric model became preeminent and it remained popular until the time of Copernicus, Galileo and Kepler.

In India, Āryabhaṭa, Brahmagupta (628 AD) and Bhāskara (1150 AD) used a version of the epicycle model to predict eclipses and the positions of planets. Gravity was understood as the attractive force exercised by the earth on a material body.

The ancient astronomers were able to realize that the earth is round. It is believed that Eratosthenes, the librarian of Alexandria, made a calculation of the radius of the earth in about 200 BC. He observed that at

Aswan on the Upper Nile at midsummer noon, a gnomon cast no shadow except for that cast by the bob itself, whereas at Alexandria, 500 miles (app 5000 stadia) to the north at the mouth of the Nile, the gnomon cast a shadow equal to 1/8 of its length at the same time of day and year. The sun is so far away that its rays may be considered to be parallel. At midsummer noon if the sun is directly overhead at Aswan, It lies south of the vertical by an angle at the center of the earth equal to that subtended by the distance between these cities. Eratosthenes estimated that 500 miles represented 1/8 of the radius of the earth which is close to its true value. But since the straight-line distance between Aswan and Alexandria was not known with accuracy, the estimate is a projection using current knowledge. Eratosthenes' estimate of the earth's circumference could have been a lucky coincidence given that Strabo's Geographica provides distances for regions in Egypt that are divisors of a large astronomical measure and, therefore, wrong.

Our idea of stade comes from Ptolemy's Encyclopaedia of geography in which it is defined as being equal to 2/15 of a Roman mile. Ptolemy believed that a degree was equal to 500 stades implying that the earth had a circumference of 180,000 stades. But stade was not a standardized measure.

The concept of momentum can be traced back to Hipparchus in the second century BC. By the fifteenth century the notions of velocity and acceleration were well understood. William Ockham of England argued that forces could act at a distance without direct contact. Leonardo da Vinci claimed that perpetual motion was impossible and that falling bodies accelerated uniformly.

In the history of natural sciences, terrestrial and celestial aspects have played an intertwined role, each defining constraints and context for the other. Celestial ideas underlying science are often left unstated in an attempt to keep the narrative straightforward. Thus the machine-like cosmology underlying classical science is not stressed, because it creates problems related to origin of consciousness and the question of free-will and agency in a causally closed world. The interplay between machine cosmology and the agency of the individual reveals new frontiers for scientific exploration.

The relationship between the terrestrial and the celestial issues is seen most clearly in the astronomical and astrological tradition of Ptolemy, Copernicus, Galileo, and Kepler. Visions of the cosmos, models of the planetary motions, astrology, and theological ideas about man's place in the universe informed this tradition. The role of astrological notions in the development of modern science is often left out in modern histories. But this is at the cost of insight into the process of discovery, because the thinker in the ancient world was motivated by the equation between the cosmic and the terrestrial.

At one level, the question of the position of the earth in the universe is central to this inquiry. The eventual abandonment of the geocentric model for the heliocentric took place over great theological resistance in Europe. This was because the physical centrality of the earth in the universe was a central belief of the Christian Church, although it originated in the earlier Aristotelian ideas. This was in contrast to India where the earth did not play a central role in cosmology. In the Purāṇas, there is mention of innumerable world systems beyond our own. The Purāṇic system was already in place before the classical siddhantic astronomy of Āryabhaṭa Why the Indian and the Greek scientific traditions moved in different directions -- the Indian algebraic and computational and the Greek geometric – is an interesting story.

Claudius Ptolemy wrote his book in Alexandria in 145 AD but its original is lost. It is known to us as the Almagest, which is its twelfth century Arabic version. This book incorporated earlier ideas from the ancient world, in particular from Mesopotamia and Egypt, and it was to become the standard textbook of astronomy in the West for centuries. The Almagest was later translated back into Greek and it is likely to have accretion of Islamic material, which is especially true of the sections concerning star locations that were given much attention by Islamic astronomers.

Ptolemy also wrote the Tetrabiblos, a book on astrology. The connection between astronomy and astrology is related to the belief that the events in the sky are mirrored by those on the earth. This idea played an important role in the work of many astronomers, including Brahe and Kepler. Astrology was connected to medicine, and parts of medical prognosis and treatment were determined by astrological information. Treatment was based on the astrologically favorable moment. Each sign of the zodiac, like the planets, was thought to rule a part of the human body.

Bloodletting, used to correct the imbalance of bodily humors, was regulated by the position of the moon. When the moon was in the zodiac ruling a particular part of the body, bloodletting from that part was to be avoided, since the attraction of the moon might cause excessive bleeding. The power of the moon's pulling power varied by its phases. Ptolemy and Kepler were astrologers, and Copernicus and Galileo had studied medicine.

The Greek astronomical tradition

Anaximander (sixth century BC) believed the stars to be condensations of air filled with fire. He took the Sun to be the highest of the heavenly bodies, followed by the Moon, the fixed stars, and planets, in that order. He assumed that the earth was a cylinder, on whose one end were situated the livable continents. The earth rested in the middle of the universe.

The Pythagoreans took the earth to be a sphere. The fixed stars moved in regular motion; however, the seven planets (Sun, Moon, Mercury, Venus, Mars, Jupiter, and Saturn) did not always do so. The Pythagoreans believed the natural world to be governed by laws. Plato (fifth century BC) focused on the certainty of mathematical ideas, so that he had much affinity to Pythagorean notions, although he was different from them in that he emphasized geometric models. He is believed to have asked if the planetary motions were actually regular and uniform like that of the stars. Regarding the creation of the world, Plato spoke of the Demiurge, whom he mentions frequently in the Timaeus as the entity who fashioned and shaped the material world. He describes the Demiurge as unreservedly good and hence desirous that the world should be as good as possible. The reason why the world is imperfect is that the Demiurge had to work on pre-existing chaotic matter.

During the period of 450-150 BC the Greeks kept astronomical and meteorological diaries called parapegmata. The early parapegmata mention the names of the astronomers Meton and Euctemon. Meton suggested that in 19 years occur almost exactly 235 months, and this could be used to correlate solar and lunar calendars. Euctemon gave 90, 90, 92, and 93 days as the lengths of the seasons. Although, not accurate for its times, it meant that the Greeks were already discovering asymmetries in the cosmic order.

Eudoxus (fourth century BC) suggested that the retrograde motions of the five lesser planets could be explained by considering four concentric spheres. The planet was located at the equator of a sphere spinning uniformly, and this sphere was embedded into a second sphere, concentric with it, that was spinning about a different axis and which carried round with it the inner sphere. The outer sphere was, in turn, carried around by a third sphere located outside it, whose spin generated the west-to-east motion of the planet along the ecliptic; and this third sphere was, in turn, carried round by a fourth sphere that reproduced the east-to-west motion of the planet around the earth. The outer two spheres thus reproduced the principal movements of the planet, whereas the two inner spheres explained (qualitatively and not quantitatively) the retrograde motions.

Eudoxus proposed three nested spheres for the Moon and the sun. The outermost sphere for the Moon generated its daily east-to-west motion; the speeds of the inner spheres were for the lunar month and the 18.6-year eclipse cycle. In total, 27 spheres were needed in this model: 4 for each of the lesser planets, 3 each for the Moon and the sun, and one for the fixed stars.

Aristotle (384-322 BC) attempted to make the scheme consistent by combining different spheres and postulating new spheres between one nest and another. Each additional sphere had the same axis as the given nest, but it had motion in the opposite direction. By this system, the peculiar motions of one planet were prevented from being transmitted down to the planets within. More details of the spheres are to be found in the works of Simplicius (sixth century AD) who wrote commentaries on Aristotle's writings.

Aristotle saw a basic difference between terrestrial and celestial regions: terrestrial phenomena were associated with impermanence and death, whereas celestial phenomena were associated with geometric perfection and circular motion. He gave several reasons for believing the earth to be spherical. Foremost amongst these is that the natural movement of the element earth is downward.

Regarding whether the earth moved, he noted that heavy bodies fell toward the center of the earth for this was their natural tendency. This would then be the natural tendency of the earth, unless it was at the center of the universe. The earth could not be thought to be floating on water or on air. He quoted the circumference of the earth as 400,000 stadia, but gave no explanation for how this figure was obtained.

Aristotle opposed the atomists, Democritus and Leucippus, who had argued for void space and a multitude of worlds. He also opposed Heraclitus who insisted change was the basic condition and the world was periodically destroyed and created, and Plato, who held that the world was created by the Demiurge. Aristotle's system was later adopted by Christian and Islamic theology, and it played an enormous influence on western science until the later Middle Ages.

Aristarchus (c. 310-230 BC) is said to have declared that the earth was in orbit about the sun, but this was not accepted by others. He argued that the sun was 19 times further than the Moon (he was wrong by a factor of more than 20). Another obscure tradition was that the earth was spinning on its axis. Archimedes ascribed it to Aristarchus in his Sand-Reckoner, mentioning that in this view the sun and the stars are at rest and the earth revolves in a circular orbit with the sun at the center. But no mention was made whether planets revolve around the earth or the sun.

Apollonius of Perga (200 BC) suggested that the earth was on one side of the center of the planetary circuits. It was due to the motion on such eccentric circles that the speed of the planet varied across the sky. By this time the idea that the planet moved on an epicycle of small radius, whose center was carried uniformly on a large carrying circle, called the deferent, with Earth as the center also became popular. This offered a simple explanation of the retrograde motion of planets.

Hipparchus made significant astronomical observations at Rhodes between 141 and 127 BC. He compiled a list of lunar eclipses observed in Babylon from the eighth century BC. He adopted the sexagesimal system of Babylonian calculations of angles, and also the division of the circle into 360 degrees. Many of his figures for the periods of the Moon and the planets are from Babylon. Hipparchus noted that the four seasons were not of equal length. The sun took 94.5 days to move from spring equinox to summer solstice, and 92.5 days to move from summer solstice to autumn equinox. The other two seasons were just over 88 and 90 days. He explained this by taking the earth to have an eccentricity of 1/24 of the radius of the sun's circle.

He is credited with the discovery of the precession of the equinoxes, the shifting of the fixed stars with time. Ptolemy informs us that Hipparchus believed the precession rate to be 1° per century (the actual rate is 1° per seventy years). He found the position of the star Spica to be 6°

west of the autumn equinox by finding the angle between it and the moon at an eclipse. One hundred years earlier, Timocharis had found Spica to be 8° west of the equinox. Hipparchus concluded that the celestial sphere rotates relative to the framework of the equator and the ecliptic about the poles of the ecliptic.

Contact between Greek and Indian astronomies

It is interesting to determine if there was contact between Indian and Greek astronomies. The picture of evolution of early astronomy that emerged in the histories of the last 150 years assumed that Indian astronomy was derived from Greek and Babylonian astronomies but this story is based on poor understanding of Indian texts. A more complex picture is emerging based on the pre-Alexandrian contact between the two civilizations.

This contact took place through the agency of the many Indic kingdoms in Persia, Mesopotamia, and West Asia that are known to have existed in the second and first millennia BC. The ruling elites of the Hittites and the Mitanni in Turkey and Syria, and the Kassites in Mesopotamia worshiped Vedic gods. The Mitanni were joined in marriage to the Egyptian pharaohs during the second half of the second millennium and they appear to have influenced that region as well. The Ugaritics list 33 gods, just like the count of Vedic gods.

Here we will provide examples of earlier Indian usage of a key idea that is seen as indicative of Greek advance.

1. Division of circle in 360 parts. This is to be found in the Ṛgveda 1.164, which is anterior by several centuries (if not over a thousand years) to its usage in Babylon or Greece. The count of 360 was apparently chosen as the average of the 354 days of the lunar year and the 366 days of the solar year.

2. The viewing of the sun's orbit in an eccentric circle, credited to Apollonius and Hipparchus. This is to be found in the Śatapatha Brāhmaṇa which is at least half a millennium earlier.

3. The sun as the center of the universe is so described in many passages in the Vedic texts.

4. The division of the zodiac into twelve parts is to be seen in the Ṛgveda 1.164.11, where mention is made of the 720 paired sons of the wheel of time which has twelve spokes. Even the original lists of 27 nakshatras contain only 24 original names, indicating that this was connected to the 24 half-months of the solar year. In Śatapatha Brāhmaṇa (11.6.3.8), it is stated that the Ādityas are the twelve months, indicating clearly a twelve part division of the circuit of the sun.

Indian thought uses the correspondence between the microcosm and the macrocosm, and this is developed extensively in the ritual and medicine. But in contrast to Greek astronomy, there is less emphasis on geometrical shapes. Perhaps influenced by its own grammatical tradition, its astronomy sought to find efficient techniques of computation. If Greek astronomy was geometrical in inspiration, Indian astronomy was algebraic and geometrical. The arithmetic and algebraic aspects of Indian astronomy are clear in the centrality of the number 360 in the various geometric altar representations that sought to harmonize the lunar and the solar years. The Śatapatha Brāhmaṇa also represents the circuit of the sun geometrically in a circular altar. Algebraic methods of calculation are described at much length in the Vedāṅga Jyotiṣa and the Siddhāntas.

It is generally accepted that scientific development in both India and Greece had a ritual basis. In particular, A. Seidenberg in his papers has argued that mathematics and geometry arose in India earlier than in Greece. The historian of science van der Waerden summarized the evidence thus:

> Seidenberg has pointed out that in Greek texts as well as in the Shulbasutras, geometrical constructions were regarded important for ritual purposes, namely for constructing altars of given form and magnitude. In Greece this led to the famous problem of doubling the cube, whereas in India it was not the volume but the area of the altar that was considered important. In both cases, one essential step in the altar constructions was the solution of the problem: to construct a square equal in area to a given rectangle. To solve this problem, exactly the same construction was used in Greece and in India, a solution based on the Theorem of Pythagoras. Also, the ideas about the religious importance of exact geometrical altar constructions were very similar in both countries.

The similarity in the approach of the Greeks and the Indians need not be due to one borrowing from the other. It is likely that the ancient world shared broad ideas that were amplified in uniquely different ways in different civilizations. The sharing of the basic ideas was due to the undoubted interaction that took place in the ancient world via trade and migrations of people.

The Almagest

The date of Ptolemy's birth and death are not known, but his works cite observations that belong to the period 127 to 141 AD. His astronomical works are dedicated to one Syrus, and his immediate teachers included one Theon, from whom he acknowledges receiving records of planetary observations. The name of his book Almagest is from the twelfth century Arabic edition of which the original is lost.

The Almagest contains geometrical models and related tables for the movements of planets. The work in thirteen books begins with a statement of reasons that are largely Aristotelian. Ordinary affairs help us attain moral insight, but to attain knowledge of the universe one must study astronomy. Following Aristotle, he places physics on a lower plane, since it deals with the changing and corruptible world. Astronomy, on the other hand, leads us to understanding gods, for it draws our attention to the first cause of celestial motions.

The Almagest starts off by asserting that the heavens are spherical. Ptolemy deduced that the earth was spherical from three facts. First, the curvature of the earth is apparent from the fact that a ship at a great distance appears below sea-level. Second, the observers further north cannot see the more southerly stars. Third, the local time recorded for an eclipse is not the same for all observers, and further west the observer the earlier the recorded time. He deduced that the earth was at the center of the universe, because if it were not, the sky would not be an exact hemisphere. He said the earth could not move, because otherwise birds could fall off the edge. The earth could not spin, because if it did, then clouds and other flying things could never move toward the east. The Almagest presents models of the motions of planets. His theory of the sun's motion is actually the earlier work of Hipparchus. We know this because his tables are accurate for Hipparchus's time, and not his own. He modified the Hipparchus theory on the motion of the Moon. Considering the data from partial eclipses, he calculated the sun's distance to be 1,210 Earth's radius (which is actually one-twentieth the correct result).

The Almagest contains a catalogue of over a thousand stars, with their longitude, latitude, and apparent brightness, arranged in 48 constellations, which some believe is really the catalogue compiled by Hipparchus with longitude reduced by 2 2/3° to account for the precession in the period between the two men. R.R. Newton showed that much of the observations in the Almagest are either invented or modified to fit his theory.

Ptolemy's other books include a digest of the Almagest called Planetary Hypotheses, Optics, Geography, and a companion book on astrology, called the Tetrabiblos, that was concerned with the influences of the celestial bodies in the sublunar sphere. The Tetrabiblos was a very popular astrological work of antiquity in the Islamic world and the medieval Latin West. It served as a compendium of astrological lore, and it spoke in general terms, collected from earlier sources. Its astrological effects of the planets are explained based upon their combined effects of heating, cooling, moistening, and drying. His Optics and Planetary Hypotheses can be pieced together from Arabic versions. His minor works on projection, Analemma and Planisphaerium, are available in Greek. His extensive writings suggest that he was assembling an encyclopaedia.

Ptolemy introduced the notion of the equant point that was taken to be located as the mirror image of the earth in an eccentric circle. He further proposed that the point on the circle did not move with uniform speed with respect to the center; rather, it moved with a speed that would appear uniform to an observer at the equant point. His abandonment of the idea of uniform circular motion with respect to the center came in for much criticism in the medieval West and the Islamic world.

To deal with the Moon's evection, that is alteration in the Moon's orbit caused by the attraction of the sun, he introduced a mechanism that varied the distance from the earth of the Moon's epicycle. This caused the distance of the Moon from the earth to vary between 33 and 64 times the radius of the earth. This should vary the apparent diameter of the Moon by a factor of two, which is never the case.

Ptolemy arbitrarily aligned the centers for Venus and Mercury with the mean Sun in order to explain why these two planets are never far from the sun. Taking the order of planets to be Moon, Mercury, Venus, Sun, Mars, Jupiter, and Saturn, in his Planetary Hypotheses, he further declared that planets through their motions shared all the possible heights, leaving no gaps. Thus, the maximum height of the Moon was 64 Earth radii, which was equal to the minimum height of Mercury, and so on. Using this logic, he arrived at a universe whose radius was 19,865 Earth radii, or about 75 million miles. Later craftsmen in medieval Europe tried to represent this model in metal.

Siddhantic and Islamic astronomies

With the rise of Christianity, Europe entered a scientific Dark Age. Meanwhile, during the reign of Caliph Mansur (753-774), Indian embassies from Sindh to Baghdad brought scholars and two astronomical siddhāntas of Brahmagupta (seventh century), the Brahmasiddhānta and the Khaṇḍakhādyaka, whose Arabic translations became famous in the Islamic world as the Sindhind and the Arkand. Edwin Sachau, the translator of al-Bīrūnī's India, reminds us that the Islamic world learned from Brahmagupta earlier than from Ptolemy. The Āryabhaṭīya of Āryabhaṭa was translated into Arabic as Arajbahar. Another influx of Indian learning took place under Caliph Harun (786-808). Greek astronomy was preserved in the Islamic world through the Almagest.

In the classical siddhāntic period of Indian astronomy starting with Āryabhaṭa, the calculations are not done with respect to the lunar nakshatras but rather with respect to the twelve signs of the zodiac. There is speculation that this change arose out of the interaction with the Greeks, but the twelve-division zodiac was a part of the early Indian astronomical tradition.

The mean longitudes were computed from the number of days elapsed from the beginning of long periods called the kalpa and the yuga, with the current yuga (Kaliyuga) having commenced on 17/18 February 3102 BC. Planetary motions were computed using epicycles and eccentric circles. Eclipses were computed more accurately by applying algebraic techniques and plane and spherical trigonometry was also used. The problems dealt with in the siddhāntas include:

1. Determination of the longitudes of planets and also of the ascending and descending nodes of the moon;
2. Corrections of these computations with the passage of time;
3. Lunar and solar eclipses;
4. Problems relating to the shadow;
5. Phases of the moon;
6. Helical rising and setting of planets;
7. Occultation of stars and planets; and
8. Astronomical instruments.

Indian astronomical texts are of three types: siddhāntas, karaṇas, and koṣṭhakas. While the siddhāntas are comprehensive and commence the calculations from the kalpa or the yuga, the karaṇas are practical manuals to facilitate calculations from a specific epoch with zero corrections at that point. The koṣṭhakas or saraṇis are astronomical tables for the casting of horoscopes by astrologers. There are also texts that focus only on instruments.

The prominent astronomers after Āryabhaṭa include his later rival Brahmagupta, Bhāskara II (b. 1114), and the many mathematician-astronomers of the Kerala school that flourished during the years of the Karnataka (Vijayanagara) empire. The two most prominent names of this school are Mādhava (c. 1340 - 1425) and Nīlakanṭha (c. 1444 -1545). Their contributions include power series for trigonometric functions, demonstration that π is irrational and contributions to calculus. Nīlakanṭha presented an improved version of the Āryabhaṭa's scheme where the five planets orbit the sun and in turn they all orbit the earth.

The Islamic calendar is lunar, and the Islamic year is 11 days shorter than the solar year. The prediction of the Moon's path with respect to the horizon becomes important in the Islamic calendar, with the month beginning with the sighting of the lunar crescent in the evening sky. Ptolemy's theory of the Moon dealt with its motion with respect to the ecliptic, therefore, additional work on spherical geometry was required. The five daily prayers for the Muslim required means to tell the time accurately. For this an Indian formula marking time with respect to the shadow length was used. Later, tables for finding the time of day from the altitudes of the sun or the time of night from the altitudes of the bright stars were developed. This required solving for the unknown sides or angles of a triangle on the celestial sphere from the known sides and angles.

By the ninth century, the concept of the trigonometric functions (such as sine, cosine) were introduced into Islamic science by the translations of the Indian siddhāntas. Trigonometric identities greatly simplified calculations involving triangles on the celestial sphere. Another consideration was the orientation of mosques and prayer towards Mecca. This was solved by the development of cartographic grids for Mecca-centered maps, giving distance and angle in an easy form.

Two noteworthy Islamic observatories were by the Persian astronomer Nasir al-Din al-Tūsī (1201-1274) in Maragha, who compiled a zij, astronomical tables in the style of Ptolemy, and Ulugh Beg (1394-1499) in Samarkand, whose tables included a catalogue of over 1,000 stars.

Ibn al-Haytham (965 - c. 1040) saw the heavens as formed of concentric spherical shells, within whose thickness other shells and spheres were located, and he rejected the Ptolemaic equant. Nasir al-Din al-Tūsī devised a planetary model that only used uniform circular motion by adding two small epicycles to each of the planetary models. This was improved in the fourteenth century by Ibn al-Shatir in Damascus. These ideas worked their way into the models that arose later in Europe.

Indian mathematics in the West

The increasing mathematization of astronomy may be seen as a by-product the spread of Indian numerals into Europe, together with the notion of negative numbers that was resisted for several decades by the Church. Georges Ifrah explains why this happened: "The Church effectively issued a veto, for it did not favor a democratization of arithmetical calculations that would loosen its hold on education and thus weaken its power and influence; the corporation of accountants raised its own drawbridges against the 'foreign' invasion; and in any case the Church preferred the abacists [the defenders of the Roman numerals] --who were most often clerics as well --to keep their monopoly on arithmetic."

Indian numerals maintained an underground status in Europe for some time. But other branches of Indian mathematics had already reached Europe through the agency of the Arabs and been assimilated. In particular, Kerala was in continuous contact with Europe and Arabia at the beginning of the sixteenth century. Although the texts of the revolutionary advances of the Kerala mathematicians have not yet been found in Europe, there are methodological similarities and plausible transmission channels. Inductive generalization was used in Kerala and then we see its usage in pre-calculus Europe. Furthermore, John Wallis (1665) gave a recurrence relation and proof of Pythagoras theorem in the same manner as Bhāskara II.

Some suggest that calendar accuracy and inadequacies in sea navigation techniques led Europeans to seek knowledge from their colonies in the sixteenth and seventeenth centuries. Indian mathematical manuscripts may have been brought to Europe by Jesuit priests such as Matteo Ricci who spent two years in Kochi (Cochin) after being ordained in Goa in 1580. Kochi is only 70 km from Thrissur (Trichur) which was then the largest repository of astronomical documents. Two European mathematicians Whish and Hyne obtained their copies of works by the Kerala mathematicians from Thrissur, and it is not inconceivable that Jesuit monks may have also taken copies to Pisa (where Galileo, Cavalieri and Wallis spent time), or Padua (where James Gregory studied) or Paris (where Mersenne who was in touch with Fermat and Pascal, acted as an agent for the transmission of mathematical ideas).

The astrolabe

Astronomical instruments tell us a lot about the conceptions about the universe that lay behind them. The astrolabe, 'star-grasper,' for showing how the sky looks at a specific place at a given time, played an important role in the development of western astronomy in the Middle Ages. The sky is drawn on the face of the astrolabe and the positions of the stars marked on it. To use it, the moveable components are adjusted to a specific date and time. Once set, the entire sky, both visible and invisible, is shown on the face of the instrument. This allows a great many astronomical problems to be solved in a very visual way. Typical uses of the astrolabe include finding the time during the day or night, finding the time of a celestial event such as sunrise or sunset and as a handy reference of celestial positions.

The plane astrolabe, made usually of brass, was used while suspended from the thumb and it gave the altitude of an object, which was measured using a ruler pivoted about its center. It had a solid plate of fixed coordinate circles, above which rotated a net of pierced metalwork on which were pointers for the brightest stars, with parts of moving circles representing the equator and the ecliptic. Some aspects of the theory of stereographic projection that underlies the astrolabe were certainly known to Ptolemy, although its origins may lie in classical Greece. In Ptolemy's Planisphaerium, there are hints that he may have had an instrument like the astrolabe.

The earliest evidence of the use of the stereographic projection in a machine is in the writing of the Roman author and architect, Vitruvius (died sometime after 27 BC), who in *De architectura* described a clock (probably a clepsydra or water clock) made by Ctesibius in Alexandria. Ctesibius' clock appears to have had a rotating field of stars behind a wire frame indicating the hours of the day. The wire framework was possibly constructed using the stereographic projection with the eye point at the north celestial pole. Similar constructions dated from the first to third century have been found in Salzburg and northeastern France, so such mechanisms were apparently fairly widespread among Romans.

Theon of Alexandria (c. 390) wrote a treatise on the astrolabe that was the basis for much that was written on the subject in the Middle Ages. Synesius of Cyrene (early fifth century) seemed to have made some improvements to the astrolabe. In a letter that has survived, Synesius claims to have been the first since Ptolemy to have written on the matter of astrolabe projection, but if so, the superior work of Theon came soon afterwards.

The astrolabe found its full development in the Islamic world, where it was introduced in the eighth and ninth centuries. Arab treatises on the astrolabe were published in the ninth century and indicate long familiarity with the instrument. The oldest existing instruments are Arabic from the tenth century, and there are nearly 40 instruments from the eleventh and twelfth centuries. The astrolabe was valuable in Islam because of its ability to determine the time of day and, therefore, prayer times and as an aid in finding the direction to Mecca.

The astrolabe moved with Islam through North Africa into Spain and from there it was introduced to European culture through Christian monasteries in northern Spain. The earliest astrolabes used in Europe were imported from Islamic Spain with Latin words engraved alongside the original Arabic. It is likely that European use of Arabic star names was influenced by these imported astrolabes. By the end of the twelfth century there were at least a half dozen competent astrolabe treatises in Latin, and there were hundreds available only a century later. European makers extended the plate engravings to include astrological information and adapted the various timekeeping variations used in that era.

The astrolabe, which was widely used in Europe in the late Middle Ages and Renaissance, peaked in popularity in the fifteenth and sixteenth centuries, and was one of the basic astronomical education tools. Several interesting astrolabe variations known as universal astrolabes, which make a single instrument usable in all latitudes, were also invented, but due to their high cost and complex operation, never gained the popularity of the planispheric type. These instruments projected the celestial sphere on the equinoctial colure and lacked the intuitive appeal of the planispheric type. But three-dimensional models called armillary spheres were built and used for observation.

Copernicus

Nicolaus Copernicus (1473-1543) was born in Poland and he studied Latin, mathematics, astronomy, geography and philosophy in the University of Krakow. At this time scientific education consisted mainly of mathematics and introduction to the ideas of Aristotle and Ptolemy regarding the universe, calculation of religious calendar, and casting of astrological horoscopes. He also studied Euclid's Elements and the Alfonsine Tables for computing the positions of the sun, Moon, and the planets relative to the fixed stars that appeared in Augsburg in 1483.

To have a career in the Church, he chose in 1496 to go to Italy to study canon law at the University of Bologna. Here he also studied Greek, mathematics and astronomy in addition to his official course of canon law. He rented rooms at the house of an astronomy professor and began to undertake research with him, assisting him in making observations. On 9 March 1497 he observed the moon eclipse the star Aldebaran.

Meanwhile his uncle proposed his name for the position of canon at Frauenburg Cathedral, and in 1497, while still in Bologna, he received official notification of his appointment as a canon and he was given leave to join as soon as he finished his studies. Copernicus visited Rome in 1500 and stayed on to lecture. Here he observed an eclipse of the moon. On his return to Poland he was installed as canon of the cathedral of Frauenburg in 1501. But since he had still not finished his studies in canon law, he asked for leave to return to Italy both to take a law degree and to study medicine. He was granted this leave and this time he went to Padua.

At Padua, Copernicus studied both medicine and astronomy which made sense because physicians used astrology. Next he moved to the University of Ferrara from where he received his canon law doctorate. He stayed in Ferrara for a few months before returning to Padua to continue his studies of medicine.

Returning to Poland, he was for some time a physician to his maternal uncle who was the Bishop of Ermland, a few miles from Frauenburg, the official residence of the Bishop of Ermland. In 1512, when his uncle died, he resumed his duties as canon at Frauenburg. He devoted himself to astronomy. His observatory was in the rooms in which he lived in one of the towers in the town's fortifications. It is here he slowly developed a heliocentric model of planets, showing how this allowed an unambiguous ordering of planets and elimination of equants, as had been done earlier by the astronomers of the Islamic world.

Around 1514, he distributed a handwritten little book now called the Little Commentary, where he set out his cosmology. His theory was presented in terms of seven axioms, of which the first four stated that the center of the universe was near the sun (not the center of the sun), and that the distance between the earth and the sun was small compared to the distance to the stars; the fifth was that the rotation of the earth accounted for the apparent daily rotation of the stars; the sixth stated that the apparent annual cycle of movements of the sun is caused by the earth revolving round it; the seventh was that the apparent retrograde motion of planets is caused by the motion of the earth from which one observes.

It appears that he began writing his major work *De revolutionibus* in the following year. By this time his fame as an astronomer was wide enough for him to be appointed by the Lateran Council of the Pope as one of the experts to improve the calendar, which was known to be out of phase with the seasons. The next few years of his life involved increasing administrative duties and he also saw the war between Poland and the Teutonic Knights towards the end of 1519. At the end of this war, he participated in peace talks representing the Bishop of Ermland. The peace talks failed and the war continued. Frauenburg came under siege. At the end of the war he became the Commissar of Ermland and given the task of rebuilding the district after the war. Still later, Copernicus returned to Frauenburg as canon, concentrating on his astronomical writing.

A summary of his work appeared in 1540, and since it did not cause any controversy in the theological circles, he allowed his complete work, *De revolutionibus orbium coelestium* (On the Revolutions of the Heavenly Spheres), to be published in 1543, the year of his death. Georg Joachim Rheticus, a young professor of mathematics and astronomy at the

University of Wittenberg who was his student, wrote the introduction to the book, where he stressed how Copernicus was driven by a desire to find mutual relationship between the motions that harmonized them, and how he had been compelled to abandon the hypotheses of Ptolemy.

Rheticus was unable to supervise the printing of *De revolutionibus*, and he asked Andreas Osiander, a Lutheran theologian with considerable experience of printing mathematical texts, to do so. Osiander replaced Copernicus's original Preface following the title page, by his own preface in which he claimed that the results of the book were not intended as the truth; rather, they merely were a simpler way to calculate the positions of planets and that the earth truly moved around the sun. The preface was unsigned and the true authorship not revealed publicly until fifty years later. It was perhaps because of Osiander's preface that book was not immediately condemned by the Church.

Since he was using circular motions, Copernicus placed a motionless sun not at the centre of the universe, but close to the centre. He was also forced to use epicycles. Because of these reasons and the opposition of the Church, many astronomers and natural philosophers did not take his model seriously.

In the Ptolemaic system, Venus and Mercury kept company with the sun and, therefore, their periods were also one year. In the Copernican system, it was easy to make sense of their periods that increased in a natural sequence from the innermost to the outermost planets. Retrograde motions became much more understandable. Strictly speaking, the Copernican theory was not sun-centric. In it, the geometry of the various orbits was not based on the sun, but rather on the centre of the earth's orbit (also called the Mean Sun). His idea of the distance of the sun from the earth was about the same as that of Ptolemy and others before him, he took the mean solar distance as 1,142 Earth radii.

After Copernicus, the accurate observations of Tycho Brahe (1546-1601) were to bring about a revolution in the work of astronomers. In 1576, the King Frederick II of Denmark granted Brahe the lordship of the island of Hven, together with the resources to build an excellent observatory. This became Uraniborg, 'castle of the heavens', the finest astronomical observatory up to that time, with instruments such as astrolabes, armillaries, sextants, octants and azimuthal quadrants. He performed a variety of observations of planets and comets. He also compiled a catalogue of 777 stars that superseded the one in Almagest. He worked at Hven until 1597, when royal funding ended.

In 1572, a supernova appeared in the sky. This was one of the eight historical supernovae that are known to have appeared in 185 (questioned by some), 385, 393/6, 1006, 1054, 1181, 1572, and 1604. Its appearance created a sensation because it challenged the Aristotelian idea of the perfection and completeness of the heavens. The 1572 supernova lasted for 18 months, fading in color to yellow, red, and livid. Brahe wrote a book on it called *De Nova Stella*. As an astrologer, Brahe predicted that the influence of the new star will persist from 1592 to 1632, and it would lead to the demise of ornate religion.

Tycho Brahe also proposed his own cosmological system. In it planets moved around the sun which, in turn, went around the earth. This Tychonian system soon surpassed the Ptolemaic in popularity and it remained a competitor to the Copernican system. Brahe's insistence on Earth being at rest flowed from two arguments. He was convinced that if the earth moved, a stone dropped from a tower will not fall vertically. He also thought that the motion of the earth would have the same effect on comets as on planets and make their motion retrograde when they are in opposition to the sun.

An astrological world-view was basic to Tycho's entire philosophy of nature. He had a long-standing interest in alchemy, particularly the medical alchemy associated with Paracelsus (1493-1541). In lectures he gave in Copenhagen in 1574, Tycho defended astrology on the grounds of correspondences between the heavenly bodies, terrestrial substances and bodily organs. He summarized his ideas in two mottos: *Despiciendo suspicion*—'By looking down I see upward,' and *Suspiciendo despicio*—'By looking up I see downward.'

Several scholars have argued that Tycho's commitment to a relationship between macrocosm and microcosm played a role in his rejection of the Copernican model.

Galileo

Galileo Galilei (1564-1642) grew up in Pisa and Florence. His father wished him to become a medical doctor, but his own interests lay in mathematics. He studied the works of Euclid and Archimedes from Italian translations. He remained officially enrolled as a medical student at Pisa but by 1585 he gave up this course, leaving without completing his degree.

Galileo began teaching mathematics and in 1586 he wrote his first scientific book *La Balancitta* (The Little Balance) describing Archimedes's method of finding the specific gravity of substances using a balance. Three years later, he was appointed professor of mathematics at the University of Pisa.

In 1591, Galileo's father died, and needing more income to provide for the rest of the family as the first born, he sought and received appointment at the University of Padua in 1592, where he stayed for 18 years. His duties were mainly to teach Euclid's geometry and standard (geocentric) astronomy to medical students to prepare them for astrology.

By 1604 he had come out against certain parts of Aristotle's view of astronomy and natural philosophy, prompted by the appearance of the supernova of 1604. Galileo used parallax arguments to prove that the New Star could not be close to the earth. He also began to study the pendulum and motion on inclined planes, formulating the correct law of falling bodies and discovering that a projectile follows a parabolic path, although these results were to be published much later.

In 1609, he heard of the use in Holland of a curved glass in a tube for magnification. Using these reports, and his skills as a mathematician and craftsman and by grinding and polishing his own lenses, Galileo made telescopes whose magnification was twice than that of the Dutch instrument. A demonstration for the Venetian Senate was arranged that led to a large increase in his salary. By the end of the year, he had turned his telescope on the night sky and began to make remarkable discoveries that were to change astronomy. These astronomical discoveries were published in a small book called the Starry Messenger (*Sidereus Nuncius*) published in Venice in May 1610:

> About ten months ago a report reached my ears that a certain Fleming had constructed a spyglass by means of which visible objects, though very distant from the eye of the observer, were distinctly seen as if nearby. Of this truly remarkable effect several experiences were related, to which some persons believed while other denied them. A few days later the report was confirmed by a letter I received from a Frenchman in Paris, Jacques Badovere, which caused me to apply myself wholeheartedly to investigate means by which I might arrive at the invention of a similar instrument. This I did soon afterwards, my basis being the doctrine of refraction.

The book made him a celebrity. Galileo claimed to have seen mountains on the moon, to have proved the Milky Way was made up of tiny stars, and to have seen four satellites orbiting Jupiter. To ingratiate himself with Cosimo de Medici, the Grand Duke of Tuscany, he named the satellites 'the Medicean stars.' He also sent Cosimo a telescope as a gift.

Cosimo was duly impressed and in June 1610, a month after his little book was published, he became chief mathematician at the University of Pisa without any teaching duties, and mathematician and philosopher to the Grand Duke of Tuscany. When he visited Rome the following year, he was treated as a celebrity and given various honors and made a member of the Accademia dei Lincei. He treasured this membership so much that he signed himself 'Galileo Galilei Linceo' from this time on.

On his return to Florence, he continued to examine the moons of Jupiter and by 1612 he was able to find their periods. He was also studying Saturn and he was puzzled by what his telescope, which wasn't very strong, showed: the rings as lobes on either side of the planet that would vanish when the ring system was edge on. He also discovered that the planet Venus showed phases like those of the moon, and therefore must orbit the sun and not the earth.

But this did not enable one to decide between the Copernican and the more popular Tychonian systems although he was favoring the Copernican system for its simplicity. The opponents of a moving Earth argued that if the earth rotated and a body was dropped from a tower it should not fall vertically. But his experiments had not shown this to happen.

Galileo also observed the sunspots. He reported his findings in Discourse on Floating Bodies (1612) and more fully in Letters on the Sunspots that appeared a year later. In 1618, he became involved in a controversy regarding the nature of comets, where he supported the incorrect theory that they were close to the earth. Meanwhile, the Jesuits began to see Galileo as a dangerous enemy.

Galileo had avoided controversy regarding the Copernican system, but he was drawn into it through his old student Castelli, the newly appointed chair of mathematics in Pisa, who was a supporter of Copernicus. Castelli defended the Copernican system at a meeting in the Medici palace with the Grand Duke Cosimo II and his mother the Grand Duchess Christina of Lorraine in Florence in December 1613, where he had been asked to explain the apparent contradictions between the Copernican theory and the Bible. Castelli wrote to Galileo afterwards telling him how he had won the argument. In response, Galileo wrote back stressing that the Bible had to be interpreted in the light of the truths of science. Galileo's opponents in Florence sent copies of this letter to the Inquisition in Rome. Though nothing came of this complaint, he was denounced from a Florence pulpit in 1614.

Cardinal Robert Bellarmine, who was responsible for the official interpretations of the Bible for the Church, seemed at this time to see little reason for the Church to be concerned regarding the Copernican theory because of the view it was only a mathematical theory that helped in calculations and not a model of physical reality. As such, it did not threaten the established Christian dogma regarding the structure of the universe.

In 1616, Galileo wrote the Letter to the Grand Duchess which vigorously attacked Aristotelian ideas, arguing for a non-literal interpretation of the Bible when the literal interpretation contradicted facts. He also affirmed that the Copernican system represented the physical reality:

> I hold that the sun is located at the center of the revolutions of the heavenly orbs and does not change place, and that the earth rotates on itself and moves around it. Moreover ... I confirm this view not only by refuting Ptolemy's and Aristotle's arguments, but also by producing many for the other side, especially some pertaining to physical effects whose causes perhaps cannot be determined in any other way, and other astronomical discoveries; these discoveries clearly confute the Ptolemaic system, and they agree admirably with this other position and confirm it.

Pope Paul V now ordered the Inquisition to decide on the Copernican theory. The Inquisition condemned Copernicus and Galileo was forbidden to hold Copernican views. Galileo was not much concerned with this because his admirer, Maffeo Barberini, was soon elected as Pope Urban

VIII. Galileo's book *Il saggiatore* (The Assayer) was about to be published by the Accademia dei Lincei in 1623 and Galileo was quick to dedicate this work to the new Pope. The work described Galileo's scientific method and contains his famous assertion regarding the centrality of mathematics in science:

> Philosophy is written in this grand book, the universe, which stands continually open to our gaze. But the book cannot be understood unless one first learns to comprehend the language and read the characters in which it is written. It is written in the language of mathematics, and its characters are triangles, circles, and other geometric figures without which it is humanly impossible to understand a single word of it; without these one is wandering in a dark labyrinth.

Due to his friendship with Pope Urban VIII, Galileo thought he was immune to attacks by the Inquisition. He started working on the Dialogue on the Two Great World Systems to discuss the relative merits of Ptolemy and Copernicus. The book was ready by 1630, but he could not obtain permission from Rome to publish it. Eventually he received permission to publish from Florence, and the book appeared in February 1632.

The book is in the form of a dialogue between Salviati, who argues for the Copernican system, and Simplicio who is an Aristotelian philosopher. The climax of the book is an argument by Salviati that the earth moves which was based on Galileo's theory of the tides. This theory of the tides was false despite being postulated after Kepler, who had already put forward the correct explanation. It is ironic that the strongest argument which Galileo gave in support of Copernicus was wrong!

Shortly after publication of Dialogue, the Inquisition banned its sale and ordered Galileo to appear before it in Rome. Illness prevented him from traveling to Rome until 1633, and when he appeared he was accused of having breached the conditions laid down by the Inquisition in 1616. The truth of the Copernican theory was not an issue at this trial since the earlier judgment of 1616 had declared it false. He was found guilty, and condemned to imprisonment for life.

Because of his connections, his imprisonment was more like house arrest. He was allowed to return to his home in Arcetri, near Florence, but had to spend the rest of his life watched over by officers from the Inquisition. Now he wrote Discourses and mathematical demonstrations concerning the two new sciences.

The Discourses was smuggled out of Italy, and taken to Leyden in Holland where it was published. His most rigorous mathematical work, it treated problems on impetus, moments, and centers of gravity. In it he stated the physical law: 'The speed acquired by the same movable object over different inclinations of the plane is equal whenever the heights of those planes are equal.' He described an experiment using a pendulum to verify this property and used these ideas to give a theorem on acceleration of bodies in free fall:

> The time in which a certain distance is traversed by an object moving under uniform acceleration from rest is equal to the time in which the same distance would be traversed by the same movable object moving at a uniform speed of one half the maximum and final speed of the previous uniformly accelerated motion.

This led to the result that the distance that a body moves from rest under uniform acceleration is proportional to the square of the time taken.

Kepler

We know a lot about the life of Johannes Kepler (1571-1630) from his correspondence. Born in the small town of Weil der Stadt in Swabia, his family moved to nearby Leonberg in 1576. He was the first child and his father was a mercenary soldier and his mother the daughter of an innkeeper. His father is believed to have died in the war in the Netherlands when Johannes was five. He lived with his mother in his grandfather's inn where he helped out in the serving.

Kepler's early education was in a local school and then at a nearby seminary, from which, intending to be ordained, he went on to enroll at the University of Tübingen, a bastion of Lutheran orthodoxy. Kepler remained a profoundly religious man. His writings contain numerous references to God, and he saw his work as fulfillment of his Christian duty to understand the works of God. Kepler believed that since man was made in the image of God, understanding the universe was possible.

At Tübingen Kepler was taught astronomy by one of the leading astronomers of the day, Michael Maestlin (1550-1631) from whom he learned that the preface to *De revolutionibus* was not by Copernicus.

It seems that in Tübingen Kepler's religious beliefs were not entirely in accord with the prevailing orthodox Lutheranism, as in the 'Augsburg Confession' (*Confessio Augustana*). These may explain why Maestlin persuaded Kepler to abandon plans for ordination and instead take up a post teaching mathematics in Graz. The Church looked at his work with disfavor and he was excommunicated in 1612. Although he became Imperial Mathematician, he never succeeded in getting the ban lifted.

Kepler set out to answer the question of the number of planets. Instead of the seven planets of the standard geocentric astronomy, the Copernican system had six, since the moon was taken as a satellite of the earth. But why was this number six? In the Ptolemaic astronomy the planetary orbits were simply assumed to be in contact. This fitted nicely with the belief that the whole system was turned by the movement of the outermost spheres beyond the sphere of the 'fixed' stars. In the Copernican system, the annual component of each planetary motion was a reflection of the annual motion of the earth, and this made it possible to calculate the size of each planet's path. It was found that there were huge spaces between planets.

Kepler's answer to these questions is described in his Mystery of the Cosmos (*Mysterium Cosmographicum*) that appeared in 1596. He suggested that if a sphere were drawn to touch the inside of the path of Saturn, and a cube were inscribed in the sphere, then the sphere inscribed in that cube would be the sphere circumscribing the path of Jupiter. Then if a regular tetrahedron were drawn in the sphere inscribing the path of Jupiter, the insphere of the tetrahedron would be the sphere circumscribing the path of Mars, and so inwards, putting the regular dodecahedron between Mars and Earth, the regular icosahedron between Earth and Venus, and the regular octahedron between Venus and Mercury. This explains the number of planets perfectly: there are only five convex regular solids. According to Platonic ideas, there existed five regular solids: tetrahedron, cube, octahedron, dodecahedron, and icosahedron. The idea was that God must have created five spaces for these solids, and these spaces separated six planetary spheres.

Kepler saw his cosmological theory as providing evidence for the Copernican theory. Before presenting his own theory he gave arguments to establish the plausibility of the Copernican theory. For example, it explained why Venus and Mercury are never seen very far from the sun (they lie between Earth and Sun) whereas in the geocentric theory there is no explanation of this fact. Kepler lists nine such questions in the first chapter of the *Mysterium Cosmographicum.*

Kepler carried out this work while he was teaching in Graz, but the book was seen through the press in Tübingen by Maestlin. The agreement with values deduced from observation was not exact, and Kepler hoped that better observations would improve the agreement, so he sent a copy of the *Mysterium Cosmographicum* to Tycho Brahe I, who was then in Prague where he was invited by the emperor, Rudolph II, after the end of royal support by Denmark. Brahe had in fact already written to Maestlin to suggest a mathematical assistant. Kepler was offered this job.

Kepler began his work in 1600. But within a year Brahe died and Kepler succeeded the old master as the Imperial Mathematician and astrologer to the emperor. He took up the difficult problem of the orbit of Mars and using the observations of Brahe, he concluded that the orbit of Mars was an ellipse with the sun in one of its foci. The actual process of calculation for Mars was immensely laborious--there are nearly a thousand surviving folio sheets of arithmetic--and Kepler himself refers to this work as 'my war with Mars,', but the result was an orbit which agrees with modern results so exactly that the comparison has to make allowance for secular changes in the orbit since Kepler's time. He made explicit use of the concept of observational error and this important notion may have been originated by Brahe.

Meanwhile, William Gilbert (1544-1603), a physician in London, had proposed in his On the Magnet that the earth itself was a giant spherical magnet, proposing further that this force may be responsible for the fall of bodies to the surface of the earth. Kepler now thought that a similar force might be exerted by the sun on planets, the nearer planets being affected more strongly than the distant ones. This physical intuition helped him make a leap beyond the framework in which Copernicus had worked before him.

He was looking for a model that had the capacity to explain the motion of the planet both in longitude and latitude. This was in contrast to earlier models where incompatible theories were proposed for these two motions.

Between 1618 and 1621 appeared his Epitome where he presented his ideas in a question and answer form for a larger public. In 1627, there appeared the Rudolphine Tables, named after the emperor Rudolf II who had commissioned Kepler to assist Tycho in the compiling of new planetary tables, more accurate than the earlier Prutenic Tables based on Copernican models. In 1631, one year after the death of Kepler, the precision of the new tables and the power of his laws became obvious when the Frenchman Pierre Gassendi was to confirm the passage of Mercury across the face of the sun. This was the beginning of the triumph of mathematics in the description of the cosmos.

In 1611, Kepler presented a new design of telescope, using two convex lenses. This design, in which the final image is inverted, was so successful that it is now usually known not as a Keplerian telescope but simply as the astronomical telescope. In 1611, his son and his wife died. Then the Emperor Rudolf was forced to abdicate in favor of his brother Matthias, who, unlike his brother, was a strict Catholic. Kepler was dismissed and he now moved to Linz.

Kepler married again in 1613. He writes in the preface of his new book titled New Stereometry of Wine Barrels (*Nova stereometria doliorum*) that appeared in 1615 that at the wedding celebrations he noticed that the volumes of wine barrels were estimated by means of a rod slipped in diagonally through the bung-hole, and he wished to investigate this problem. This new book was a study of the volumes of solids of revolution, where basing himself on the ideas of Archimedes, he used a resolution into 'indivisibles,' that is part of the ancestry of calculus.

Although Kepler's main task as Imperial Mathematician was to write astronomical tables, he worked to complete The Harmony of the World (*Harmonices mundi libri V*), that went beyond the Mystery of the Cosmos. The Harmony appeared in1619, and it presented a more elaborate mathematical model using polyhedra. The mathematics in this work includes the first systematic treatment of tessellations, a proof that there are only thirteen convex uniform polyhedra (the Archimedean solids) and the first account of two nonconvex regular polyhedra.

Working on Tycho's observations on Mars, Kepler had proposed his 'first law' that the planetary orbit is an ellipse with the sun at one focus in his 1609 book New Astronomy (*Astronomia nova aitologetos*). This was to liberate astronomers from their futile attempts to look for perfect circular orbits. In his 'second law,' Kepler proposed a variant of the Ptolemaic equant, later to be recognized as the empty focus. He took the speed of the planet to be inversely proportional to its distance from the sun, with the rule that the line from the sun to the planet traces out equal areas in equal times.

Later, in The Harmony of the World he explored the relationship of one planetary orbit to another. Looking for connection in the arithmetic ratios, he made the discovery of his 'third law' that the square of the period of a planet is in a fixed ratio to the cube of the radius of its orbit. The 'third law' was not actually discovered until the work was in press. This is how he described his discovery:

> It was conceived mentally on 8th March in this year one thousand six hundred and eighteen, but submitted to calculation in an unlucky way, and therefore rejected as false, and finally returning on the 15th of May and adopting a new line of attack, stormed the darkness of my mind. So strong was the support from the combination of my labour of seventeen years on the observations of Brahe and the present study, which conspired together, that at first I believed I was dreaming, and assuming my conclusion among my basic premises. But it is absolutely certain and exact that the proportion between the periodic times of any two planets is precisely the sesquialterate proportion of their mean distances.

Kepler never stated these three laws systematically in the form that we know them today. To get a flavor of the times, note that Kepler's mother was charged with witchcraft while he was writing the Harmony. He enlisted the help of the legal faculty at Tübingen and he was successful in getting his mother released, partly as a result of technical objections arising from the authorities' failure to follow the correct legal procedures in the use of torture.

By the time the Rudolphine Tables were published, Kepler was working for Albrecht von Wallenstein (1583-1632), one of the few successful military leaders in the Thirty Years' War (1618-1648). Wallenstein, like the emperor Rudolf, expected Kepler to give him astrological advice.

Although Kepler's extensive and successful use of mathematics makes his work look modern, his metaphysical views show that at heart he was an astrologer and a neo-Platonist. He is termed a natural philosopher, for whom understanding the universe meant understanding the nature of its creator. In the Harmony of the World, Kepler argued that the human soul was endowed by God with the ability to intuit the harmony in the universe. His favorite analogy was that the sphere of the universe was created in the image of the Trinity. This book is the most eloquent example of Kepler's belief that astronomers were the priests of almighty God with respect to the Book of Nature and that their business was to praise God's glory.

Traditional astrology recognizes five significant relationships based upon the twelve fold division of the zodiac signs. These five relationships were derived by analogy with the ratios of the musical scale. The conjunction is equivalent to the same two notes played in unison. The opposition divides the circle in the ratio 1:2, which corresponds to the octave. The sextile (5:6) corresponds to a minor third, the square (3:4) to a perfect fourth and the trine (2:3) to a perfect fifth. Kepler rejected the twelve divisions of the zodiac, and doing so he wished to synthesize a new astrology of music, geometry and astronomy.

Using correlations of planetary angles with weather, and from his collection of 800 horoscopes, Kepler concluded that when planets formed angles equivalent to particular harmonic ratios a resonance was set up, both in the archetypal 'Earth-soul' and in the souls of individuals born under those configurations. He said that 'in the vital power of the human being that is ignited at birth there glows that remembered image,' and the geometric-harmonic imprint constitutes 'the music that impels the individual to dance' as the movements of planets, by transit and direction, echo and re-echo the natal theme.

In addition to the five classical aspects, Kepler proposed the quintile (72°), bi-quintile (144°) and sesqui-quadrate (135°). Seen in the analogy of the musical scale, the quintile is equivalent to an interval of a major third (4:5), the sesqui-quadrate to a minor sixth (5:8) and the bi-quintile to a major sixth (3:5). He rejected other aspect configurations on aesthetic grounds.

Historians believe that Kepler's astrological ideas played an important role in his discoveries. The historian John North put it this way: "Had he not been an astrologer he would very probably have failed to produced his planetary astronomy in the form we have it." Kepler believed in astrology in the sense that planetary configurations physically affected humans as well as the weather on Earth. To put astrology on a surer footing, he wrote a book on astrology (1601). Later, in The Intervening Third Man, or a warning to theologians, physicians and philosophers (1610), he took a position between the two extreme positions for and against astrology, advocating that a definite relationship between heavenly phenomena and earthly events could be established.

Kepler predicted the transit of Mercury across the face of the Sun in 1631, but he died before he could observe it. Gassendi made this observation and he was astonished at the small angular diameter of the planet. Horrocks (1618-1641) observed the transit of Venus of 1639, and by projecting the sun's image upon a white screen in a camera obscura, he found the size of 76" + 4", close to the correct value. He was pleased that the diameter of the planets seemed to be proportional to their distance from the sun, in consonance with the spirit of Kepler's doctrine of harmonies.

More accurate measurements of the planetary diameters were made in the late 1630s by the use of a Keplerian telescope fitted with a micrometer, with its cross-wires moved, by a screw, in the focal place of the eyepiece. The relative distances of the planets were fixed by Kepler to high precision. When the size of the earth was set somewhere in between Mars and Venus, it was discovered that the sun was at an astonishingly large distance of twenty or thirty thousand Earth radii. Huygens suggested 25,086, implying a solar parallax of 8.2", which is quite accurate, but it was based on ad hoc reasoning. The improvement in the estimate of the solar system is seen by comparing this figure to the traditional value of 180" and Kepler's 60".

A major element in the understanding of the universe is a correct idea of its physical size. Initially, this was in terms of relative angular distances, but when an understanding of the nature of light was achieved and its velocity determined, scientists had found the measure by which the cosmos could be ranged. Kepler's mathematical theories and Galileo's use of the newly-invented telescope set the stage for the modern phase of natural science. Now it became possible to use mathematics more comprehensively than ever before in the computation of the movements of the heavenly bodies, and also examine phenomena that had been hidden to the naked eye. With the work of Newton, it became possible to explain celestial phenomena in terms of physical principles. And beyond Newton, with the speed of light measured, a correct understanding of the size of the solar system became possible. Kepler's laws led to the discovery of the law of gravitation. Astronomy had become a part of physics. Terrestrial and celestial worlds had become two aspects of the same underlying principles. But to know the cosmos it was essential to know the nature of the smallest particle, which is a particle of light.

Although the journey from Ptolemy to Kepler can be seen also as a story of the dethroning of Earth as the center of the Universe, and replacing it by the sun, or as one where perfect circles together with epicycles were replaced by ellipses, it is more importantly a replacement of the idea of absolute position and time by relative position. In modern astronomy, the sun is not stationary either, since it is part of a galaxy that is moving with respect to other galaxies.

It is instructive to compare the scientific journey from Ptolemy to Kepler to the different path of the astronomical tradition of India, where there is nothing similar to the dramatic struggle between the astronomers and the Church over the centrality of the earth. What made the European experience unique by the time of Copernicus, Galileo, and Kepler was that it had become the administrative centre of far-flung empires, which required organization and a bureaucracy supported by a university system. This set up a struggle between the new secular authorities and the old Church administration which was reflected in the resistance to the new ideas of the astronomers.

There is another aspect to this story that provides lessons regarding the process of scientific discovery. Astrological reasoning played a role in the critical advances, especially of Kepler, and we know that Newton devoted as much time to alchemy as to physics. Science does not always advance based on logical thought and specific conceptual leaps may be a consequence of a leap of intuition.

To focus on the most important single factor, the new understanding was more a consequence of new technologies that were created in the scientific revolution than the attempt to find a common basis to terrestrial and celestial phenomena. Once the telescope confirmed that planets were like the earth, it was natural to seek the application of terrestrial laws to their motions. It was clear that the earlier division of the universe into Earth and the heavens, with their separate motions, was incorrect. In this sense, the technological advance of the telescope played a much greater role in scientific advance than theological views and the opposition to them. It became possible, also, to determine the correct size of the solar system, and soon discover how, in spite of the relative smallness of Earth, terrestrial laws were universal.

Ptolemy believed that the earth did not rotate because something thrown directly up returned to the same spot. Pierre Gassendi in the seventeenth century showed that this argument was wrong by means of an experiment in which he dropped stones from the top of a mast of a moving ship and found that the stones landed at the foot of the mast directly underneath.

Galileo Galilei was the first to define momentum as the product of the mass m and the velocity v of the body. He found that freely falling bodies acquired velocities proportional to their times of fall, i.e., v is proportional to t, or $v = a\ t$, where a is the constant acceleration. He recognized the appearances of a centrifugal type of force on rotating bodies. He showed that a pendulum has a period dependent on its length and not its weight. But he failed to recognize that circular motion is accelerated motion. He broke with tradition in ascribing force to be acting on a body only when its motion changes.

Rene Descartes (1596-1650) believed that forces are transmitted only by contact. He considered the motion of planets to be caused by the pressure created by the vertical motion of material and ethereal elements of space. He and Christian Huygens (1629-1695) noted that circular motion is accelerated motion.

Robert Hooke (1635-1703) wrote about the representation of the motion of an orbiting body in terms of inertial and centripetal components. The inertial component forces the body to move along the tangent to the orbit at each moment. The centripetal component pulls the body away from the straight line trajectory of the inertial component into the orbit. In a letter in 1679 to Isaac Newton (1642-1727), Hooke suggested that the centripetal force drawing a planet toward the sun varies inversely as the square of the separation. Newton integrated the ideas of Galileo and Hooke with Kepler's laws of planetary motion by means of the concept of mutual attraction summed up in his third law of motion: to every action there is equal and opposite reaction. Newton published his gravitational theory in 1687 in the book Principia.

Roger Boscovich (1711-1787), a Croatian philosopher who taught at Rome, extended the Newtonian system to describe the structure of matter. He postulated a point atom, with finite mass but no dimensions. All such atoms were identical, the varied forms of matter resulted from the different arrangements of the atoms.

Boscovich claimed that at very small distances the force between these atoms was repulsive, and as the distance was reduced to zero the force increased without limit, so that the particles could never touch. At large distances the force was attractive and declined as the square of the distance: it was equivalent to gravitation. At intermediate distances the force was alternately attractive and repulsive.

Newton's three laws of motion dealt with velocity, acceleration, and force respectively. But measurements of velocity and acceleration are clearly relative to some frame of reference. For example, a car moving on the surface of the earth with a speed of 50 miles per hour has a much higher speed relative to the sun and a still higher speed relative to the center of the galaxy.

Consider a stone being whirled around in a circle by a string tied to it: relative to the center of the circle the stone is moving at a uniform angular speed which gives rise to the constant acceleration v^2/r. The tension in the string is the force which equals mass into this acceleration. Relative to the stone, the picture is entirely different. The stone is at rest and the string is going around it in a circle. The string still experiences a tension, while the use of the second law of motion suggests there is no force on the stone. Since the forces do not balance out any more it appears that Newton's second law does not apply in this reference frame.

Newton was aware of this problem and this led him to postulate the idea of absolute space, where the laws of motion apply unconditionally. In a frame that is accelerated relative to absolute space Newton's method required invention of fictitious forces to balance the equations of motion. Thus, in the example of the whirling stone, relative to the stone one invents the fictitious centrifugal force which balances out the tension of the string. The fictitious forces are called inertial forces because they are proportional to the inertia of the system. Reference frames that are in uniform motion relative to absolute space do not need any inertial forces. Such reference frames are called inertial frames.

Consider the earth's motion relative to absolute space. On the surface of the earth one would first observe the fictitious centrifugal force due to the earth's rotation. But the magnitude of this force is small because the angular speed of the earth is small. A larger force called the Coriolis force arises when we view a pendulum swinging to and fro in a vertical plane. At the North pole the earth's rotation with respect to absolute space (Newtonian frame) will make the plane of oscillations of the pendulum, which is fixed with respect to the Newtonian frame, appear to rotate in a direction opposite to that of the earth's rotation at the same rate. The rate of the earth's rotation thus found is the same as would be obtained if the motion were measured relative to the distant 'fixed' stars.

It was argued by Ernst Mach (1838-1916) that the result of the experiment with the pendulum was more than a coincidence and the distant stars should be considered a Newtonian frame. He conjectured that since inertia is proportional to mass therefore the inertial force produced on the pendulum should itself somehow depend on the matter in the distant stars. In other words the mass of an object is not an intrinsic attribute but depends on the distant matter in the universe. This statement of Mach's principle had great influence on the development of new ideas in understanding the phenomenon of gravitation.

Gravity and Geometry

It was realized by Riemann that the physical world might be non-Euclidean. William Clifford (1845-1879) was greatly influenced by Riemann's work and in 1876 in a brief note entitled 'On the space theory of matter' he speculated on how curvature of space might be related to matter. He wrote: "Riemann has shown that as there are different kinds of lines and surfaces, so there are different kinds of space of three dimensions; and that we can only find out by experience to which of these kinds of space in which we live belongs. In particular, the axioms of plane geometry are true within the limits of experiment on the surface of a sheet of paper, and yet we know that the sheet is really covered with a number of small ridges and furrows, upon which (the total curvature not being zero) these axioms are not true. Similarly, he says although the axioms of solid geometry are true within the limits of experiment for finite portions of our space, yet we have no reason to conclude that they are true for very small portions; and if any help can be got thereby for the explanation of physical phenomena, we may have reason to conclude that they are not true for very small portions of space.

> "I wish here to indicate a manner in which these speculations may be applied to the investigation of physical phenomena. I hold in fact
> (1) That small portions of space are in fact of a nature analogous to little hills on a surface which is on the average flat; namely, that the ordinary laws of geometry are not valid in them.
> (2) That this property of being curved or distorted is continually being passed on from one portion of space to another after the manner of a wave.
> (3) That this variation of the curvature of space is what really happens in that phenomenon which we call the motion of matter, whether ponderable or ethereal.
> (4) That in the physical world nothing else takes place but this variation, subject (possibly) to the law of continuity."[2]

Einstein's mathematical theory related matter and space. The first step in the formulation of this theory was the introduction in 1911 of the principle of equivalence. According to this principle, gravitational and inertial forces are indistinguishable. Consider a windowless spacecraft that is moving freely in a region of space without any significant gravity. Experimenters within the spacecraft can announce that they are unaccelerated and therefore an inertial frame. If the spacecraft now enters the gravitational field of a star its trajectory would become curved and it might swing past the star. By the equivalence principle the experimenters within the spacecraft would not know of the change in their trajectory because they would still be in free-fall motion. In fact, they would believe that they are still an inertial frame.

Consider a rocket that leaves the surface of the earth with an acceleration, in empty space, that is equal to the gravitational acceleration on the surface of the earth. The equivalence principle states that no experiments can be designed by the passengers of the rocket to determine whether they are accelerating in space or at rest on the surface of the earth.

Since it is not possible to distinguish between inertial systems and those in free-fall, it follows that the conclusions of the theory of relativity should also apply to systems in free-fall motion. Furthermore, laws of physics do not make any distinction between two systems one of which is in a field of constant gravity and the other is undergoing uniform acceleration. In a gravitational field objects should behave as they do in space free of gravitation if one introduces a reference system that is accelerated relative to an inertial system.

Einstein's theory of gravitation via general relativity reached its final form in 1915. In this theory spacetime becomes curved due to matter. Our universe then consists of spacetime of varying curvature. Einstein showed that the minimum formal structure that quantified these ideas was in terms of ten gravitational potentials that determine the metric of spacetime and define the geodesics (minimal paths) along which objects will tend to move. The curved orbits of freely moving objects in the Newtonian picture become the straight paths in the curved spacetime of Einstein's picture. The amount of the curvature is proportional to matter.[3]

An analogy that helps in viewing curvature in spacetime is that of a stretched rubber sheet with a heavy metallic ball placed on it. The rubber sheet stretches and sags around the ball. If a small, light ball is rolled along the sheet, not aimed at the heavy ball, it would move in a curved path. One can even visualize how at the right speed and angle the smaller ball would move in an elliptic trajectory on a frictionless rubber sheet. The depression produced by the lighter ball would also interact with the one produced by the heavier ball.

Einstein, in introducing his theory, described three observational implications. These were a precession of the orbit of the planet Mercury, the slowing down of clocks in a gravitational field, and the deflection of light by a massive body. The predictions of the theory were soon confirmed by measurements within experimental error.

Precession of the orbit of Mercury

According to Newton's theory of gravitation a planet should move about in elliptic paths around the sun. The elliptic path closes upon itself and retraces itself indefinitely. However, in the solar system, owing to the planets affecting each other, the ellipses do not in fact stay fixed in space; they rotate very slowly in the plane of the solar system. According to Newtonian theory, if the effect of the interplanetary forces could be subtracted away we should be left once again with stationary closed orbits. Actual calculation does not bear this out exactly, however. In the case of Mercury, for which the discrepancy is the largest, the calculated precession of the orbit is an angle of about 8.85 minutes of arc per century relative to the fixed stars; the observed amount is about 9.551, leaving an unaccounted discrepancy of about 0.7' or 43" of arc per 100 years.

Einstein's theory, while requiring that scales of time and distance be altered in a gravitational field, amounts to a modification of Newton's inverse-square force law in ordinary spacetime. This, modification amounts to a small additional term in the force law, corresponding to an extra attractive force varying as $1/r^3$, that is sufficient to account for the discrepancy in the precession of the perihelion of Mercury.

Gravitational redshift

According to the general theory of relativity, the rate of a clock is slowed down when it is in the vicinity of a large gravitating mass. Since the characteristic frequencies of atomic transitions are in effect clocks, one concludes that the frequency of such a transition occurring on the surface of the sun should be lower than a similar transition observed in a terrestrial laboratory. In other words, one should observe a redshift in the wavelengths of spectral lines.

Another way to view this is to note that radiation emitted from a body will lose energy due to the pull of gravity. Similarly, radiation falling on a body will gain energy. Since energy of light is universally proportional to its wavelength, light escaping from a star would have its wavelength increased which is a redshift.

Gravitational redshift can be explained by the principle of equivalence. Consider an observer in a free falling laboratory above the earth's surface. Due to free-fall there is no effect of gravity within the laboratory and a single frequency radiation from the earth would thus appear to have a constant wavelength. On the other hand, to an observer outside the laboratory it appears that the radiation waves entering the laboratory from the floor get compressed in wavelength as they move to the ceiling which is due to the constant increase in the velocity of the laboratory by gravity. Since the wavelength inside the laboratory is constant the only conclusion to be drawn is that the emitted radiation from the earth gets longer and longer in wavelength the farther it moves across its gravitational field.

Since the radiation emitted from the earth appears to have longer wavelength to an observer on, say, a distant spacecraft, such an observer would conclude that clocks on the earth are going on at a slower rate. To a person on the earth the transmissions from the spacecraft would be blueshifted or reduced in wavelength and therefore, the clocks in the spacecraft would appear to be going faster.

The bending of light

Soldner in 1801 suggested that if light were treated as a stream of particles of finite mass travelling at the speed *c* it should be deflected by a massive body. The value of the prediction by Newtonian theory is, however, only half as much as in general relativity. Observations of bending of starlight by the sun have confirmed Einstein's theory.

There is, of course, a fundamental difference in the way this bending manifests itself in general relativity. The light waves continue to move in straight lines but matter having caused the spacetime to have become curved around it makes this path appear bent to the observer. In the presence of matter the angles of a triangle spanned by light rays add up to more than 180 degrees.

Another test of general relativity was predicted by Irwin Shapiro in 1964 who pointed out that the time required for radar waves to make a round-trip from the earth to a spacecraft or a planet should be somewhat more when the waves pass close to the sun.[4] This prediction has been confirmed.

Black holes

John Mitchell in 1783 and Pierre Laplace in 1799 first conceived the possibility of black holes, objects that are so dense that they prevent the escape of light. If one views light as consisting of particles of mass m, the escape speed from the surface of a spherical body of mass M and radius R satisfies:

$$(1/2)\, mc^2 = GMm/R$$

If $R = R_S < 2GM/c^2$, even Newtonian theory allows for the existence of a black hole.

It turns out that the limit R_S discovered by Laplace is exactly the same that general relativity gives for the occurrence of a trapped surface around a spherical mass. However, the basis of this trapping of the surface in general relativity is different as it corresponds to a closing of curved surface upon itself. For the sun, the radius R_S is about three kilometers, while for the earth it is about 1 centimeter.

To visualize a black hole in general relativity it helps to consider spacetime as a stretched rubber sheet. Objects with mass produce depressions in the sheet. If an object were heavy enough, it would sink deep into the sheet to which it would remain connected by means of a highly stretched rubber neck. To a distant observer this stretching of spacetime is equivalent to reduced speed of light. Therefore, a sufficiently massive body would produce a stretching that would make the speed of light in the vicinity of the black hole to be zero. A black hole would, therefore, not emit any radiation but it would continue to have gravitational effect on matter close to it.

Schwarzschild in 1916 showed that a solution to the general relativity equations indicates an infinite red-shift when a non-rotating mass M contracts to a radius $R_s = 2GM/c^2$, now known as the Schwarzschild radius. This radius is the same as obtained using Newtonian theory.

Objects do not ordinarily collapse into black holes due to internal forces that counteract the attraction of the gravitational force. It is believed that stars form when clouds of Interstellar gas and dust shrink together. This shrinking causes the inner core of the star to get heated to temperatures that can support nuclear fusion. In the beginning this fusion converts hydrogen into helium releasing energy that keeps the star in equilibrium against the attractive force of self-gravity. When hydrogen gets depleted, the inner core shrinks further raising the temperatures still higher so that a new process of fusion can take place. This converts helium into carbon. The next steps in the sequence are carbon to oxygen to neon etc. The final stages in the sequence are the iron group of nuclei which consist of iron, cobalt, and nickel. As the nuclear energy of a star diminishes the pull of gravity causes the central region to contract and heat up to very high temperatures. This causes the outer regions to swell up and cool down. To the outside observer the star appears to become larger in size and redder in appearance owing to the cooling. Stars at this stage are red giants.

For stars with mass less than about 1.4 M_o (where M_o is the mass of the sun) the final state is one where the matter in the star contracts to size roughly equal to that of the earth where the pressure of the electron waves balances the force of gravity. Such stars are called white dwarfs. If the contraction should proceed further, which is possible if the mass of the star is roughly in the range 1.4 M_o to 3.0 M_o, matter is compressed into a state more dense than in white dwarfs. The density is higher by a factor of about 100, and the matter is in the form of neutrons, waves of which counteract gravity. Such stars are called neutron stars.

When the star is still heavier it becomes a supernova and explodes. In one scenario the core rushes inwards and the mantle rushes outwards. A tremendous shock wave is developed that produces heating in the mantle triggering fusion in it. It also accelerates the matter in the mantle to velocities beyond the escape velocity which is consequently blown off into interstellar space. The core, if its mass is less than 3 M_o, becomes a neutron star, otherwise the gravitational force causes it to become a black hole.

The event horizon

We have seen that light rays passing a body get red-shifted and deflected. Light rays leaving the surface in a perpendicular direction are not deflected, while those that leave in a direction tangential to the surface are deflected the most. When the body contracts and the spacetime around it becomes extremely curved the situation is altered. When the body has contracted to a radius 1.5 times the Schwarzschild radius all light rays emitted tangentially get curved into circular orbits. This is called the radius of the photon sphere.

With respect to the observer, we can speak of a light cone which represents a spherical sheet of light emanating from the observer. Since the speed of light cannot be reached by any material body, the world line of the body cannot cross its light cone. As an object approaches a black hole its light cone tilts toward the black hole due to the curvature of spacetime. At the Schwarzschild surface, the future light cone is completely tipped into the black hole so that all light emitted by the particle falls into the black hole. Its past light cone is tipped away in such a fashion that it can receive light only from the outside world. Consequently an observer cannot have advance warning of the existence of the black hole unless that inference is made indirectly.

From a distance the object appears to approach the black hole rapidly and then disappears. In the spacetime of the object nothing untoward happens and it moves smoothly into the black hole.

Since the light emitted just outside the Schwarzschild radius is radiated out, and that emitted just inside the radius falls within, this radius forms a surface where the photons are static from the point of view of the distant observer. Owing to the fact that the special theory of relativity should apply in small regions, the conclusion to draw is that space falls inwards at the speed of light. The surface at which space falls inwards with the speed of light is the event horizon.

It was shown by Price in the 1960s that during collapse the object's irregularities are lost. The surviving attributes for the black hole are mass, charge, and angular momentum. Solutions of Einstein's equations for this kind of a black hole were found in the 1960s. Such a black hole is commonly called a Kerr-Newman black hole. Whereas the Schwarzschild black hole does not have any charge or angular momentum, the rotating (Kerr-Newman) black hole has two characteristic surfaces. In one of these, space flows inwards with the speed of light: this is the static surface. In the other the space rotates with the speed of light: this is the event horizon. The event horizon lies inner to the static surface. The region between the two surfaces is termed the ergosphere. The static surface sphere is flattened along the axis of rotation. It was shown by Penrose in 1969 that energy can be extracted from a rotating black hole by injecting a mass into its ergosphere. The injected mass splits into two parts: one component moves against the rotation of the space in the ergosphere and falls into the black hole through the event horizon. The second component moves along with the space, gains energy and is ejected out of the static surface with a net gain in energy. By this process nearly 30 percent of the total energy of the black hole can be extracted, which is the maximum rotational energy fraction that a black hole can have. When all the rotational energy is lost, the static surface and the event horizon become a single spherical surface, and this is a non-rotating Schwarzschild black hole.

Stephen Hawking did a quantum mechanical analysis of black holes in 1974 and showed that they emit thermal radiation. To understand this one must view vacuum in a quantum mechanical fashion, i.e., as a sea of virtual particles and anti-particles. These particles are continuously created and destroyed. By the uncertainty principle energy can be borrowed so long as it is repaid in time. More the value of the energy of a particle antiparticle pair that is created, the less time can this pair exist. This fluctuation about the 'zero state' of vacuum can have influences on physical processes, and it has been experimentally verified for electromagnetic processes.

Vacuum fluctuations interact with the gravitational field of the black hole. This creates virtual particle pairs. Some of these fall into the black hole; for some the particle and the antiparticle of the pair annihilate each other as they normally do in vacuum. Both these happenings have no overall effect on the black hole. The third possibility where one member of the pair falls into the black hole and the other member escapes is the one which causes the black hole to lose energy. To the distant observer, this corresponds to the emission of a particle by the black hole. Hawking showed that the radiation from black holes is of the same form as for hot bodies. One can, therefore, associate a temperature with a black hole. Curiously this temperature is higher if the mass of the black hole is smaller.

A black hole is supposed to radiate away all its energy in a time approximately 10^{66} $(M/M_o)^3$ years. As it becomes smaller its radiation increases due to rise in temperature. At the very end it shoots out a lot of high energy particles and photons. Astronomers have been looking for these sources of high energy radiation created by evaporating black holes but have found no evidence. Of course the only black holes that would evaporate completely would be the miniholes that are assumed to have been created at the big bang because for large black holes the evaporation time is larger than the estimates of the epoch at which the big bang took place.

Objects of different sizes need different densities before black holes can form. A star of mass equal to the sun will have to be compressed to about nuclear densities (app 10^{16} grams per cubic centimeter) before a black hole will form. For a billion solar masses the required density is below that of water. If enough stars were brought together, a black hole may form without the stars touching each other.

The large scale structure of the universe

The earth is a part of the solar system which consists of the sun, the planets and their satellites, asteroids, meteorites, and comets. The solar system in turn belongs to our galaxy, which contains about 10^{11} stars. This galaxy is shaped like a bun and has a diameter of about 10^5 light-years. The solar system lies at a distance of about 3×10^4 light-years from the center of the galaxy, thus not occupying any privileged position. The stars in the galaxy take about 200 million years to complete one orbit around the galactic center. It is estimated there are about 3×10^9 other galaxies in the observable universe, which is as far as the best telescopes can probe. While on the scale of galaxies and clusters of galaxies the universe is irregular, on a larger scale the distribution of galaxies seems to be fairly uniform. The diameter of the observable universe is estimated to be about 10^{10} light years. If M_0 represents the mass of the sun, the estimate of the mass of the matter in the universe is $3 \times 10^{20} M_0$.

Since stars are generally electrically neutral, only gravitation appears important in cosmology. In the nineteenth century and the early part of the twentieth century most astronomers believed the universe as a whole to be static. Newtonian gravitation could not explain this static picture, however. As gravitation is an attractive force all matter in the universe should eventually collapse which runs counter to the static picture. Einstein's gravitation theory suffered from the same difficulty and therefore he modified his equations by introducing a new repulsive force that became important only over cosmological distances. Between this repulsive force and the force of gravitation the universe could be held static.

In 1928, Hubble discovered that the wavelength of the radiation from galaxies outside of our own exhibited a lengthening or a shift toward the red end. The lines from distant galaxies appeared at longer wavelengths, compared with the lines of our own galaxy or of nearby ones.

The distance of the galaxies was estimated by their brightness; the fainter a galaxy, the more distant it is. Hubble found a linear law relating $z = (\lambda - \lambda_0)/\lambda_0$, the red-shift of the absorption lines of known processes to the distance d:

$$z = dH/c$$

where H is now called the Hubble's constant, $H \approx 1.5 \times 10^{18}$/sec and c is the velocity of light.

One might argue that the red shift is produced by a strong gravitational field close to which most stars are located. It is difficult to reconcile all experimental evidence with this hypothesis, however.

The galactic red shift was originally interpreted as being due to the Doppler Effect. This is the effect which makes the whistle of an approaching train sound high-pitched because of a bunching up of sound waves. The same reason makes the whistle of a departing train sound low-pitched. The galactic redshift could then imply that the farther a galaxy is, the faster is its velocity of recession. More recently, however, the redshift has been primarily attributed to an expansion of space. We may thus imagine the galaxies to be embedded in a space which is itself expanding. All galaxies move away from one another, not unlike dots on a balloon that is inflated.

Two assumptions are generally made to construct theoretical models of the universe and these are the Weyl postulate and the cosmological principle.

The Weyl postulate: According to this postulate galaxies move in spacetime in regular tracks that do not intersect each other. This means that the galaxies can be taken to be stationary in a space (surface *V*) that is perpendicular to the world lines. The point X may be considered the moment when the universe was created.

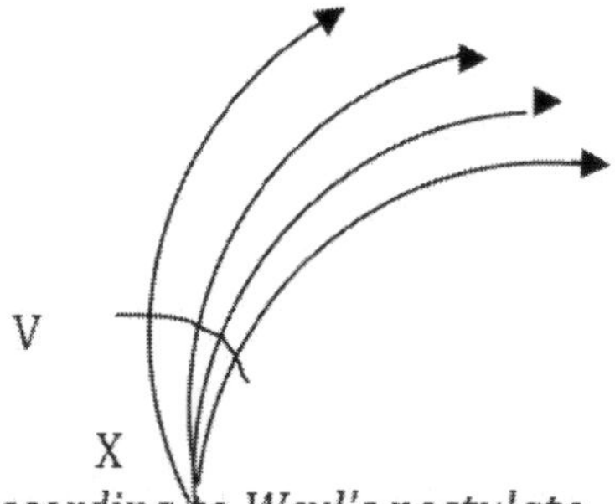

Motion according to Weyl's postulate

Weyl's postulate permits a synchronization of the clocks on different galaxies. We can also say that on the surface V that intersects the galactic tracks at right angles the clocks record the same time. This time is termed a universal or cosmic time that may be used as a reference for the universe as a whole.

The cosmological principle: According to this principle the universe is spatially homogeneous and isotropic. This means that at any cosmic time *t*, the universe looks the same, no matter what galaxy it is viewed from.

Using the above assumptions, the universe may be described in terms of two physical quantities; the curvature of the *V* space and the expansion factor *S(t)*. If the expansion factor S(t) increases with time, it means that the universe is expanding; if S(t) decreases with time, the universe is contracting; if S(t) remains unchanged, the universe remains static.

In his 1917 paper that described some cosmological implications of the general theory of relativity, Einstein obtained a static model of the universe by introducing the long-range repulsive force to counteract the force of gravity. This was done in an ad hoc way by introducing a cosmological constant into the relativity equations. Einstein tried to justify this constant by appealing to Mach's principle. He argued that doing this allowed one to relate global and local effects. The local mass density was made dependent to the cosmological constant. This universe had uniformly distributed matter and a uniformly curved spherical space.

The same year de Sitter showed that the use of relativity theory and the cosmological constant was also in consonance with an isotropic universe that contained no matter. This demonstrated that one could not talk of a unique universe. The de Sitter universe had the further property that any objects introduced into it moved away from each other. It was shown by Friedmann in 1922 that an expanding model of the universe could be obtained from Einstein's equations without the Λ-force. The Einstein equations relate the behavior of these models, as characterized by the expansion factor S and the curvature parameter k to the distribution of matter and energy in the universe. The solutions can be described by means of Fig. 3.2 which plots the expansion factor against time for different value of *k*, the curvature of the *V*-surface. In the case of zero or negative curvature, *S(t)* continuously increases with t, thus representing an ever-expanding universe. When *k = 1*, the universe first expands and later starts contracting to a singularity represented by *S =0*.

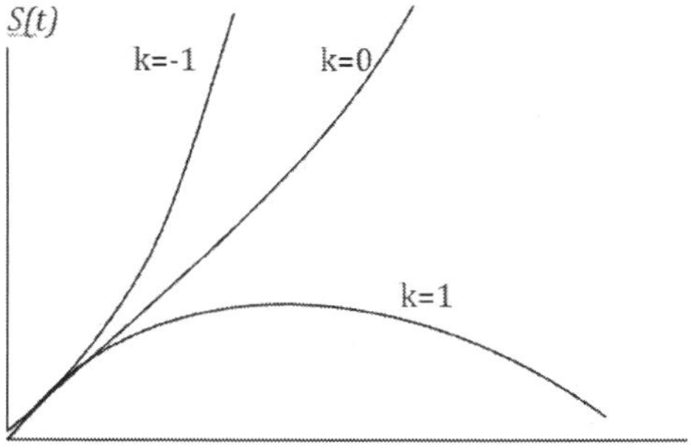

Plot of S(t) versus time

The three models start with *S = 0*, or from a state where the matter state is infinite. This is generally called the big-bang model of the universe where creation occurs at time *t=0* out of a primordial singularity containing infinite energy. The age of the universe is defined as the cosmic time which has elapsed since *t=0*, and it is estimated to be about 15 billion years. The big bang model of the origin of the universe was proposed soon after the discovery of the expansion.

Gamow speculated that the early universe was largely high intensity radiation, and subsequent development of the universe reduced the intensity of the radiation much more rapidly than it reduced the density of matter, so that the current state of the universe is matter dominated. According to Gamow a background of radiation should also exist at the present time. It was speculated that the temperature of this radiation should be between 5 and 50 degrees Kelvin. In 1965, Penzias and Wilson detected a background radiation in the microwave region which was isotropic and corresponded to black-body radiation at about 2.7°K. This radiation is generally taken to be a relic of the big bang.[5]

The steady-state theory

An alternative to the big-bang model called the steady-state model was proposed by Bondi and Gold, and Hoyle in 1948. The approach of Bondi and Gold was different to that of Hoyle, although the overall picture was substantially the same. Bondi and Gold modified the cosmological principle to arrive at their model, while Hoyle modified Einstein's equations.

Bondi and Gold named their modified principle the perfect cosmological principle. According to it the universe looks the same at all cosmic times. They argued that to accept the big-bang model would be to accept that the laws of physics have changed with time, since a changing universe should imply changing physical laws. They claimed that a study of distant galaxies by our physical laws when the radiation from these galaxies was emitted millions of years ago, when the laws were different, is incorrect.

Using their new principle, Bondi and Gold were able to deduce several properties of a steady-state universe, including that the universe must continually expand. To provide for the matter density to remain constant in an expanding universe they postulated a continuous creation of the matter. Hoyle proposed that this matter was created out of a reservoir of negative energy associated with space. The reduction in the density of this negative energy upon expansion of the space was cancelled out by the creation of new matter. It was suggested that if the creation and expansion processes were not in exact balance, the universe would fluctuate around a steady-state picture. This fluctuation may exhibit itself in terms of matter concentrated in galaxies.

The steady-state theory is not taken as a serious alternative to the big-bang theory ever since the background microwave radiation was discovered.

Newtonian cosmology

Consider a Newtonian universe with a finite amount of matter. Starting from the center of the distribution, concentric spheres can be drawn that include increasingly greater amount of matter. Consider also that in Newtonian theory a distribution of matter within a sphere acts gravitationally as if it were all concentrated at the center without regard to the radius of the sphere. Matter distributed in the outermost fringes would be attracted to all the remaining matter and the universe must collapse. This is the gravity paradox. But it is a paradox only if the universe is static and infinitely old. If it is accepted that matter upon extreme compression somehow tends to explode, then one has the picture of a cyclic universe.

A finite Newtonian universe cannot be in static equilibrium. If matter did explode out at the big bang it should eventually fall back into a singularity. Such a model can in fact explain galactic redshifts if the earth is taken to be somewhere close to the center of the galaxy. Then the gravity at the earth and the solar system would be low, while the gravity in the outlying regions would be high. This would cause the starlight received at the earth to be red shifted. The further a luminous object from earth, the greater is the redshift. This red-shift will be enhanced if the galaxies are moving away from each other. If the universe entered a phase of contraction, so long as the contraction blueshift did not compensate the gravitational redshift, one will still infer that the universe was expanding. Such a model has not found favor with physicists because it places the earth in a distinguished position.

Newton was looking for a stable universe and he was thus compelled to consider an infinite universe. For an infinite universe that has existed infinitely long one encounters another paradox called the Olbers' paradox. The radiation from all the stars in such a universe would make the sky bright at night. The paradox disappears when we consider a finite, expanding universe.

In 1934, it was shown by Milne and McCrea that Newtonian theory could be used to give precisely the same results as obtained using general relativity about the dynamic evolution of the universe. They considered a model where the universe is taken as a cosmic ball that is expanding.

The standard picture of matter and motion leaves us with several puzzling questions. For example, the theory of relativity was supposed to have banished absolute space yet astronomers can now talk of the absolute velocities of the earth and the sun through the background microwave radiation.

The speed of light is the upper limit of motion according to the relativity principle. Yet for black holes inside the event horizon space appears to flow faster than the speed of light.[6]

To an object that has just entered a black hole, the radiation from the rest of the universe gets extremely blue-shifted. The events on the outside appear speeded up and in fact the entire future of the universe flashes instantaneously. Does this mean that objects do not actually reach the singularity once they have crossed the event horizon? What is the size of a black hole in local spacetime?

Another interesting problem is the explanation of anomalous red shifts of certain extragalactic star-like objects called quasars. For many quasars there are components that seem to be moving away from each other at speeds exceeding that of light. Since this is at variance with the special theory of relativity, the apparent superluminal motion is taken to be an illusion. Several explanations for this illusion have been proposed but none of them is completely satisfactory.[7]

Observations over the last twenty years have shown that the universe is expanding and the galaxies are receding at a quickening rate. In order to explain this and other discrepancies in the structure of the cosmos, dark matter and dark energy, which do not interact with visible matter and energy, have been postulated. It is estimated that dark matter accounts for 23% and dark energy about 73% of the mass-energy density of the observable universe. This means that ordinary matter accounts for only 4% of the mass-energy density of the observable universe. Dark matter was postulated by Fritz Zwicky in 1934 to account for the evidence of 'missing mass' in the orbital velocities of galaxies in clusters. The current estimate that 96% of the universe is dark suggests that perhaps the way we are looking at the universe is wrong and our conception is ready for a drastic revision.

IV WAVES AND FIELDS

Waves and light

Light waves are electromagnetic and their position is at one end of the electromagnetic spectrum. The wavelength of visible light ranges from 4000 angstrom for blue light to roughly 7600 angstrom at the red end of the spectrum. These wavelengths correspond to frequencies of the order of 10^{14} cycles per second. At the other end, microwaves are at 10^{10} cycles per second and radio communication occurs in the range of 10^{7} cycles per second.

A wave is a disturbance that propagates through space. A stone thrown into a lake will generate a train of ripples which spread out from the point of impact. In contrast to particle motion, wave propagation does not involve a transfer of matter but rather the propagation of a disturbance. Water molecules oscillate up and down perpendicular to the surface of the water. These molecules have both potential and kinetic energy which is transmitted onwards.

If a long string is fastened at one end and the free end given a sharp snap, a pulse travels down its length. The speed of propagation of the pulse depends on the mass-density and tension of the string. The total effect of two or more waves propagating simultaneously on the same string can be obtained by adding the effects of the individual waves at all points. This is similar to the principle that when two or more forces act upon a single particle the resultant force is the vector sum of the two, and the acceleration of the particle is proportional to the resultant force, which is a consequence of the linear superposition principle.

An infinitely long string may propagate waves with any frequency, and propagate them all simultaneously. It is possible that if the waves had the proper amplitudes a superposition of these would yield a single spike that has a well-defined position as a function of time.

Sound waves are pressure waves. If the source and the observer move toward each other, the observer encounters more wave pulses than if they were a fixed distance away and measures a higher frequency. If the relative motion is away from the source, the observer measures a lower frequency. This change in frequency due to motion of the source or observer is the Doppler Effect. A popular illustration of the effect is the increase in the pitch of the whistle of an approaching train and the decrease in the pitch when the train pulls away. A similar phenomenon is true for electromagnetic waves.

Newton pictured light as a stream of particles. He argued that when a ray of light is incident on to a glass surface, the transmitted ray in the glass is bent nearer to the normal than the original because the particles gain speed as they enter the glass. He claimed that the speed gain was due to the glass attracting the particles. According to this picture, the speed of light is greater in the denser medium.

An experiment was performed by Foucault in 1850 which showed that the speed of light through water, a material denser than air, was actually lower than the speed in air. Earlier in 1803, Thomas Young performed an experiment the results of which tilted the evidence strongly in favor of a wave theory. In this experiment, a screen with two slits was placed between a light source and a wall that illuminated the wall with alternating bands of light and darkness. The center band was the brightest, and the intensity of the illuminated bands decreased as one moved away from it. The interference pattern disappeared when either of the slits was shut. The result can be easily explained on the basis of the wave model. The alternating light and dark bands are due to interference that results when the waves of light diffracting from the two slits produce effects that interfere with each other. In areas where one wave crest overlaps another wave crest, the result is an intensification of light. In areas where a crest meets a trough, a cancellation takes place and no light reaches the wall. Since light beams do not interact with each other, this cancellation occurs in the detecting material of the wall.

Accelerated charges emit electromagnetic waves and it is believed that the analogous situation of accelerated masses should lead to gravitational waves. Two neutron stars, orbiting each other, or a non-spherical neutron star during its collapse should produce gravitational waves in the range of a few kilohertz that could just be detected in the laboratory. In the past twenty five years several experiments were designed to detect gravitational waves that might be generated in other regions of our own galaxy and recently their discovery was announced.[1]

Interconnected fields

Electric phenomena were known to man from early time. It was known that amber rubbed by wool will attract small and light bodies. The physicist William Gilbert (1540-1603) showed that a number of substances had properties similar to amber; he termed them electric bodies after the Greek electron for amber. Later Steven Gray (1670-1736) discovered the fundamental difference between insulators and conductors, and the Du Fay (1698-1739) explained the dual nature of electricity in terms of two constituents, the glass and the resin electricity. He also showed that electric forces were repulsive for the same kind and attractive for different kinds of electricity.

Benjamin Franklin (1706-1790) originated the convention of using the terms positive and negative for the two kinds of electricity. Franklin, and independently Watson, showed in 1747 that in every electrical process equal amounts of positive and negative electricity are formed. Thus when a glass rod is rubbed with a piece of silk, the glass rod becomes charged with positive electricity; an exactly equal negative charge is established on the silk piece. Thus friction only separates the two kinds of charges.

The idea that electric forces act like gravitation at a distance is due to Aepinus (1759). The exact law was found independently by J. B. Priestley (1733-1804) and Henry Cavendish (1731-1810). The first verification of this law was made by Coulomb in 1785 by direct measurement and it is known after his name. The force between two charges q_1 and q_2 is proportional to the product of the charges and inversely proportional to the square of the distance *r* between them.

Electric charge is quantized. There exists a smallest charge that cannot be subdivided any further, and all charges are integer multiples of this value $e = 1.6 \times 10^{-19}$ coulomb. But no similar quantization occurs for mass.

Many elementary particles carry just one unit of electric charge. The lightest of these particles is the electron, which carries a negative charge $q = -e$ and has a mass $m_e = 9.1 \times 10^{-28}$g. It is instructive to compare the gravitational attraction $F_g = G\, m_e^2 / r^2$ with the electrostatic repulsion $F_e = k_1 e^2 / r^2$ between two electrons at distance *r* from each other. The result is $F_e / F_G = k_1 e^2 / G M_e^2 = 4 \times 10^{42}$, showing the extreme weakness of the gravitational force as compared to the electric force.

The study of current electricity began with Luigi Galvani, a professor of anatomy in Bologna. He discovered that electrical sparks produced by a nearby machine caused muscular contraction in a dissected frog. In another experiment, Galvani found that whenever a metal connector connected the frog's nerve and the frog's muscle, a similar contraction took place. Galvani concluded that a fluid, which he identified with electric charge, was transported by the metal from the nerve to the muscle causing the contraction. In 1792, a year after publication of Galvani's results, it was shown by Alessandro Volta that one could construct a pile of layers of copper, moist pasteboard, and zinc that produced an electric shock. Soon it was accepted that current electricity as well as electrostatics were manifestations of the same phenomenon.

Magnetic phenomena have been known since antiquity. Lodestones were known in ancient times and the mariner's compass is an old invention. There is a radical difference between magnetic and electrical phenomena: there are no free magnetic charges. The basic entity in magnetism is the magnetic dipole, i.e., a pair of materially connected opposite poles (charges) of equal strength. There exist two kinds of poles, and similar poles repel and opposite poles attract. By convention one calls the kind of pole which on a magnetic compass needle tends to point toward the geographic North pole of the earth a magnetic N-pole and the opposite a magnetic S-pole. The behavior of the magnetic compass can then be explained by saying that the earth itself behaves like a giant magnet, with a magnetic S-pole near the geographic N-pole, and vice versa. It was Gilbert who first made this observation.

The force law for magnetic poles is analogous to that for electric charges. The force between two magnetic poles P_1 and P_2 is proportional to the product of the pole strengths and inversely proportional to the square of the distance between them.

Due to the connections between electricity and magnetism, one expects magnetic poles to be quantized. If that is indeed so is unknown. Then there is the apparent impossibility of isolating single magnetic poles. Even the electron possesses a complete dipole, but the only magnetic quantity accessible to measurement in such an elementary dipole is the dipole moment $p = P\ell$ where ℓ is the distance separating the two poles of strength P.

The concept of field to explain electric and magnetic forces was introduced by Michael Faraday (1791-1867). According to him the capability of a charge q_1 for exerting a force on another charge q_2 was the result of the field E present throughout space even in the absence of charge q_2. By convention, the field at any point in space outside a positive charge is a vector pointing away from that charge, and in the case of a negative charge, pointing toward the charge.

By following the direction of the field one can trace out lines of force for a pair of opposite charges. A similar concept of the magnetic field applies to magnetic phenomena. The lines of force in magnetism can be made visible by scattering iron filings over a sheet of paper and holding a magnet closely over these. By convention, magnetic field lines are taken to point away from a N-pole and toward a S-pole. The lines of force for both electric and magnetic fields are vectors and they have magnitude and direction defined at each point in space.

Electric and magnetic fields can be derived from electric and magnetic potentials. The electric potential is a scalar function defined in terms of a single variable throughout space. It is the potential difference between two points and not the absolute value that determines the electric field intensity between the points. The magnetic potential is a vector variable, in contrast, owing to the magnetic field lines being always closed. If the gradient of an arbitrary scalar function were to be added to the magnetic potential, the field remains unchanged. Such a choice is expressed by stating that the magnetic potential can be gauge transformed.

A connection between electricity and magnetism was noted by the Danish physicist Hans Christian Oersted (1777-1851) who observed the presence of a magnetic field in the vicinity of an electric current, with closed magnetic field lines encircling the current. Biot and Savart in 1820 and later Ampere in much more elaborate and thorough experiments established the basic experimental laws relating the magnetic field strength to the current and explained the law of force between one current and another. Each of two long, parallel, current-carrying straight wires a distance *d* apart, experiences a force per unit length directed perpendicularly towards the other wire which is directly proportional to the currents and inversely proportional to the distance *d*. The force is attractive if the currents flow in the same direction and repulsive otherwise.

An important application of the property of magnetic field surrounding current is the electromagnet, obtained by letting a current pass through a number of loops wound into a solenoid. In an early demonstration a magnet driven by a small battery supported more than a ton of iron.

The equivalence of the magnetic field produced by a current loop with the field of a magnetic dipole made Ampere suggest that all magnetism observed in nature is the result of elementary circulating charges. This mechanism along with magnetism associated with spin angular momentum is sufficient to explain magnetic properties of atoms.

There is a parallel to the Ampere's law of magnetic potential around a moving charge. According to this principle, called Faraday's induction law, an electric potential is set up in a wire if it intersects changing magnetic potential.

While no forces are set up between an electric charge and a magnetic pole if they are at rest with respect to each other, a magnetic field exerts a force on a moving charge. The direction of the force F is always perpendicular to both the velocity v and magnetic field B, so that for a positive charge the three vectors v, B, F form a right-hand system. The magnitude of this force depends on the angle θ between v and B and is given by

$$F = q \times \frac{v}{c} B \sin \theta$$

The fact that a given charge has no magnetic field around it when viewed by an observer at rest with respect to it and at the same time it has a magnetic field when viewed by a moving observer suggests further grounds for considering electric and magnetic fields to be aspects of a comprehensive entity, the electromagnetic field, whose decomposition into electric and magnetic components depends on the state of motion of the observer.

It was Maxwell who in 1865 saw a way to achieve a consistent unification by first generalizing Ampere's law by adding to moving charges causing magnetic fields another term which he called the displacement current. This generalization is necessary when the fields are fluctuating. Displacement current is defined as the rate of change of the induced electric field in the medium. Maxwell surmised that light was an electromagnetic phenomenon, and that electromagnetic waves of all frequencies could be produced. When electromagnetic energy propagates, the electric and magnetic field vectors are oriented at right angles to the direction of propagation. One can associate with the passing of an electromagnetic wave past a point in space three mutually perpendicular vectors since the magnetic and the elective field vectors are themselves at right angles to each other. A rough visualization of this process producing electromagnetic waves is a coherent train of alternating magnetic and electric fields generating each other as they spread out.

Heinrich Hertz in 1888 produced electromagnetic waves by making sparks jump across the gap between two charged spheres. When these waves encountered a circular wire with a small gap, they produced in it a current that in turn produced sparks at the gap. Hertz measured the velocity of these waves and showed that it was equal to the velocity of light.

The initial models of electromagnetic phenomena took the ether as the carrier of the electric and magnetic fields. The ether was supposed to have several mechanical properties, and Maxwell's first interpretations of his equations were also based on these properties. The most popular model of the ether was as a fluid whose rate of flow represented the electric field and whose vortices represented the magnetic field. Electric charges were imagined as pulsating spheres in the ether fluid and it was visualized that such spheres exerted force on one another. These models suggested experiments which led to the discovery of new phenomena.

Heinrich Hertz considered assertions regarding properties of the ether as superfluous. He believed there was no basis to extrapolate from the mechanical behavior of terrestrial objects to ether behavior. Lacking knowledge of the properties of ether, he believed that the best thing to do was to speak of the phenomena directly. This abandonment of the mechanical explanation had a profound influence on the development of twentieth century physics.

There exist issues of global and local symmetry in Maxwell's equations. Global symmetry refers to physical phenomena that remains invariant when the variables in question are transformed everywhere at once. Thus if all the charges in the universe were changed in polarity at once the field would remain unchanged. Local symmetry, on the other hand, refers to changes required in fields everywhere, if the variables are transformed in a limited region of space.

The basis to the understanding of the theory of electromagnetism is the observation that an electric charge is surrounded by an electric field stretching to infinity, and that the movement of an electric charge gives rise to a magnetic field also of infinite extent. We noted that for a system of fixed charges a global symmetry exists in the sense that all charges can be reversed in polarity simultaneously without altering the field. If the electric potential of a small charge system was raised, the field within the system would remain unchanged, but at its boundary with the environment the fields will be modified. When the potentials in the system are modified we are constrained to modify the global symmetry into a local one. The same thing occurs when we permit the charges in the system to move. Moving charges produce a magnetic field which restores the local symmetry.

It is in the system of potential fields that local transformations can be carried out leaving the original electric and magnetic fields unaltered. The system of dual, interconnected fields has an exact local symmetry even though the electric field alone does not. Any local change in the electric potential can be combined with a compensating change in the magnetic potential in such a way that the electric and magnetic fields are invariant.

The dual nature of light

Maxwell's equations and the explanation of the two-slit experiment take light as a wave. Yet there are experimental situations where the only explanation requires that light is a particle phenomenon. An example of this is the photoelectric effect that describes the emission of electrons when a metal plate is irradiated with ultraviolet or X-rays. It is seen that the energy of the released electrons is determined by the color (or frequency) of the incident radiation. The intensity of this radiation does not determine the energy of the individual electron, but the rate at which electrons are released. Since energy is proportional to the frequency of the radiation one can theorize that the energy of an emitted electron is the incident energy minus the energy needed to liberate it. What is required to make the explanation complete is the hypothesis that light of a particular color consists of discrete, energy carrying entities called photons, all of which have the same energy. Thus electrons in a metal absorb individual photons completely. An electron cannot absorb a fraction of a photon. The photoelectric effect shows up even when the intensity of the radiation is so weak that it takes minutes before an electron is emitted.

In this corpuscular model of light photons of infrared light have lower energies than photons of visible light, while photons of ultraviolet light have higher energies. At frequencies higher than those of the visible spectrum such as for X-rays the energy is still higher. In 1923, A. H. Compton used X-rays to demonstrate that photons carry momentum. He designed an experiment showing that photons can transfer part of their momentum to electrons and be scattered in a fashion similar to the collision and subsequent scattering of billiard balls.

But if photons are represented as particles and the motion of the photons through each slit is represented in classical probabilistic terms then in the two-slit situation the probabilities for single slits should be added up when both slits are open. But in the two-slit case bands of zero intensity are obtained on the screen, implying that photons are behaving differently than in the single-slit case.

We are compelled to accept that each photon in the double-slit experiment is somehow traveling through both the slits and interfering with itself to form the interference bands since such bands are formed even if the particles are go through the slits one at a time.

Both sides on the debate on the nature of light being waves or particle are partly right. But neither of the two descriptions is completely correct. We need a description that transcends those of waves and particles and still is consistent with both so that different effects such as the photoelectric and the two-slit interference can be explained.

This new description is provided by quantum mechanics, and it is valid not only for light but also for electrons, protons, and all other entities that compose the universe. This new description is mathematical with a probabilistic core. In the photoelectric effect one cannot predict with certainty as to which electron will absorb a photon: one can assign a probability to this event. In the two-slit experiment one can have no certain knowledge as to which slit a given photon will pass but one can determine the probability of finding it at a certain point on the screen.

The conception that a particle can go simultaneously through two slits can obviously not be understood in logical terms. This means that one must abandon classical notions and look at the issue from a new perspective.

V THE WORLD OF QUANTA

New rules and interpretations

The ancients believed that properties of time, space, and motion could be determined as attested by the school of Vaiśeṣika although they were perplexed by the conceptualization of these categories. If considering space to be either continuous or discrete leads to paradoxes, so does the idea of divisibility. If matter is subdivided endlessly, do the smallest fragments have zero mass? If so, how does adding these fragments lead to finite mass? On the other hand, if the smallest atom has finite mass, and thereby a finite volume, why is it impossible to subdivide it further? Kaṇāda's resolution[1] to these paradoxes also leads to difficulties. His resolution was that the smallest atoms were point objects which somehow behaved as if they had finite size and mass, which implicitly considered the dichotomy of the object and the observer. In reality, the atom is a point, but its perception is different. The resolution of the paradox of divisibility in modern physics[2] is similar to that of Kaṇāda.

The phenomena of mechanics and electromagnetism are coupled by the Lorentz law which states that a charged particle moving in electric and magnetic fields experiences a force. By the end of the nineteenth century, scientists felt that a picture of the world with matter consisting of particles, and radiation consisting of waves could provide a framework for a description of all physical phenomena. In this picture, the elementary particles were protons and electrons, each of which had mass and unit electrical charge, and their interactions were through electromagnetic and gravitational forces. Soon it was discovered that many processes did not conform to this picture.

Historically, the first indication of a breakdown of the classical concepts occurred in the phenomenon of black body radiation, which is concerned with the thermodynamics of the exchange of energy between radiation and matter. Classically it is assumed that this exchange of energy is continuous, in the sense that waves of frequency ν can give up any amount of energy on absorption, the actual amount depending on the energy intensity of the beam. It was shown by Planck in 1900 that a correct formula is obtained only if it is assumed that the energy exchange is discrete. Specifically, Planck postulated that radiation of angular frequency ν can only exchange energy in units of $\hbar\nu$ where $\hbar$ is now called the Planck's constant. This can be taken to mean that radiation of frequency ν behaves like a stream of particles of energy $\hbar\nu$.

A simpler example of the particle aspect of radiation is the photoelectric effect that was explained by Einstein in 1905. If a beam of monochromatic light of frequency ν is projected on the surface of a metal, electrons may be emitted. If $\hbar\nu$ is less than the threshold W, a characteristic of the metal, no electrons are emitted. If $\hbar\nu > W$, electrons are emitted with kinetic energy T where $T = W - \hbar\nu$. The energy of the emitted electrons depends only on the frequency of the radiation and not its intensity, and W is the work which is required to free the electron from the attractive potential produced by the metal. Both black body radiation and the photoelectric effect show that energy exchange takes place by quanta $\hbar\nu$.

The atomic nucleus was discovered in 1911 by Rutherford. In the planetary model of the atom, electrons orbit about the positively charged nucleus. According to classical electrodynamics an accelerating charge like the electron in orbit must radiate energy, so one cannot explain the inherent stability of the atom. It was not clear why the radiated energy was not over a continuous range of frequencies. There also existed considerable amount of puzzling data from spectroscopy, which was clarified to some extent by Ritz's combination rule of spectra, showing that the frequency of each spectral line can be expressed as a difference of two terms. In 1913, Bohr introduced his model of the atom to explain some of the above difficulties. According to this model, the atom has stable orbits such that an electron moving in them does not radiate electromagnetic energy. But in making a transition from an orbit of higher energy to one with lower energy, the electron radiates. The frequency of this radiation is related to the difference between the energies of the electron in these two orbits. Both of Bohr's principles were in the nature of postulates. But it was possible with their aid to explain, in excellent agreement with experiment, the observed spectrum of the hydrogen atom. The nature of these postulates was a revolutionary step beyond classical mechanics.

After the introduction of Bohr's stationary states, new developments showed the need for having quantities connected with two states. Ritz's combination law, which results in Bohr's frequency condition, showed that the frequencies of the spectral lines are each connected with two states. Then Einstein introduced coefficients for emission and absorption each connected with two states, as were the quantities in the Kramers-Heisenberg dispersion formula.

It was suggested by Louis de Broglie in 1923 that the wave-particle duality applicable to light should also apply to electrons and other particles. In 1927, Davisson and Germer showed that a beam of electrons reflected from the surface of a nickel crystal formed diffraction patterns, exactly analogous to the diffraction of light by a grating. The pattern persists even when the intensity of the electrons is so low that they pass through the apparatus almost one at a time. Diffraction is essentially a wave phenomenon, and its appearance showed that a wave must in some way be associated with the motion of a single electron.

The above seemingly contradictory observations could only be explained in the framework of the new paradigm of quantum mechanics. This paradigm had its beginnings in Heisenberg's conception in 1925 of representing physical quantities by time-dependent complex numbers. Soon afterwards this approach was elaborated by Born, Jordan and

Heisenberg into what was matrix mechanics, the earliest consistent theory of quantum phenomena.

In 1926, Schrödinger showed that the usual rule for quantization can be replaced by the requirement for the finiteness and single-valuedness of a certain function. Using this approach Schrödinger was able to derive a time-dependent wave equation and apply it to several situations. He also demonstrated a formal equivalence of this wave mechanics and Heisenberg's matrix mechanics.

In addition to the difficulties in the interpretation in terms of classical concepts of the two-slit experiment, an important distinction exists between classical and quantum views. In the classical description, given two points A and B in the path of a particle and given all forces acting on the particle in its path as well as its previous interactions, one can determine the exact trajectory between A and B. In the quantum description, it is impossible to localize a particle at specific points in its path. Even if one should assume that two points in the path have been determined, all one can do is to indicate a large bundle of paths each with its own probability that can potentially be the trajectory of the particle.

For the two-slit experiment, say for electrons, the interference persists so long as no attempt is made to see which of the two slits each particle went through. If any attempt is made to determine the path of the electron, the interference vanishes. Even if this determination is sought long after the particles have gone through the slits (delayed choice), as in experiments where light from a distant star reaches us from two paths due to gravitational lensing, the interference patterns disappear. Wheeler interpreted this to mean that the photons, emitted billions of years earlier, decided to travel as particles as they *knew* that an attempt would be made to find the path they would take, indicating that past and present are intricately intertwined.

During the early development of quantum theory a principle which proved very useful was Bohr's Correspondence Principle: The quantities obtained from quantum theory, and hence containing $\hbar$, must transform into corresponding classical quantities by the limiting process $\hbar \to 0$. It is a statement of the universality of the laws of nature and rejects the idea that there are separate laws for the microscopic and the macroscopic realms.

Each quantum state corresponds to a whole family of classical states. An important property of the quantum states is that they have a superposition relation between them which means that they may be viewed as vectors or as wave function. The basis of the standard interpretation of quantum mechanics consists of the following statements:

1. The state of a physical system is described by the wave function Ψ.
2. If Ψ_1 and Ψ_2 represent two states of a system, then a linear combination of the two also represents a state of the system.
3. The wave function of a system obeys a continuous equation of motion, the Schrödinger equation.

4. The process of measurement is described by the action of an appropriate operator on the state. A measurement sends the system into a new state.[3] In general, the process of observation brings about a discontinuous change of Ψ, which is the *reduction of the wave packet.*

The most surprising result about the dynamical variables in a quantum description is that their values are expressed in terms of probabilities. In other words, if an experiment were repeated several times one would be able to predict the outcome of the measurements in a probabilistic sense only. Quantum mechanics provides a probabilistic picture of reality.

The wave function for a particle may be symmetrical or anti-symmetrical. Particles with symmetrical wave functions are called bosons after Satyendra Nath Bose who investigated their statistics first. When the wave function is anti-symmetrical the particles are termed fermions after Enrico Fermi. Boson have integer angular momentum 0, $\hbar$, $2\hbar$, ... while fermions have half-odd integer angular such as $\hbar/2$ and $3\hbar/2$. Photons and mesons are bosons whereas protons, neutrons, and muons and neutrinos are fermions. Several bosons can be in the same state. As the number of bosons in a particular state increases, the probability that more will enter the state also increases. Fermions behave differently in that the probability of finding two identical fermions in the same state is zero. The property that the presence of one fermion in a state excludes all other identical fermions is termed the Pauli Exclusion Principle after Wolfgang Pauli who first suggested it based on empirical grounds.

The uncertainty principle

A periodic waveform can be viewed as a sum of a suitable number of sinusoidal functions of different frequencies that are multiples of the fundamental frequency of the waveform. On the other hand, pulses or transient signals can be represented by the sum of sinusoids of all conceivable frequencies, which is a frequency band extending from zero to infinity. If the pulse is not of finite duration but has most of its energy concentrated in a certain time interval, T, it may happen that the frequency function has most of its energy concentrated in a finite band, F. In fact it can be shown that the product TF is always greater than a certain constant.

Position and trajectory are not defined precisely in quantum mechanics; also momentum is defined in terms of the frequency band associated with the probability distribution of the location of the particle. It follows that a lower bound should be associated with the product of position and momentum values.

In general, if the position of a particle were specified to limits Δx and the momentum to limits Δp, then

$$\Delta x \, \Delta p \geq \hbar/2$$

A similar restriction is defined to the measurement of energy of a particle at a definite point of time:

$$\Delta E \, \Delta t \geq \hbar/2$$

These relations were derived by Werner Heisenberg in 1927 and they have since come to be known as the uncertainty relations. The restriction in the simultaneous measurement of certain variables is known as the uncertainty principle.

The act of observation always disturbs the system. When we measure the temperature of a hot liquid by inserting a thermometer, heat flows from the liquid to the thermometer till their temperatures are equal. The liquid cools somewhat to this common temperature, and the thermometer reading therefore measures the disturbed system. In large systems the effect of the measurement can be made so small so as to be negligible. This is not so in the atomic world. The uncertainty is fundamental here because whereas in the Newtonian picture one can talk of the precise value of position, momentum or some other attribute even before a measurement, one cannot do so except after a measurement has been made. Such measurement, however, disturbs the system and variables such as position and momentum cannot be measured simultaneously with total precision.

The law of conservation of energy also requires a reinterpretation in view of the energy-time uncertainty relation. To assert that energy is conserved requires energy measurements to be made at different instants of time. The energy-time uncertainty relation requires that the energy checks be not made at instants too close together lest the energy measurement become very imprecise. This leaves open the possibility that over very short durations of time the law of conservation of energy can be violated. Thus particles of definite energy can be created out of nothing so long as they disappear within the time allowed by the uncertainty relation. This time is so small at everyday energies so as to be totally insignificant. But for elementary particles, this has important consequences.

Mathematically, let the state of a system be described, at a given moment by a definite, in general complex, function $\Psi(q)$ of the coordinates. The square of the modulus of the function determines the probability distribution of the values of the coordinates: $||\Psi||^2 dq$ is the probability that a measurement performed on the system will find the values of the coordinates to be in the element dq of the configuration space.

The state of the system, that is the wave function, varies with time. If the wave function is known at some initial instant then from the very meaning of the concept of complete description of a state, it is in principle determined at every succeeding instant.

The sum of the probabilities of all possible values of the coordinates of the system must, by definition, be equal to unity. It is therefore necessary that the result of integrating $||\Psi||^2$ over the entire space should be equal to unity:

$$\int || \Psi ||^2 \, dq = 1$$

This is the normalization condition for wave functions. If the integral of $||\Psi||^2$ converges, then by choosing an appropriate constant coefficient the function Ψ can be normalized. If the integral of $||\Psi||^2$ does not converge, then $||\Psi||^2$ does not, obviously, represent the absolute values of the probabilities of the coordinates; the ratio of the values of $||\Psi||^2$ at two points may represent the relative probability of the corresponding values of the coordinates.

All quantities calculated by means of the wave function, and having a direct physical meaning, have a form in which Ψ is multiplied by Ψ^*. This means that the normalized wave function is determined only to within a constant phase factor of the form $e^{i\alpha}$ (where α is any real number), whose modulus is unity. This indeterminacy is in principle irremovable: it has no effects on any physical results, however.

As mentioned before the principle of superposition of states holds. It follows from the principle that all equations satisfied by wave functions must be linear in Ψ.

If the states do not interact, their joint wave function can be represented as the product of the individual wave functions. Since a system, consisting of two particles, that are far apart and moving towards each other, would have these particles interact with each other eventually, the above condition causes logical difficulties that recur in quantum mechanics. One of these areas of difficulty is the measurement problem.

If the quantum laws only provide probability connections between the results of consecutive measurements on an apparatus then the question arises that why is the concept of consecutiveness non-relativistic.

A disquieting feature of the preceding discussion is the fact that the state function of an object seems to evolve in two different ways. Firstly, it evolves in time according to Schrödinger's equation $H\Psi = i\hbar \dfrac{d\Psi}{dt}$. Secondly, it changes discontinuously, according to probability laws, if a measurement is carried out on the system. This latter change is the reduction of the wave function. While the state function evolves in a causal manner, no matter what the time period, so long as no measurement is made on it, the process of measurement requires a definite choice to be made regarding the wave function that defines a puzzling duality. This duality may be expressed clearly with the help of the following paradox.

Consider a closed room which consists of an experimenter studying the motion of an electron with the help of an apparatus. One may associate with the room a wave function which will evolve with time. Given the initial wave function one can without ambiguity determine it for all future time. This wave function, however, is a product of the wave functions of the experimenter, the apparatus and that of the electron, and we know that upon his measurement the experimenter within the room would modify the wave function of the electron. If the experimenter within the room communicated his observation to us later, we would need to modify our earlier results as well. This however leads to a contradiction since a Schrödinger type equation should have completely described the evolution of the room wave function.

This difficulty was pointed out by Schrödinger himself in a scenario that is now known as the cat paradox. Consider a closed chamber containing a cat and a small amount of a radioactive substance, the probability of decay per minute of one atom of which is exactly 0.5; the decay, if it occurs, activates a Geiger counter, and closes a circuit that electrocutes the cat. The entire system can be represented by a wave function which is a superposition of two waves, one denoting the state 'cat alive' and the other the state 'cat dead.' At the end of the experiment, when the chamber is opened, the cat is thrown into a definite alive or dead state only through the act of observation. According to quantum mechanics one cannot speak of the cat being either dead or alive before the act of observation, when surely the cat must have been in one of these two states even before the chamber was opened. In another version of this paradox, due to Wigner, the cat is replaced by the experimenter's friend to circumvent the objection that the cat might not possess full awareness of its own existence. Then the question arises: is the experimenter's friend alive or dead before the act of observation, because being 'dead-alive' is definitely meaningless.

Wigner and others believe that the only way to get out of the above paradoxes is to assume that the wave function of the object is reduced due to its interaction with the consciousness of the experimenter. And since the dynamics of consciousness are not known, the problem of the room with an experimenter inside it lies outside the pale of quantum mechanics and of present-day physics. This view-point makes the following situations symmetric. We know matter affects consciousness; therefore consciousness also affects matter. Wigner's view assigns to sentient beings a central role in the organization of the universe.

A quite different resolution of the Schrödinger's cat paradox is provided by the man-worlds interpretation of quantum mechanics proposed in 1957 by Hugh Everett.[4] According to this interpretation, the wave function represents objective reality. This is in contrast to the usual understanding of the wave function where it defines a sum of potentialities and a computational procedure. According to the Everett view, the states of the wave function are the description of the system in the many universes that co-exist with ours, without interacting with each other. An act of observation does not cause the wave function to collapse, but merely-shows up one of the actualities. Each moment the universe splits into countless near copies of itself, and the electron through a slit reaches different positions on the screen in the copies, so that the distribution is according to what the wave function predicts which circumvents the paradox of measurement. The Schrödinger's cat would, in the many-worlds interpretation, be dead in some worlds and alive in others. This interpretation is far removed from a commonsensical view of reality.

The complementarity interpretation

Bohr in 1927 gave an interpretation of quantum mechanics that elevated duality, such as that between waves and particles, to a fundamental attribute of physical reality.

In this view, mutually exclusive aspects are a part of reality's comprehensive description. For light the basic reality is the wave aspect which corresponds to the classical description while its conception as photon is symbolic, which is required to express the exchange of energy and momentum between matter and radiation. For electrons and protons, the situation is reversed. Bohr believed that "however far the phenomena transcend the scope of classical physical explanation, the account of all evidence must be expressed in classical terms."

Bohr pointed out that from an operational point of view it is not possible to come up with experimental arrangements that measure position and momentum exactly and such measurements require complementary experiments. The thought experiment that Bohr used to illustrate this is the setup of an electron passing through a slit in a diaphragm. If the diaphragm were rigidly connected to measuring devices like scales and clocks, the exact position of the electron would be ascertainable, while the information concerning the energy or momentum exchange would be lost owing to the rigid connection of the diaphragm with the frame. On the other hand, if the diaphragm were suspended by weak springs, the momentum transfer would be ascertainable while the information concerning the exact position of the passing electron would be lost owing to the indeterminate location of the diaphragm.

The complementarity interpretation is consistent with the Vedic view that reality has a unity but this unity cannot be apprehended in logical terms. The Vedic view has additional elements related to consciousness that are not a part of the quantum mechanical framework.

The EPR argument and Bell's theorem

Einstein, Podolsky and Rosen (EPR) in 1935 advanced an argument to show why quantum mechanics is an incomplete theory. This argument is closely related to the interpretation of the measurement process and is not generally accepted as sound. The following premises, which are to a degree interrelated, are fundamental in the EPR paper for a theory to be locally realistic and complete:[5]

1. The reality criterion. Regularities in observed phenomena are caused by a physical reality whose existence is independent of the human observer.
2. The completeness criterion. A physical theory is complete only if every element of the physical reality has a counterpart in the physical theory. To these two criteria one may add the following two assumptions implicit in the EPR paper.
3. The induction assumption. Inductive inference is a valid mode of reasoning and is applicable to statistical predictions as well.
4. The locality assumption. If at the time of measurement two systems no longer interact, no real change can take place in the second system in consequence of anything that may be done to the first system. Put differently, no influence of any kind can propagate faster than the speed of light. This assumption is also called Einstein locality or Einstein separability.

We now look at the measurement process in light of the EPR argument. Consider a system consisting of two spin one-half particles to be in a singlet state (total spin zero) and let the two particles move freely in opposite directions. Once the particles have separated without change of their total spin and ceased to interact, any desired spin component of particle-one may be measured. The total spin being zero, one knows immediately, without in any way interfering with particle-two, that its spin component in the same direction is opposite to that of particle-one. On the basis of the EPR criterion of physical reality it must be concluded that the inferred value presents an element of physical reality and must have existed even before the measurement was carried out. But since any other direction could have been chosen equally well, all three spin components of particle two must have simultaneously definite sharp values after its separation from particle one. Since quantum mechanics, because of the non-commutativity of the spin operators, allows only one of these components to be specifiable at a time with complete precision, it does not provide a complete description of physical reality. Indeed other EPR premises could also be similarly questioned.

The EPR argument is criticized on its assumption that the two particles, once they have separated sufficiently, are two independent systems. Bohr questioned the reality criterion itself. He believed that since quantum mechanics can be regarded as a computational device for obtaining the probability of every measurement involving both the system to be observed as well as the measuring instruments, no attributes of physical reality can be ascribed to the former alone. In accordance with his complementarity interpretation, Bohr claimed that quantum mechanics can speak neither of particles with attributes that exist but cannot be accurately observed, nor of particles where the attributes are a priori indefinite. Rather, it described experimental arrangements where complementary expressions such as position and velocity, or spin in two orthogonal axes can never be employed simultaneously.

It was shown by J.S. Bell in 1964 that particles that are governed by a locally realistic theory must satisfy a certain inequality that was to be named after him. Consider a spin one-half particle with its spin defined in three different axes A, B, and C. The value of the spin when measured in each of these axes can be +1/2 or -1/2; we label the former by A^+, B^+, C^+ and the latter by A^-, B^-, C^-. If a particle has been found in the states A^+ and B^-, then it must be a member of the class $A^+B^-C^+$ or $A^+B^-C^-$. Now, If $N(A^+B^-)$ represents the number of particles with spins A^+ and B^-, then

$$N(A^+B^-) = N(A^+B^-C^+) + N(A^+B^-C^-)$$

and so on. Algebraic manipulations show that the above leads to

$$N(A^-B^+) \leq N(A^-C^+) + N(B^+C^-)$$

Extrapolate now from the case of single particles for which two properties are known to that of pairs of particles, each particle of which is tested for one property. The pairs are created in such a way that there is always a strict negative correlation for any property considered separately, as in the preceding example illustrating the EPR argument, so that both properties of both particles can be deduced. For spins along A and B, designate by $n[A^+B^+]$ the total number of particles with the spins A^+B^- and A^-B^+ respectively, or $n[A^+B^-] = N(A^+B^-) + N(A^-B^+)$. Using this argument repeatedly we deduce

$$n[A^+ B^+] \leq n[A^+C^+] + n[B^+C^+]$$

which is the Bell inequality.

The Bell inequality predicts a relation between correlations obtained amongst three attributes. The prediction by quantum mechanics is different to that of Bell inequality.

One can measure correlations between polarization states to test the prediction of Bell's inequality. One can visualize a gas that emits light when it is electrically excited. The excited atoms in the gas emit photons in pairs. The photons in each pair have the same polarization and they move in opposite directions. One can place such a light source in between two polarizers that lets through photons with polarization in definite directions. An experiment was performed in 1972 which showed that actual observations are in agreement with quantum mechanics and in violation of the Bell inequality and, thereby, a locally realistic interpretation of quantum mechanics.

The paradox inherent in the violation of the Bell inequality can be explained in several ways. One way is to adopt the positivist attitude towards measurement whereby the question of the particle having spins before the measurement is meaningless but this will be in conflict with the EPR reality criterion. One may similarly bring to question the induction assumption but this too would conflict with the reality criterion.

If one wished to retain the essence of the reality criterion, it becomes imperative to give up the assumption of Einstein separability. This implies that one should be prepared to accept that certain influences can travel instantaneously, so that the measurement on one particle influences the measurement on another particle even if it were far removed.

Quantum mechanics and relativity

The wave function Ψ completely determines the state of a physical system in quantum mechanics. The mathematical expression of this is the Schrödinger equation which is an equation of motion with one derivative with respect to time. For a relativistic theory all the space-time coordinates should be equally preferred, however. A relativistic theory for a single particle is possible, but this requires introduction of a spin of half quantum and such a theory was introduced by P.A.M. Dirac in 1928.

Dirac's starting point was the use of the correct relativistic expression for energy in the formulation by Schrödinger of the dynamics of a free-particle. The relativistic expression for the square of the energy is

$$E^2 = c^2p^2 + M_0^2c^4$$

where M_0 is the rest mass, p is the momentum of the particle, and c is the speed of light. This leads to

$$E = \pm (c^2p^2 + M_0^2c^4)^{1/2}$$

Dirac argued that this relation implied two free particle states with definite momentum p, one with positive total energy, and the other with negative total energy.

Why do not electrons in a positive energy state make a transition to the negative energy states releasing energy equal to at least 2 M_0c^2 = 1.02 million electron volts, for this spontaneous transition process is not observed. It was suggested that the answer to this is due to the Pauli Exclusion Principle. Since electrons are fermions, no more than one can occupy a given state. Therefore, if it is assumed that the negative energy states are already filled, then no spontaneous transitions from the positive energy states will be possible.

The negative energy electrons are normally unobservable. However, if a negative energy electron absorbs sufficient energy it can make a transition to one of the unfilled positive energy states, leaving a vacancy in the sea of negative energy electrons. The existence of the vacant state means that another negative energy electron can make a transition, filling the original vacancy but leaving another vacancy in its initial state. This change in the position of the vacancy appears like the movement of a real particle. The vacancy moves in the same direction that a positively charged particle would move if subject to a field. The vacancy acts exactly as if it were the charge-symmetric counterpart of an electron, or its antiparticle and called a positron. Dirac's theory predicts the existence not only of anti-electrons, but of charge-symmetric antiparticles corresponding to all of the fundamental particles. Positrons were first observed in 1932, anti-protons in 1955, and anti-neutrons in 1956. Since then other antiparticles have also been detected.

When a negative energy electron gains enough energy that should appear as a creation of an electron positron pair. Likewise, when an electron in a positive energy state makes a transition to a vacant negative energy state not only the electron but also the vacancy disappears. The electron and the positron annihilate each other leaving photons as the only trace. The same is true of other particle/antiparticle annihilations.

Bosons also have negative energy states available to them. Hence anti-bosons also exist that may be created and annihilated in pairs. Since these particles are not subject to the Pauli Exclusion Principle, any number of bosons should be able to make transitions from negative to positive energy states without leaving any vacancies behind. The Dirac explanation of the antiparticle as a vacancy is not considered to be the correct explanation. Antiparticles are taken to have a real existence and the particle antiparticle interaction is facilitated by the creation of virtual particles by the uncertainty principle.

R. P. Feynman in 1949 gave another very different interpretation of the relation between particles and antiparticles. The state function for a particle has the term Et, a product of energy and time. Feynman noted that when t is changed to -t the conventional order of time is reversed. If in addition E is changed to -E, the term $(-E)(-t) = Et$ remains unaltered. The same state function should then describe a positive energy electron going forward in time and a negative energy electron or a positron going backward in time. This allows for the interpretation of an electron of a particular energy going backward in time as a positron of the same energy going forward in time. Similarly, a positron going backward in time becomes an electron going forward in time.

To derive a relativistic theory for particles with integral spin, such as photons, is more difficult. We can set up a quantum theory for them by considering how the states change when we change the direction of the time axis. These changes turn out to be non-local. For an assembly of the particles we can setup field quantities which do not change in a local way, but when we interpret them in terms of probabilities of particles, we again get non-local behavior.

Because of such results and others it is claimed that a satisfactory rapprochement of the quantum and the relativity theories has not yet taken place.

The basic ingredients of particle theories include not only particles and forces but also fields. A field is simply a quantity defined at every point throughout some region of space and time. In the physics of electrically charged objects, the field is a convenient device for expressing how the force of electromagnetism is conveyed from one point to another. Charged particles emanate an electromagnetic field, and each particle interacts with the sum of all the fields rather than directly with the other particles.

In quantum mechanics, particles can also be represented as fields. Conversely, it is convenient sometimes to represent the quantum mechanical field as a particle. The interaction of two particles is then viewed as an exchange of a third particle, called the quantum of the field. When two electrons approach each other and bounce apart they are said to exchange a photon, the quantum of the electromagnetic field mediating this interaction. The exchanged quantum is reabsorbed within a finite time and cannot be detected which is why it is a virtual particle. The life span of a virtual particle is inversely proportional to its energy, and the range of the interaction is inversely related to its mass. For massless virtual particles like photons, the interaction range is infinite.

The number of quantum mechanical states of the field quantum defines the number of components of the field. The number of these states is in turn related to the intrinsic spin angular momentum of the particle. Both the magnitude of the spin and its direction or orientation is quantized. The number of possible spin states equals twice the magnitude of the spin plus one. Thus an electron, which has a spin of one-half, has two spin states: parallel or anti-parallel to the motion of the particle. A spin-one particle has three orientations: parallel, anti-parallel and transverse.

Since a scalar field has just one component, its quantum is represented by a spin-zero (scalar) particle. A three-component vector field requires a spin-one particle. A photon with spin-one represents the quantum of the electromagnetic field, while a graviton with a spin of two units is the quantum of the 5-component gravitational field. Furthermore, since the photon and the graviton are massless particles that travel with the speed of light, only their transverse spin states exist.

The freedom that one has in the choice of the phase of the wave function of the electron defines gauge invariance. The finding that the phase of an electron wave is inaccessible to measurement has a corollary: the phase cannot have an influence on the outcome of any actual experiment. If it did, that experiment could be used to determine the phase. The electron matter field exhibits symmetry with respect to arbitrary changes of phase. Any phase angle can be added to or subtracted from the electron field and the results of all experiments will remain unchanged.

The symmetry of the electron matter field described above is a global symmetry and it is not invariant to local gauge transformation. Thus shifting the phase of the electrons in one of the beams in the two-slit diffraction experiment shifts the diffraction pattern. This phase shift can be accomplished by applying an electromagnetic field, and it can be used to ensure the gauge invariance of the electron field.

The theory that results from combining electron matter fields with electrodynamics is quantum electrodynamics. Certain difficulties are associated with this theory. One problem is to calculate the result of even the simplest electromagnetic interactions, such as that between two electrons. Such interaction can be visualized as taking place through an exchange of one virtual photon, or two photons and so on. The total probability of interaction is determined by the sum of the contributions of all such events.

Feynman introduced a systematic procedure of tabulating these contributions by visualizing these events in one spatial dimension and one time dimension. However, difficulties arise when one considers loops, events where a virtual photon is emitted and later reabsorbed by the same electron. Since the maximum energy of a virtual particle is limited by the time needed by it to reach its destination, loops have infinite energy. This means diagrams with loops have an infinite contribution to the strength of the interaction.

The infinities can be eliminated through the technique of renormalization, which consists of finding a negative infinity for each positive infinity, so that the sum of the contributions to the infinities cancels. A finite result can be obtained if it is required that all interaction probabilities be finite and positive. Renormalization is based on the view that when a measurement is made on an electron, what is actually measured is not the mass or the charge of the pointlike particle with which the theory begins but the properties of the electron together with its enveloping cloud of virtual particles. Only the net mass and charge, the measurable quantities, are required to be finite at all stages of the calculation. The properties of the pointlike object, which are called the bare mass and the bare charge, are not well defined. The philosophy of this approach is similar to the one used by Kaṇāda to resolve the divisibility paradox.

The logic and the internal consistency of the renormalization method leave a lot to be desired. However, the best defense of the theory is that it works well. It yields results that are in agreement with experiments to an accuracy of about one part in a billion, which makes quantum electrodynamics a very accurate theory.

VI THE BUILDING BLOCKS

Elementary particles and their interactions

Since the nucleus of the atom consists of protons and neutrons, the stability of the nucleus can only be explained by postulating a strong short-range attractive force between the nucleons to counteract the electric repulsion between the protons. Furthermore, since the neutron is not a stable particle, disintegrating eventually into a proton, an electron and a neutrino, one may view this disintegration as resulting from another short-range force which is called the weak force owing to its weakness relative to the electromagnetic and the strong forces. The table below sums up the relative strengths of these forces.

Fundamental forces of nature with strength and range

Interaction	*Strength(at 10^{-13} cm)*	*Range of potential*
Electromagnetic	10^{-2}	Infinite
Gravitational	10^{-38}	Infinite
Strong (nuclear)	1	short ($\approx 10^{-13}$ m)
Weak (nuclear)	10^{-13}	short ($\approx 10^{-16}$ m)

When accelerated protons are directed at other protons at low energies, they bounce off like billiard balls. However, once a threshold is reached, the protons may come off quite slowly accompanied by a third particle--a π-meson. The π-meson has a rest mass of about 140 MeV. As soon as this much of kinetic energy is available, meson creation in the p-p collision is possible. Yukawa predicted the existence of such a particle as the quantum of strong force in 1935. Being massive its range is short.

If the energy of the proton-proton collision is increased further, many more sub-nuclear particles are produced. At even higher energies, the corresponding antiparticles start to appear. When antiparticles subsequently collide with particles they get annihilated, losing their mass to lighter particles and kinetic energy.

The classification of a physical entity as being fundamental rests on pragmatic grounds as well as the state of knowledge. The earliest belief was that all matter was fundamental, though transformable, and that the total amount of matter in the universe remained constant. This proposition was proved by Antoine Lavoisier in the late eighteenth century who showed that the total mass of the end products of a chemical reaction was exactly equal to the mass of the reacting substances. This led to the acceptance of the principle of conservation of matter. The principle of conservation of energy was established separately. Upon the demonstration of the equivalence of mass and energy, the two principles became the new principle of conservation of energy. In the early nineteenth century, John Dalton's atomic hypothesis represented matter in terms of basic indivisible units called atoms. The atoms of each element were assumed to be identical and so the number of types of atoms was equal to the number of elements. By the end of the nineteenth century it was believed that the number of elementary atoms was ninety two.

The discovery of the structure of the atom demonstrated that all atoms can be viewed as being composed of neutrons, protons, and electrons. Out of these the neutron is unstable and decays into a proton, an electron, and an antineutrino with a half-life of twelve minutes. Since the interactions of a neutron cannot be completely described in terms of the interactions of its decay products, it is taken to be an elementary particle. The same criterion is applied to determine which of the unstable particles should be taken to be elementary.

Only eleven elementary particles are completely stable in their free states. These are the electron, the proton, the neutrino (in three different flavors), their antiparticles, and the photon. The other particles appear either in high energy interactions or as products in the decay of heavier particles. The half-lives of these unstable particles range from 12 minutes for the neutron down to 10^{-23} or 10^{-24} seconds.

The elementary particles are divided into three classes on the basis of their interactions. These classes are the hadrons, the leptons, and the photon. Hadrons take part in all the four interactions, viz. the strong, the weak, the electromagnetic and gravitational. The hadrons are of two types: the baryons, and the mesons. Baryons are fermions and range in mass from proton upward, while mesons are bosons that are usually lighter than baryons. Leptons are fermions that do not participate in strong interactions. There are twelve leptons known: the electron, three types of neutrinos, the muon, the tau particle, and their corresponding antiparticles. The photon belongs to the last class; it is a boson which participates only in electromagnetic interactions.

During the past few years a great deal of effort has been put into devising a single master theory incorporating all known forces. Three of the four forces are now described by theories that have the same general form. In fact the weak force and electromagnetism can be understood in the context of a single theory.

The weak force was discovered in 1896 by Henri Becquerel as mediating the radioactive decay of an atomic nucleus. As we know it now, such decay results in the creation of two particles: an electron and a neutrino. The electron could be readily observed in the experimental equipment of Becquerel's day, but the neutrino having no mass and being electrically neutral escaped detection. It was not until much later that the neutrino was finally observed indirectly through its interaction with matter.

An exchange of particles is invoked to explain the fundamental forces, and the particle that has been assigned to carry the weak force is the intermediate boson or the W particle (W for weak). As the range of a force is inversely proportional to the mass of the exchanged particle, it is evident that the W particle must be very massive. In 1961, a second, neutral vector boson, now called Z, was introduced to complement the electrically charged W.

Maxwell's theory of electromagnetism and Einstein's theory of gravitation are both based on local gauge symmetry. Due to the elegance and success of these theories attempts were made to obtain a similar framework for the strong and the weak forces.

One reason it was possible to construct a single theory for electromagnetism and the weak force in spite of their seemingly different orders of magnitude is that they share important similarities. First, it was observed that the strength of the weak interaction increases as the energy of the experiment is increased, and it is possible to visualize that at some high enough energy the strength of the electromagnetic force and the weak force is the same. Second, the interaction probabilities of both forces follow the same rule. Third, the two interactions are universal in comparison with the strong interaction. All particles, including hadrons, participate in the weak and electromagnetic interactions but only hadrons are affected by the strong force. There are several striking differences as well. Thus the range of the forces is different, as is their strength, the charge of the currents and their relation to parity. Also only particles with a left-handed spin are affected by weak interactions in which electric charge is changed, whereas particles with right-handed spin are unaffected. However the fact that the currents in a weak interaction are heavily dependent on the electric charge of the particles makes it imperative that a deep connection should exist between the two forces.

The first important step in unraveling this connection was taken in 1954 by C. N. Yang and R. L. Mills and independently by R. Shaw. Their work started with an established global symmetry and explored the consequences if it were made a local symmetry. The symmetry they examined was the isotopic-spin symmetry according to which the strong interactions of matter remain nearly invariant when the identities of protons and neutrons are interchanged.

As in other instances where a global symmetry is converted into a local one, the invariance can be maintained only if something more is added to the theory. It turns out that six new fields need to be introduced. They are vector fields and they have infinite range. Two of these can be identified with the ordinary electric and magnetic fields and thus describe the field of the photon. The remaining fields can be taken in pairs and interpreted as electric and magnetic fields but the particles they describe differ in a crucial respect from the known properties of the photon: they are massless spin-one particles that carry charge. One particle is negative and the other positive.

The Yang-Mills theory had several shortcomings. In this theory the protons and neutrons are indistinguishable. Furthermore, it predicts electrically charged photons.

Meanwhile it was found that some of the Yang-Mills fields could be endowed with mass while retaining exact gauge symmetry. The technique is generally called the Higgs mechanism, which is an example of the process of spontaneous symmetry breaking. The fundamental idea of the Higgs mechanism is to include in the theory an extra field, one having the peculiar property that it does not vanish in the vacuum. The vacuum is generally defined as the state in which all fields have their lowest possible energy. The energy of the Higgs field is smallest when it has some uniform value greater than zero.

The Higgs mechanism also leads to the Yang-Mills field quanta becoming massive. The Higgs field is a scalar quantity and so the quantum of the field has a spin of zero. The Yang-Mills fields are vectors, like the electromagnetic field, and are represented by spin-one quanta. Each Yang-Mills quantum coalesces with one Higgs particle in the process gaining mass.

It was in 1967 that a model of the weak interactions based on a version of the Yang-Mills theory in which the field quanta gain mass through Higgs mechanism was proposed. In 1971 it was shown that such a theory could be renormalized.

The assumption on which the electroweak model is ultimately founded is local invariance with respect to isotopic spin. To preserve this invariance four photon-like fields are introduced rather than the three of the original Yang-Mills theory. The fourth photon could be identified with some primordial form of electromagnetism. It corresponds to a separate force which is added to the theory without explanation.

At the outset all four fields in the electroweak model are of infinite range and therefore must be conveyed by massless quanta; one field carries a negative electric charge and the other two fields are neutral. Spontaneous symmetry breaking introduces four Higgs fields, each field represented by a scalar particle. Three of the Higgs fields are absorbed by Yang-Mills particles, so that both of the charged Yang-Mills particles and one of the neutral ones take on a large mass. These particles are collectively named massive intermediate vector bosons, and they are designated W^+, W^- and Z^0. The fourth Yang-Mills particle, which is neutral, remains massless: it is the photon of electromagnetism. Of the Higgs particles, three lend mass to the Yang-Mills particles and they are unobservable, but the last Higgs particle is not absorbed and it should be seen if enough energy is available to produce it. The other prediction of the model, the neutral Z^0, introduces a new kind of weak interaction, the neutral-weak-current event. Neutral weak currents were first observed in 1973. The W and Z particles were detected in 1983. The masses of the W and Z particles are 81 and 93 times that of the proton. In 2012, a particle consistent with the Higgs boson was observed and identified as this particle.

A theory of the strong force

A promising theory of the strong force began to emerge only after it was realized that hadrons, the particles that interact through this force, could be viewed as constructed out of more fundamental entities. In order to understand this it is necessary to see the invariants of strong interactions.

A striking feature of the hadrons is that they often appear in multiplets of different charge but very nearly equal mass. Thus there are two nucleons, three Σs, and two Ξs. It appears likely that the mass differences within a multiplet are electromagnetic effects, and that as far as strong interactions alone are concerned their effective mass is the same in each multiplet.

It may also be assumed that strong interactions are invariant under interchange of particles within a mass multiplet. As an example we assign numbers + 1/2 and -1/2 to proton and neutron to identify them as different isotopic-spin states I_3 of the same nucleon. Another useful quantum number which is actually derived from charge and isotopic-spin is hypercharge Y:

$$I_3 = Q - \frac{Y}{2}.$$

In 1962, it was shown that charge multiplets are organized into supermultiplets that reveal relations between particles that differ in properties apart from charge. The grouping of hadrons into supermultiplets involves eight quantum numbers and it was called the eightfold way. The group that generates the eightfold way is SU(3), which stands for special unitary group of matrices of size 3 × 3. The theory requires that all hadrons belong to families corresponding to representations of SU(3). The families can have one, three, six, eight, ten or more members. If the eightfold way were an exact theory, all the members of a given family would have the same mass. The eightfold way is only an approximation, however, and within the families there are significant differences in mass.

The construction of the eightfold way begins with the classification of the hadrons into broad families sharing a common value of spin angular momentum. Each family of particles is then represented by plotting the distribution of the quantum numbers of isotopic spin and hypercharge.

The regularity and economy of the particle families obtained this way defines a kind of a periodic table of elementary particles. The known hadrons fit into such families. In 1963, Gell-Mann and also Zweig showed that this regularity could be understood if all hadrons were built up of more fundamental constituents, which Gell-Mann named quarks. Gell-Mann labeled the three quarks u, d and s, for the arbitrary labels up, down and sideways. The SU(3) model is nothing but a notation for describing the various ways of combining quarks to form hadrons.

The mechanics of the original quark model are specified by three simple rules: (1) mesons are made of one quark and one antiquark; (2)

baryons are made of three quarks and antibaryons of three anti-quarks; (3) no other assemblage of quarks can exist as a hadron.

Many properties of the quarks can be deduced from these rules. Thus it is clear that each of the quarks be assigned a baryon number of +1/3 and each of the antiquarks a baryon number of -1/3, because this would make any aggregate of three quarks have a baryon number of +1, and thus define a baryon. Similarly a meson, made of a quark and an antiquark, will have a baryon number of 0.

In a similar way the quarks are assigned half-integral units of spin. Therefore a particle made of an odd number of quarks, such as a baryon, will also have half-integral spin. A particle made of an even number of quarks, such as a meson, will have integral spin.

The u quark and the d quark have nearly the same mass and identical properties excepting that of charge, which has values of 2/3 and -1/3 respectively. The u and d quarks have strangeness (another quantum number) of 0 whereas the s quark has a strangeness of -1. The s quark is also heavier than the u or the d and it has an electric charge of -1/3. The antiquarks u, d and s have values of charge and strangeness opposite in magnitude to that of the quarks.

Just two of the quarks, the u and the d, suffice to explain the structure of all the hadrons encountered in ordinary matter. The proton, for example, can be described by assembling two u quarks and a d quark; its composition is written uud. A quick accounting will show that all the properties of the proton determined by its quark constitution are in accord with the measured values. Its charge is equal to 2/3 + 2/3 - 1/3, or +1. Similarly, its baryon number is +1 and its spin 1/2. The third quark, s, is needed only to construct strange particles, and indeed it provides an explicit definition of strangeness: a strange particle is one that contains at least one s quark.

The structure of the isotopic-spin doublet for the nucleon was the starting point of the theory of the weak force. Consequently, considerations of multiplets via SU(3) have a bearing on this theory and it was realized that another quark with a property named charm should exist. The charmed quark was invoked to explain the existence of the J/Ψ particle discovered in 1975.

Since quarks have half-integral values of spin, they must obey Fermi-Dirac statistics and no two of them within a particular system can have exactly the same quantum numbers. In the original scheme quarks seem to violate this principle. Thus in making up a baryon it is often necessary that two identical quarks occupy the same state. To avoid this difficulty it was proposed that each kind of quark comes in three varieties identical in mass, spin, charge and other measurable quantities but different in an additional property, which has come to be known as color. The term color was chosen because the rules for forming hadrons can be expressed succinctly by requiring all allowed combinations of quarks to be white, or colorless. The quarks are assigned the primary colors red, green and blue; the antiquarks have the complementary anticolors cyan, magenta and yellow. Each of the quark flavors comes in all three colors, so that the introduction of the color charge triples the number of distinct quarks.

From the available quark pigments there are two ways to create white: by mixing all three primary colors or by mixing one primary color with its complementary anticolor. The baryons are made according to the first scheme: the three quarks in a baryon are required to have different colors. In a meson a color is always accompanied by its complementary anticolor.

The theory devised to account for the above interactions is called quantum chromodynamics (QCD). The strong force is then a residue of the long-range color force of QCD. The quanta of the color fields are the gluons. Like the photon, they are electrically neutral with a spin of 1, and they are therefore vector bosons. Also like the photon they are massless. They are not color neutral, however. Each gluon carries one color and one anticolor. There are nine possible combinations of a color and an anticolor, but one of them is equivalent to white and is excluded, leaving eight distinct gluon fields.

The gluons preserve local color symmetry in the following way. A quark is free to change its color, however each such change must be accompanied by the emission of a gluon. The gluon, moving at the speed of light, is then absorbed by another quark, in the process getting its own color changed. Suppose, for example, a red quark changes its color to blue. In this process it will emit a gluon with the colors red and antiblue. The gluon is then absorbed by a blue quark, changing its own color to red. Because of the continual arbitration of the gluons there can be no net change in the color of a hadron, even through the quark colors vary freely from point to point. All hadrons remain white, and the strong force is just the system of interactions needed to maintain that condition.

The phenomenon of color confinement is inherent to QCD. The color force somehow traps color objects in such a fashion so as to render the composite objects colorless. It is not known whether color confinement follows from the framework of QCD, but it *explains* why quarks or gluons are never seen in isolation.

That QCD has not helped in reducing the number of fundamental entities remains a perplexing issue. Quarks and leptons are generally grouped into three families. The u and d quarks, the electron and its neutrino form the first family; the c and s quarks, the muon and its neutrino form the second family; the b and t quarks, the tau and its neutrino form the third family. The entities of the first family appear sufficient to build all atoms and molecules in the world. It is not clear then what the significance of the other two families is: their constituents are seen only occasionally in cosmic rays and in the high-energy particle accelerators. Then there are the other apparently fundamental particles such as the gluons and the W and Z bosons.

The synthesis provided by the current theories does not yet yield a picture that can be the final answer. These theories cannot fix several parameters in the system like the mass of the Higgs particle, the strengths of the electric charge or the color force. Neither is the pattern of quark and lepton masses explained or the fact that although the weak transitions usually observe family lines, they occasionally cross them. Then there are problems related to neutrinos: one relating to their mass, and the other to the fact that far fewer neutrinos are emitted by the sun than suggested by the theory of thermonuclear reactions to explain its energy radiation. One idea to explain the deficit in the measurements is that the identity of the neutrino changes or oscillates continuously between its three flavors of the electron-type, the muon-type, and the tau-type.

It appears that a more comprehensive theory dealing with a more sweeping symmetry of nature needs to be found to answer these questions. The problem of a reconciliation of the quantum field theories with the general theory of relativity remains. At extremely small scales of distance (10^{-33} cm) and time (10^{-44} second) quantum fluctuations of space-time itself become important, and they call into question the very meaning of a spacetime continuum.

More unification

SU(5)[2] is a theory which unifies the weak, the strong and the electromagnetic forces. The five particles (three quarks and two leptons) in each generation can transform into each other by emitting intermediary particles. Twenty-four particles suffice to provide for all possible transitions. Out of these are eight gluons that carry the color force and transform the colors of the quarks; two of the gluons mediate the strong interaction. Four other particles are the intermediaries of the lepton transitions, namely the photon, and the three intermediate vector bosons Z^0, W^-, and W^+. The remaining twelve particles are labeled X and they mediate the interconversion of leptons and quarks.

What might be the size and the mass of the X particles? A clue to this question is provided by the measurement of the magnetic moment of the electron which agrees with the calculations of quantum electrodynamics to an accuracy of ten significant digits. Since this calculation takes the electron to be pointlike, it is clear that the shape of the electron, if indeed not pointlike, can only affect the eleventh digit of the result. This constraint can be shown to imply that the size of the electron must be less than 10^{-16} centimeter. Now if the X particle is a constituent of the electron one should be able to pry it loose only if one is able to probe distances several orders of magnitude smaller than 10^{-16} centimeter. Since probe energy is inversely proportional to the probing distance the energy required to see an X particle would be immense. The mass of an X particle would also be huge since its interaction range is so small. There is some evidence that the mass of an X particle should correspond to a distance that is at most 10^{-29} centimeter. This amounts to energy of 10^{15} GeV or roughly 10^{15} times the mass of the proton. The heaviest particles that could be created in particle accelerators in the foreseeable future could have masses of 100 to 1000 times the proton mass. It appears that an X particle will never be created in the laboratory.

The relative strength of the strong, the weak, and the electromagnetic forces is given by coupling constants which are very different in value. The coupling constants change as the energy of the physical processes in which they are measured changes. For instance the coupling constant for the strong force decreases slowly with the increase of energy. If the trends of changes in value of the three coupling constants were to be extrapolated, they are expected to have the same value at energy of 15 GeV or about 10^{-29} centimeter.

The unification scale of 10^{-29} centimeter is so small that if a single proton were as large as the sun, the unification scale would still be less than a micrometer. It appears that not only would man never be able to create energies in a laboratory approaching this scale, but also that perhaps no process anywhere in the universe can generate such energies. It is believed that at the start of the big bang such energies did indeed exist, and X particles must have existed freely. Theorists are at work to see what remnants of that state could be observed today to provide evidence for the X particles.

Another consequence of the SU(5) theory is that the proton should decay with an average life time of 10^{31} years. This amounts to the decay of about one proton a year in a collection of 10^{31} protons. Thus in 10,000 tons of matter which contains about 5×10^{33} protons and neutrons one would expect about 500 decays a year. The theory indicates that decay would convert a proton into either a positron and a neutral meson or to an antineutrino and a positive meson. Experiments to observe such decay have been negative.

One complication that the SU(5) theory does not address is that of gravitation becoming a significant force at very small distances. In fact at about 10^{-33} centimeter, gravitation may become as strong as the other forces. It is not clear what effect that might have on the coupling constants of the other forces.

Preon models

As we can see, research on unification consists of trying out different combinational arrangements of hypothetical particles that are consistent with properties of stable elementary particles. In that spirit, in some models quarks and leptons are represented as combinations of more fundamental entities called pre-quarks or preons.[3] In the simplest of these models just two kinds of preons, labeled A and B, are postulated. Both these preons have a spin angular momentum of 1/2. Furthermore the A preon has an electric charge of +1/3, whereas the B preon is electrically neutral. Their antiparticles will be represented by $\bar{A}$ and $\bar{B}$, and these have charges of -1/3 and zero respectively.

The model proceeds by representing a quark or a lepton by combining either three preons or three antipreons. There are eight ways two kinds of preons can be combined together taken three at a time, and another eight ways the antipreons can be combined. These combinations can be identified with the eight quarks and leptons together with the antiquarks and the antileptons of the first generation. The other generations are taken to be the excited states of the first generation.

The combinations of preons and their particle identifications are as follows. The triplet AAA has a charge of +1 and it is identified as the proton. The three combinations AAB, ABA, BAA all have a charge of +2/3 which are taken to represent the three color states of the u quark. Similarly ABB, BAB, BBA each with a charge of +1/3 are the three color states of the d antiquark. The triplet BBB is neutral and represents the electron-type neutrino. Exactly the same combinations of the antipreons give the remaining particles of the first generation, namely the electron ($\bar{A}\bar{A}\bar{A}$), the u antiquarks ($\bar{A}\bar{A}\bar{B}, \bar{A}\bar{B}\bar{A}$, and $\bar{B}\bar{A}\bar{A}$), the d quarks ($\bar{A}\bar{B}\bar{B}$, $\bar{B}\bar{A}\bar{B}$, and $\bar{B}\bar{B}\bar{A}$), and the electron-type antineutrino ($\bar{B}\bar{B}\bar{B}$).

In this model the quarks and the leptons have, on an average, equal number of preons and antipreons that provides an explanation for the longstanding cosmological puzzle about why matter is more abundant than antimatter in the universe.

The pre-quark approaches at their current state of development do not make predictions that can be checked experimentally.

Symmetries and the uncertainty principle

A valid question to ask is whether there are limits or bounds associated with the interaction symmetries in a quantum description. In other words, is it possible to predict the amount of information in strong and weak interaction symmetries using the uncertainty principle alone? The fact that the uncertainty relations are generally taken to represent the divide between classical mechanics and quantum mechanics suggests that such a prediction should be possible provided we extend the applicability of the correspondence principle to information as well. Such an extension would imply the following equation

$$I(\text{classical m.}) = I(\text{quantum mechanics}) + \text{uncertainty}$$

where I denotes information. Now since uncertainty implies negative information, the above equation would require positive information to be associated with the quantum description.[4]

Exploiting this equation to yield useful results is not easy, however. In addition to several ways one could define information associated with an object in classical mechanics and in quantum mechanics, there exist difficulties in quantifying the uncertainty in quantum mechanics in an information theoretic sense.

In one proposal the problem of defining information in classical mechanics and in quantum mechanics was sidestepped by determining only the difference between the two. The nature of this difference depends on the choice of information measure to quantify the uncertainty in quantum mechanics. Furthermore, space time was discretized. This helped deduce that a finite amount of additional information was associated with a quantum mechanical description.

Further research is necessary to determine if the application of the correspondence principle to quantum information can provide new insights.

VII ORDER AND CHAOS

The arrow of time

The very process of measurement of time by clocks or the observation of other physical phenomena presupposes change, and the universe is changing from moment to moment. Nevertheless, the laws of classical mechanics and electromagnetism do not distinguish a direction of time.[1] If we reverse a series of photographs of billiard balls colliding and moving away one could determine this fact by careful measurements of speeds at different instants because friction on the billiard table slows down the ball. In other words if the effect of the rest of the universe were eliminated then a classical object behaves in a time-symmetric fashion. The continual change in the universe imprints into irreversible dynamics of objects.

Isolated classical objects have T (T for time) symmetry. In quantum mechanics, although the Schrödinger equation is time symmetric, the process of measurement introduces asymmetry due to the collapse of the wave function. Laws of physics have spatial symmetry.

Two other symmetries that are relevant are parity (P) and charge conjugation (C). Parity refers to spatial reflection or replacing a system by its mirror image, while charge conjugation means replacing a particle by its antiparticle which is identical in mass but opposite in charge.

In the 1950s it was discovered that weak interaction is not symmetric with respect to spatial reflection. Specifically, neutrinos which interact with matter through the weak interaction have a fixed relation between direction of motion and direction of spin. The neutrino always spins in the clockwise sense in the direction of its motion. There are no neutrinos which spin the other way. Since the thumb indicates the direction of this motion when the fingers of the left hand are curled in the way the particle rotates, neutrinos are said to be left-handed. Experiments have shown that antineutrinos are always right-handed.

Experiments with K-mesons indicate that the CP symmetry - sequential application of C and P symmetries - is violated. This means that if CPT holds, then breaking of CP would also indicate a breaking of the T symmetry. This may be the reason for the arrow of time.

Time asymmetry was first emphasized in physics by the second law of thermodynamics. This law was first a refinement and generalization of the hypothesis that heat cannot, of itself, pass from the colder to the hotter body. In 1865 the law was restated in terms of the new concept of entropy which is defined as heat received divided by the temperature (in degrees Kelvin) at which the heat is received. The restatement of the second law is that the entropy of a closed, or isolated, system never decreases. Every reversible change in a closed system leaves its total entropy unaltered, for the gain of entropy in one part is balanced by its loss in the other part. On the other hand, every irreversible change in the system increases its entropy. Irreversible changes occur when heat passes of its own accord from one part of a system to another at lower temperature.

Since thermodynamics can be reduced to statistical mechanics, the significance of the second law of thermodynamics at the molecular level becomes important. One can talk of the problem of the partitioned box where all the molecules of a gas are initially in one compartment. After the partition is removed the gas molecules spread to the entire volume of the box. The question of whether all the gas molecules would at some future time find themselves in the first compartment is an interesting one. Classical physics suggests that this should be possible but from experience we know that it is unlikely ever to happen.

This difficulty is presented as the Loschmidt's reversibility paradox. Since the laws of mechanics are symmetrical with respect to the inversion of time, to each process there belongs a corresponding time-reversed process. This is in contradiction with the existence of irreversible processes.

The answer to Loschmidt's paradox is that one cannot invert time keeping the system unchanged. The system is subject to random effects of the rest of the universe even if great care is taken to isolate it. It can be shown that if in a system velocities of molecules were suddenly reversed and then small random fluctuations added to these values, the system would not retrace its history in reversed sequence. In other words, if the random changes in the system under study are all lumped together there is no paradox.

The generation of electromagnetic radiation presents another type of irreversibility. Electromagnetic waves always travel out from the source, such as an antenna. The time-reversed version of this phenomenon, where an antenna draws in electromagnetic energy around it, is never observed. An appeal to Maxwell's equations, that describe electromagnetic radiation, does not help because these equations are symmetric with respect to time. In fact Maxwell's equations allow the possibility of both outgoing and incoming radiation. This problem also exists in other wave phenomena such as water waves.

The large scale characteristics of the universe provide another example of time asymmetry. The universe is expanding and the galaxies are moving away from each other. Given a set of records with information on the relative positions of galaxies at different times, one can therefore determine the time sequence of these records.

The thermodynamic arrow of time is viewed as being related to the cosmological arrow of time. The electromagnetic arrow of time is also related to the inherent continual change in the universe. Considering a source, S, of electromagnetic waves, Maxwell's equations permit two kinds of waves to be associated with the source, called retarded and advanced waves, respectively. Examine the source at time $t=0$. The retarded wave spreads outwards beginning at this time reaching a point one light-second away at t=1 second, a point two light-seconds away at t=2 seconds, and so on. The advanced wave, on the other hand, moves outwards from the source at progressively earlier times. Thus it is one light second away at t=-1 seconds, etc. An advanced wave can also be viewed as being an incoming wave which reaches the source S at t=0. Advanced waves are never observed.[2]

The question of asymmetry in electromagnetism then becomes the question of why advanced waves are always absent. To answer this, remember that to measure time one needs to mark change. Change in turn presupposes a recognizable movement in time, a transformation that splits it into past and future. We come full circle, therefore, and see that any description in time must satisfy causality. This implies that it is incorrect to claim that the equations of theoretical physics indicate time symmetry because causality is an unwritten postulate that goes along with these equations.

Statistical description of nature

There was debate between proponents of matter continuity and atomicity in ancient India and Greece. The differing views were attempts to explain the perplexing nature of everyday reality qualitatively.

In the latter part of the eighteenth century, Joseph Black and Henry Cavendish in Britain took the first steps toward an understanding of matter undergoing transformation, as in chemical reactions, by performing quantitative experiments that demonstrated that the total mass of reacting substances remained unchanged. Soon thereafter the school of French chemistry led by Antoine Lavoisier properly identified and distinguished between the common gaseous elements.

The stage was set for demonstrating that matter was atomic when it was established that chemical elements combined in definite proportions yielded homogeneous compounds. Thus oxygen and hydrogen combine to form water when their masses are in the ratio 8 to 1. If the gas weights are not exactly in this proportion then at the conclusion of the combining process, which may be induced by an electric spark, the excess will remain uncombined.

The phenomenon of Brownian motion also makes the concept of atoms particularly appropriate and compelling. In this motion that one can see through a microscope, a suspension of fine particles in a fluid dart about in a rapid, erratic motion. It was discovered first by Robert Brown, a botanist, who noticed little particles of plant pollens jiggling around in a liquid that he was examining through a microscope. The phenomenon was later explained to be one of the effects of the molecular motion which produces an unequal buffeting of the larger particles.

From the time of Boyle in 1661 to that of Gay-Lussac in 1802, scientists carried out investigations that eventually established that the pressure exerted by a given quantity of a gas on the walls of its container is inversely proportional to the volume it occupies and directly proportional to the temperature on an appropriate scale. If the masses of the samples of the different elements in gaseous form are chosen to be equal to the molecular weights, the proportionality constant in the expression relating the measured pressure, volume and temperature is the same for all gases. Thus the following simple expression for this relationship, known as the perfect gas law, provides an excellent approximate description of the gross properties of a gas such as pressure (P), temperature (T), and volume (V):

$$P \propto T/V \text{ or } PV = RT.$$

The numerical value of the constant R depends on the units chosen for the quantities appearing in the equation. There are slight departures from this law for gases because there are small residual forces between molecules that vary from one molecular type to another.

Since masses of gases in proportion to their molecular weights occupy equal volumes at the same pressure and temperature, it is clear that there must be the same number of molecules per unit volume for all gases under the same external conditions.

This result is the Avogadro law. Avogadro did not determine the numerical value of this number but subsequent experiments showed it to be 6.0225×10^{26} molecules per kilomole, where a kilomole is a mass in kilograms equal to the molecular weight of the gas. Since pressure and temperature refer to properties of large-scale matter, which cannot be defined for a single atom or molecule, the perfect gas law and the Avogadro law represent statistical truths.

It is the motion of molecules that gives rise to the property of temperature. The average kinetic energy of a molecule is a function of the temperature and the scale that gives a constant conversion factor is the Kelvin scale. The constant of proportionality is called the Boltzmann's constant and it is equal to $k = 1.38 \times 10^{-23}$ joule per degree Kelvin. If T is the temperature in degrees Kelvin, this implies that the mean molecular kinetic energy is 3/2 kT. In fact, the mean energy in any direction of space is taken to be 1/2kT; the three independent directions involved make it 3/2 kT.

Irreversibility, structure and life

If the second of law of thermodynamics is the principle that an isolated system moves into a state of increasing disorder, how is one to explain highly organized structures in the universe?

A detailed analysis of any isolated biological system shows that entropy does actually increase. Organized structures with increasing order are always open systems that use energy and order of an input medium ejecting an output with a greater entropy increase than the decrease produced in them. Since a system in equilibrium is in a state of maximum entropy, highly organized structures are in states far from equilibrium.[3]

The earliest scientific thinking regarding life could be summed up into two points of view. The first was that a vital force was present in all living things; the second was that life arose by natural processes from non-living matter. In the beginning, adherents of both these views held that simple forms of life could arise spontaneously. It was believed that living organisms originated in sea slime by the action of heat, sun and air. This generation of life was not considered a primary phenomenon, however, since the entire universe was conceived to be living.

Some believed that living things could originate from other living animals or from lifeless matter. It was thought that life was produced by the union of a passive principle matter with an active principle form, the latter being the soul of living things.

By the beginning of the nineteenth century chemists were beginning to recognize two broad classes of chemicals. One class consisted of substances found only in living things or in the dead remains of once-living things. These were named organic substances. Other substances like minerals found in the soil and ocean, together with the gases of the atmosphere were named inorganic substances. The hypothesis was proposed that it was not possible to synthesize organic substances from the inorganic ones as the former required a vital force occurring in life which could not be duplicated in a test tube. By 1828 this hypothesis was shown to be incorrect. Organic chemistry is now defined as the chemistry of compounds containing carbon atoms in their molecules, no matter what the origin of these molecules. The narrower concept of organic chemistry, the study of substances found primarily in living tissue, is now known as biochemistry.

Earlier, in 1668, Francisco Redi had demonstrated that organic matter does not in itself have the power of creating life. By eighteenth century the notion of spontaneous generation had been modified to that of heterogenesis, according to which all living matter consist of organized particles essentially indestructible but capable of entering into different combinations, implying different life-forms. This notion of heterogenesis was superseded when it was shown by Pasteur in 1860s that generation of life can occur only if one started with appropriate germs or microorganisms. Thus organic matter could not in itself create life, and if all microorganisms are removed and excluded from an organic substance, no microorganisms appear.

The hypothesis generally accepted by the scientific world is that while spontaneous generation does not take place ordinarily, at some early stage in earth's history conditions existed that were suitable for the beginnings of life which have slowly evolved into forms of great variety and complexity. No success has yet been obtained, however, in synthesizing simple living organisms in laboratories trying to approximate conditions on primeval earth. Another hypothesis suggests that even if conditions were never appropriate on earth for the first synthesis of life, spores might have been carried here in meteoric dust, under the action of light and gravity, after life evolved on some other celestial body.

Evolution and reproduction

The principle of evolution forms the basis of the system of Sāṅkhya but that did not lead to the development of a scientific theory. The Mahābhārata (pre-400 BC) and the Purāṇas have a chapter on creation and the rise of mankind. It is said that man arose at the end of a chain where the beginning was with plants and various kind of animals and giant animals (*asuras*). Here's the quote from the Yoga Vāsiṣṭha:[4]

> I remember that once upon a time there was nothing on this earth, neither trees and plants, nor even mountains. For a period of eleven thousand years (four million earth years) the earth was covered by lava. Then demons (*asuras*) ruled the earth; they were deluded and powerful. The earth was their playground. And then for a very long time the whole earth was covered with forests, except the polar region. Then there arose great mountains, but without any human inhabitants. For a period of ten thousand years (4 million earth years) the earth was covered with the corpses of the *asuras*.

Vedic evolution is unlike Darwinian evolution. The urge to evolve into higher forms is taken to be inherent in nature. A system of an evolution from inanimate to progressively higher life is taken to be a consequence of Nature's intelligence that responds to the different proportions of the three basic attributes of sattva, rajas, and tamas.

A clear picture of evolution to explain differences between organisms of different groups was presented by Charles Darwin (1809-1882) and Alfred Russell Wallace (1823-1913). According to this theory of natural selection, evolution is basically a process of adaptation of successive generations of organisms to changes in their environments. Man can thus be seen at the end of a long chain of evolutionary changes where species modified through random mutation; those mutant species survived that were biologically stable and suited for the environment where they arose.

Living forms have great variety and all organisms are made up of microscopic units called cells. Life is directed by a program which is a substance called DNA (deoxyribonucleic acid) whose chemical structure carries the instructions for the activities of the organism, its external and internal forms, and performance in different environments. The set of instructions specified by DNA consists of genes, which are informational entities that determine specific characteristics of the organism by presiding over the synthesis of individual chemical components of the cells of the organism.

DNA is a double-stranded helical molecule which is coiled up and occupies a small volume of the cell nucleus. Each strand of the DNA molecule is an alternating sequence of sugar and phosphate units. The sugar units of the two strands face each other and are connected to paired purines and pyrimidines that are linked together by weak hydrogen bonds. In the pairing of purine and pyrimidine, adenine (A) always pairs off with thymine (T), and guanine (G) always pairs off with cytosine (C). DNA strands are divided into many segments which are the same as chromosomes, of which there are forty-six in a human cell.

Genes exert their control over cellular activities by producing enzymes that control the biochemical reactions of the cell. The DNA code is based upon information in the nature of the base sequences composed of varying arrangements of the four nucleotides in the molecule. Within the chemical storehouse of the cell there are twenty different amino acids which may be synthesized into proteins of various sizes and levels of complexity. Sequences of three nucleotides specify each amino acid. This implies that more than one combination of the nucleotides can specify an amino acid.

Proteins are formed on ribosomes of the cytoplasm. Ribonucleic acid (RNA) is an integral component of polypeptide synthesis.

The genetic information of DNA is passed on to RNA molecules which serve as templates for the formation of proteins, in other words, DNA → RNA → proteins. Proteins are essential to the functioning of cells. They may act as catalysts to accelerate chemical reactions, carry small molecules, or serve as units that make up the structural elements of cells and organisms. Experiments show that DNA is not like an archival computer data tape. Rather it is an interactive dynamic structure where transposition of certain structural features can occur within a chromosome.

The DNA of each cell of an organism carries the genes as well as other segments that regulate the functions of the genes. Not all genes may actively perform their functions in each cell. The genes that are active are said to be expressed.

Reproduction of an organism is either asexual or sexual. The most primitive way of multiplying, which is the method used by the simplest organisms, is through splitting into two halves, each of which grows into a new individual. This method of asexual reproduction is known as binary fission. Other related methods of asexual reproduction are multiple fission, where a single individual divides into many small ones or a method where the products of the division are unequal.

In sexual reproduction, the reproductive cells must melt together before they can give rise to new individuals. These cells, called gametes, are of two kinds: active, smaller male gametes or sperm-cells, and passive larger female gametes or egg-cells.

Since an individual's offsprings arise out of the gametes, therefore these reproductive cells could be considered potentially immortal. The German biologist Weismann coined the term germ-plasm for this part of the organism, in contrast to soma which is the mortal remainder. The soma is the individual who will live and die; the germ-plasm may go on indefinitely. Biological evolution may be seen as the evolution of the germ-plasm.

The principles of inheritance were first formulated by Gregor Mendel (1822-1884), though his work went unrecognized until 1900. Working on pea plants, he first studied the inheritance of a single trait. Crossing pure lines of tall and short pea plants, P, he found that the off-spring generation, F_1, contained all tall plants. When the pea plants of this off-spring generation were cross-pollinated, the next generation, F_2, had approximately three-fourths of the plants that were tall and one-fourth that were short. Mendel concluded that some factors, now called genes, were present which determined the inheritance of height and that the genes occurred in pairs because mating within the first offspring generation produced both tall and short plants, and, therefore, the off-spring generation F_1 must have contained both short and tall factors. Mendel concluded further that one gene, referred to as dominant, may mask the expression of the other because when tall and short pea plants of the P generation were crossed, all the F_1 plants appeared tall, but both tall and short plants appeared in the F_2 generation. Thus, the F_1 plants must have carried the gene for shortness, but it was recessive to the gene for tallness. Another conclusion reached by Mendel was that when gametes are formed, the genes separate from each other.

While genetic studies made after Mendel confirmed his general conclusions, it was found necessary to modify somewhat his conclusions. For instance it was seen that while recession and dominance occur in many cases, they are rarely, if ever, absolute. It is also observed that many inherited traits are controlled by more than one gene.

Experiments on bacteria, which are relatively simple, unicellular organisms, show that they, like higher organisms, have individuality. The ability of bacteria to control their movements has been known for over one hundred years. The movement is like a biased random walk, with the bias in the direction towards higher concentration of an attractant, or lower concentration of a repellant. In a medium with uniform concentration, the movement of the bacterium is random but without any apparent direction. Recently, it was shown that a bacterium also has a rudimentary memory that allows it to respond differently to different time varying concentrations of attractants or repellants. The three components of heredity, environment, and the random distribution of molecules in a cell determine the individual. This means that even when the environment and the heredity are constant, the bacteria exhibit individuality. A similar conclusion is valid for higher organisms.

The fact that biological structure is determined by the genetic code of DNA indicates that physiologically living organisms can be considered to be machines. In fact there is an interesting analogy between computers and living organisms. A computer works according to a program which specifies a set of precise instructions it must perform. The code of DNA is a program that specifies the development of the organism and its response to different environments. A computer program that alters its strategy and nature in response to the nature of the problem is an even better analogy. Thus if a computer program is designed to play the game of chess, the program of DNA is designed to play the game of life.

There is an important difference between computers and living organisms in as much as the latter have self-awareness. Some people believe that self-awareness or consciousness arises when a machine becomes sufficiently complex. According to this view, computers, in future, will have consciousness. On the other hand, there is the view that life can never be completely understood as a mechanistic phenomenon. According to Neils Bohr, "the existence of life must be considered as an elementary fact that cannot be explained, but must be taken as a starting point in biology, in a similar way as the quantum of action, which appears as an irrational element from the point of view of classical mechanical physics, taken together with the existence of the elementary particles, forms the foundation of atomic physics."

Several problems arise in the application of physics to the study of biological processes. Physical processes associated with reproduction, growth, aging, and so on are well understood but there remain puzzling issues. As an example take the question of the apparent increase of the complexity and organization of a living organism: this growth seems outside the pale of statistical physics. If the potential for this organization were assumed to exist in the DNA molecule itself, then the great stability of biological structures becomes a source of wonder. At the same time to define life unambiguously is not easy and perhaps no definition exists which would not in principle be satisfied by certain machines. On the other hand, if it were assumed that a living organism owes its characteristics to its complexity being above a certain threshold, why complexity should lead to such characteristics remains perplexing. In some sense the behavior of a living organism is greater than the sum of its parts. Many believe that currently known laws of physics do not embrace all physical phenomena and certainly not life, but this sentiment may be a reflection of the fact that complexity introduces new and surprising relationships amongst gross variables.[5]

Amongst the current controversies on the origin of life is the one on the origin of genetic information. There is a chicken-egg question regarding what came first: the proteins or the nucleic acids? Contemporary biology or biochemistry cannot answer this question. There is yet no conclusive evidence in support of the view that life began with spontaneously formed self-replicating nucleic acid. On the other hand, a proteins-first theory is problematic because a flow of information from proteins to nucleic acids is forbidden by the central dogma of molecular biology. To get around this dilemma, a suggestion is made that perhaps some other crude replicating mechanism existed at the beginnings of life. Once DNA created an efficient mechanism, the primitive mechanism simply died out. This hypothesis is an extension of the concept of evolution to include replicating molecular processes. At present there is no experimental evidence to support such a view. It also leads to further questions such as what other replicating mechanisms could exist?[6] If for atmospheric conditions that exist on the earth now, the DNA mechanism is unique, then are there other mechanisms that are more efficient in other atmospheric conditions?

The program of reducing biological phenomena to those of physics and chemistry is at the basis of modern science. But this program is unsuccessful in the reduction of Mendelian genetics to molecular genetics. The problem here is that often a Mendelian predicate term (such as *dominant*) must be associated with several molecular mechanisms (such as those that produce an active enzyme). Conversely, the same types of molecular mechanisms produce phenomena characterized by different Mendelian predicate terms. The complexity of these relationships makes such a reduction artificial. This difficulty is the result of an intricate underlying structure leading to a few simple gross features. The difficulty is compounded by the fact that biological systems are dynamic; they change with time and their features are defined approximately.

The problems of reduction are illustrated by the different ways one uses language to describe similar phenomena in the inanimate and the living worlds. A physicist might say that heating a gas causes it to expand, while a biologist might say that heating a mammal causes it to sweat. The biologist might add that the mammal sweats to keep the temperature constant, but no physicist would say that a gas expands to keep its temperature constant, even though that is exactly what happens. The reason why teleological terminology does not sound appropriate for heating a gas is because it is a relatively simple system. Biological systems are, on the other hand, equipped with several feedback loops which allow for a variety of responses to a stimulus. The mammal exposed to heat could also move away from its source or shield itself. But the interaction between the molecules of the gas is no different from feedback loop excepting that each molecule is interacting with every other molecule.

There are no logical difficulties in explaining the physical aspects of biological systems as being machinelike. The individuality of organisms is not surprising considering their complexity and the fact that their structure is influenced by the continuously changing environment. The riddle that remains is that of self-awareness.

VIII THE LOGIC OF PHYSICS

Are laws of nature evanescent?

A law of nature is a principle that must be obeyed without exception. This definition does not rule out the possibility of the law itself changing with time which is plausible if the interaction is a function of some changing aspect of the universe.

So long as the universe was believed to be infinitely old and infinite in extent, there was no point of reference to relate change. The universe is now taken to be finite in size and age and attempts have been made to relate the constants of physical laws to the epoch and the size of the universe.

It is possible for us to know something about the past history of the universe by observing the stars. The light coming from the more distant stars is from an earlier epoch. If it is assumed that stars go through similar life histories, one can examine the radiation from the distant stars to see what physical processes it corresponds to. There is no conclusive evidence at present to indicate that constants have changed in value over time. This negative result may be due to the limitations of our models, and also due to the relatively short time period over which these studies have been made.

A case for the laws of nature not being immutable can be made on additional grounds. General relativity suggests that the universe is closed. However total energy and total angular momentum cannot be defined for a closed universe for which they are meaningless concepts. When matter collapses into a black hole all laws of conservation of particle numbers lose applicability. In the words of John Archibald Wheeler, "I have not been able to find any more reasonable way to state the situation than this: nature conserves nothing; there is no constant of physics that is not transcended; or, in a word, mutability is a law of nature."

A proposal that relates the gravitational constant to the age of the universe is the Large Numbers hypothesis of P.A.M. Dirac. The starting point of this proposal is the observation that the various dimensionless constants occurring in physics have an interesting characteristic. They are either of the order of unity or of 10^{40}. To the former category belong the fine-structure constant, $e^2/\hbar c$ which is about 1/137, and the ratio of the mass of the proton to the mass of the electron, m_p/m_e, which is about 1800. To the latter category belongs the ratio of the electric to the gravitational force between the electron and the proton, e^2/Gm_pm_e, which is about 10^{40}. Similarly the estimates of the present age of the universe and the total number of protons in the universe are respectively 10^{40} atomic units (with speed of light and radius of electron taken to be 1) and 10^{80}. According to Dirac there must be some logic to explain these enormous numbers in the second category. And if there is a relationship between them, it is most likely governed by the age of the universe. And as the universe is progressively getting older, it follows that gravitation should progressively become weaker and the mass of the universe should increase as the square of the age of the universe.[1]

Other proposals have been made regarding the mechanism of the continuous creation of matter. In one model, matter creation at a point is taken to be in proportion to the matter already existing there. To some this provides the mechanism that explains, amongst other things, the current state of the earth. In this view the outermost layer of the earth was of relatively light material and of uniform thickness in the early stage of earth's development. This layer cooled and solidified and became the skin which had to resist the pressures of the newly created excess matter in the core of the earth. The skin eventually ruptured leading to the continents being separated by the oceans.[2]

Limits to unification

The logic of physics is based on the underlying unity in nature. This logic, which is immensely successful, does not mean that one should be able to explain all phenomena based on the properties of elementary particles alone. One needs to make additional assumptions relating gross behavior to the behavior of elementary constituents in larger and more complex systems. There is also the inability to separate completely behavior at different levels of observation owing to interconnected phenomena. A behavior at an integrated level has influence on the primitive levels as well.

If we accept for a moment that the unification program of physics is completely successful and the relationship between the four basic forces fully revealed, it would still not be clear what new phenomena are exhibited by more complex structures and organisms. The materialist position has no proper explanation for consciousness and who is to say that even more puzzling phenomena remain outside the pale of current scientific understanding.

An incomplete description must lead to paradox. If we view the universe as an engine governed by a unified law there can be no intervention in the workings of this engine even at small scale. If the universe has a dual nature in terms of the physical world and consciousness then how do the two aspects interrelate? If an overmind interpenetrates the universe and the consciousness of each sentient being is only a fragment of this overmind, then it might be possible to demonstrate effects of such a linkage. If these effects are physical then they will fall within the framework of the physical laws and thus have alternative explanations. If these effects relate to comprehension then they cannot be conclusive by virtue of being subjective and intuitive. It appears, therefore, that the unification program will remain incomplete.

Mathematical truths

Since physics is ultimately an explication of the universe in terms of mathematics, the problem of the meaning of mathematics is relevant. Mathematics is the language in which assertions about the physical reality are made. There are two aspects of the language that are of interest here. One aspect is that of relating definitions of primitives in the language to corresponding physical concepts. Second is the question of grammar which allows one to manipulate the primitives and construct complex sentences.

One primitive concept that has been debated considerably is that of infinity. George Cantor (1865-1918) introduced the theory of infinite sets in 1873 which allowed one to distinguish between different kinds of infinite sets. The idea at the basis of Cantor's theory is that of one-to-one correspondence which is quite obvious for finite sets. We say that two sets are of the same size if their elements can be put into one-to-one correspondence. Thus the sets of 5 books and 5 boys are equal in size because each book can be paired off with a different boy. Cantor argued that since one can set up a correspondence between the whole numbers and the even numbers:

1 2 3 4 5 6...
2 4 6 8 10 12...

where each whole number has been paired off with one and only one even number, the two infinite sets are of the same size. This definition was rejected by many on the grounds that it made a part of the set equal to the whole. Cantor countered that infinite sets followed laws that did not apply to finite collections.

Cantor called infinite sets that can be put in one-to-one correspondence with the whole numbers as countable and represented this size by $\aleph_0$ (aleph null). He next showed that the set of all fractions and whole numbers (rationals) is countable. To prove this he represented the numbers in an array as shown:

1/1	1/2	1/3	1/4	1/5	.	.	.
2/1	2/2	2/3	2/4	2/5	.	.	.
3/1	3/2	3/3	3/4	3/5	.	.	.
4/1	4/2	4/3	4/4	4/5	.	.	.
.	.	.	.	.	.	.	.
.	.	.	.	.	.	.	.

Note that some numbers are repeated as in the main diagonal where each number is 1. Now in a diagonal zigzag path going from 1/1→1/2→2/1→3/1→2/2→1/3→1/4→ 2/3→3/2→... , each number in the array is crossed just once. If repetitions of numbers are deleted one can pair off each rational in the path with a unique whole number in sequence. This establishes the result.

Cantor next showed that some infinite sets are not countable. An example of this is the set of all points on the real line, that includes rational and irrational numbers. Given an infinite set one can, by considering all its subsets, construct another set of larger size. Cantor thus arrived at a sequence of aleph numbers, $\aleph_0$, $\aleph_1$, $\aleph_2$... called transfinite numbers that represent progressively a higher measure of infinity. Cantor believed that no transfinite number existed between those representing the infinites of the whole numbers and the real line. In other words, he took the infinity of the real line to be $\aleph_1$. This is known as the continuum hypothesis.

Cantor's work was severely criticized by his contemporaries. The mapping of the part to the whole had been anticipated by Leibniz who had said that the "set of all numbers contains a contradiction, if one takes it as a totality." Cantor defended himself by claiming to be a Platonist, for whom ideas have an objective reality of their own. He did recognize, however, that one had the paradoxical situation of not being able to talk of a set of all sets, since the aleph numbers could be constructed recursively without end. Russell, upon reflection on this observation, produced a paradox dealing with classes which had a great influence on the mathematical world. This situation was described earlier in the form of the catalog and the barber paradoxes. Since classes of sets are often invoked in mathematical argument, this pointed to the care that was needed in using this concept. Later in their book, Principia Mathematica, Whitehead and Russell introduced the theory of types to avoid such difficulties. Individual objects, sets, sets of sets, and so on were classified as belonging to different types. Relations were defined for each type separately. They also introduced the axiom of reducibility, according to which any proposition of higher type is equivalent to one of first order. This axiom has received considerable criticism on the grounds that it is not self-evident.

There are three main schools of mathematical philosophy: logicism, intuitionism, and formalism. The logicist thesis developed from the view that the concept of number is derived from pure thought and not from intuitions of space and time. According to it all mathematics is reducible to logic. The exposition of this view was begun by Frege, and developed by Russell and Whitehead. Apart from the usual logical axioms, the logicist mathematicians have used the axioms of reducibility, infinity, and choice to develop their program. The reducibility axiom states that propositions regarding classes of objects are equivalent to those regarding objects themselves. The axiom of infinity states that for every natural number there is a greater one. The assertion that, given a class of mutually exclusive non-empty classes, there exists a class composed of exactly one element from each class and of no other elements is called the axiom of choice. Critics claim that the axiom of reducibility and choice may be self evident for finite classes, but there is no way to establish them for infinite classes. The infinity axiom cannot be established either, they add. To give a simple example where use of infinity creates a counter-intuitive situation, consider the surface generated by rotating $y = 1/x$, $1 \leq x < \infty$, around the X-axis. The resulting 'infinite horn' has finite volume, but infinite surface area. Thus one could fill up the inside of this surface with a finite amount of paint, but no amount would suffice to paint the outside surface. Similarly, there are solids whose volumes are arbitrarily large, but whose surfaces are arbitrarily small.[4]

The formalists believe that in addition to logical relations, mathematics also deals with extralogical relations such as those that relate to visual and aural images, physical objects, or other concepts. The formalists claim that it is unreasonable that a mere elaboration of pure thought, as in the logicist portion, can represent a variety of natural phenomena such as mechanics, electromagnetics and elementary particle physics. The formalists only require a consistency of a mathematical structure without concern for how the structure arose. They do not insist that the structure should fit within a unifying theory.

Leopold Kronecker (1823-1891) is generally credited with the rise of intuitionism. He once quipped, "God made the integers; all else is the work of man." This thesis was formally presented by L.E.J. Brouwer (1881-1966) who remained its lifelong champion. This view claims that mathematics is an activity of the human mind and the mind recognizes certain intuitions like that of integers, processes of addition, multiplication, and mathematical induction. According to the intuitionists, the concept of actual (as against potential) infinity, where the infinity of elements are defined to be existing all at once, should be rejected. The intuitionists do not accept Cantor's theory of transfinite numbers. Neither do they accept several modern constructions of real numbers, calculus and analysis. The intuitionists claim that only logical principles should be used as conform to and properly express correct intuitions. In their view, the law of excluded middle cannot be used where potential infinity is involved, even though it works fine for finite problems. According to them there are propositions that are neither provable nor disprovable. As an example of this belief they cite the question of the occurrence of a specific pattern of digits in the expansion of an irrational number which no amount of computation may be able to address.

One reason why classical logic is not strictly correct is because no physical object is defined precisely. When it is said that an object is out of a box we are assuming that the object has no influence within the box which is only an idealization. In other words, since all objects in the universe are actually connected by forces and influence, one can never localize exactly.

The reason to look for meaning in mathematics arises from the question whether a given mathematical technique or theory is correct. If mathematics could be created within the intuitionistic program one would be sure of the correctness of one's methods, but this rebuilding of mathematics is a very difficult program and it has had limited success.

The high priest of the formalist approach in the early twentieth century was David Hilbert who recognized the validity of the criticism against his approach. But he argued that since the procedures of different mathematical systems are well defined, their use in the solution of physical problems was appropriate. To validate this use he believed it was necessary that each branch of mathematics be an axiomatic system that can be shown to be consistent and complete. Consistency implies that the axioms are such that no contradictions can arise in the deductions from the system. The idea of completeness is that any statement in the language of the system is provably true or false. It was shown by Kurt Gödel in 1931 that, for mathematical systems of sufficient complexity (as for the system of natural numbers), consistency is incompatible with completeness. In other words, such systems, if consistent, must necessarily be incomplete. Gödel's result implies that Hilbert's program cannot be fulfilled. Earlier it was shown by Lowensheim and Skolem that no complete foundation can ever be achieved for the theory of sets, which was used by some to base entire mathematics. The Lowensheim-Skolem theory says that neither logic nor the theory of sets is unique; one can develop varieties of logics and set theories!

So even natural numbers defy definitive definition. No doubt, this is partly due to the fact that axiomatic systems leave some terms undefined; these undefined terms can be interpreted differently in alternative axiomatic systems. Morris Kline presented an excellent review of the problems of foundations in contemporary mathematics.[5]

The development of mathematics is guided essentially by intuition. The uncertainty with regard to the structure of mathematics does not create a major problem for the advance of physics for two reasons. First, physicists always check for plausibility of results using a mathematical technique before adopting it. Second, if a formal system generates useful physics then the structure of the system reveals some truths about the physical phenomenon. Physicists use finite techniques to obtain their results, before these techniques are cast in the framework of classical mathematics by their mathematically oriented colleagues. Intuition is used to either derive results or validate them.

The search for mathematical truths is closely tied up with the search for the logic of physical reality. Mathematics and physics complement each other and ultimately both are empirical sciences. Due to this several mathematicians and physicists have downplayed the importance of rigorous proofs, which start from foundations. Perhaps, the dual aspects of mathematics arising out of finite and continuous formulations cannot be completely reconciled. It is possible that both approaches will keep on yielding correct results just as wave and particle formulations do in the description of physical phenomena.

Knowledge representation

Descriptions of reality are in terms of mathematics and natural language and having examined interpretations of mathematics, we turn to the question of knowledge representation by natural language. This question is the focus of study not only by philosophers but, more recently, also by computer scientists seeking techniques to design machines that can understand language or translate from one language to another. The discussion that follows is mainly related to knowledge representation using computers. It is an excursus from the main theme of the book, but it is relevant because computers are increasingly employed in situations where data can neither be gathered nor analyzed without their use. Logical machines have become essential in the continuing uncovering of the structure of the physical world. While current applications are limited to numerical tasks, people visualize computers performing tasks with cognitive component. Several questions then arise: What are the limitations of computers, especially in regard to mimicking the cognitive processes of man? Can computers be used to represent linguistic information, and if yes can they then process this information autonomously to find meaning? Current research indicates that computers may never be able to process language with the same facility as that of a human.

Computer processing of a natural language went through two distinct phases in the past several decades. It was first thought that machine translation (MT) of a language into another should be an easy matter once one has compiled dictionaries and obtained mathematical representation of the grammars of the languages. It was believed that actual translation would proceed by replacing the words in the text by their equivalents, followed by a rearrangement and modification of these new words according to the grammar of the target language. But it was found that this task was not easy since a word can have several equivalents, where the correct one can only be decided by the context. The mathematical representation of the grammar of a natural language so that the sentences are unambiguous was given up as an intractable problem. Machine translations were often incomprehensible, or they totally distorted meaning. By the mid-1960s the MT program, as envisaged originally, was dead. The focus in the recent years has shifted away from MT to providing a preliminary translation, which can then be worked upon by an editor to produce the finished work. The other area to which attention is given is the definition of a constrained language form and vocabulary, more flexible than in artificial languages, so that there is no ambiguity in meaning. These efforts have brought the problem of knowledge representation to the fore. Such a representation assumes certain knowledge of the application environment, and knowledge of the intended audience. Various techniques of knowledge representation have been incorporated in current systems: these include semantic networks, first order logic, frames, and production systems. Each of these techniques offers special advantages for specific situations.

These techniques of knowledge representation suffer from many shortcomings. In the semantic network approach, where relationships between objects and classes are specified, it is not known how to distinguish between information related to an object as against that of a class and how to deal with exceptions. The first order logic approach cannot deal with incomplete knowledge or with situations where non-deductive inference is called for. In the frames approach the knowledge base is decomposed into highly modular chunks, a procedure not always possible. In the production system approach rules connecting 'patterns' and 'action' (say in human reasoning) are defined. However, the memory required to define a pattern may be so large so as to be impossible to have in practice.

If there are limits to the nature of natural language processing by the computer, what is the nature of these limits? It appears that the best one can do is to devise actual systems -- in other words, use a constructive approach. The greatest success in devising a constructive approach to the description of a natural language is Pāṇini's grammar for the Sanskrit language, an achievement termed by the famous linguist L. Bloomfield as 'one of the greatest monuments of human intelligence.'[6] The knowledge representation methodology in the grammar of Pāṇini and his successors is, in many ways, equivalent to the more powerful currently researched AI schemes. It includes rules about rules, analogs of which are not known for modern languages. Some elements of the Pāṇinian approach have already been incorporated in the current computer understanding systems. We will review the 'standard' approach to natural language processing, so that one may appreciate the commonality between the two as well as main points of difference.

A discourse may be analyzed in terms of primitives that deal either with being or becoming. In other words, a primitive either describes categories and objects and their relationships, or if the context is clear it describes agents and transformations. These two kinds of primitives are complementary and yet each can serve as a knowledge representation scheme. One may describe transformation implicitly by means of description of the objects at successive times, and categories and objects in a domain can be defined as new objects. At another level, one may name an object from a root related to its most significant function, or one may have separate labels for objects and functions without any apparent relationship between the two. Often, languages have features related to both these ideas.

Perhaps the earliest example of a debate about the being-becoming dichotomy is the one between the schools of Gārgya and Śākaṭāyana, two ancient Indian philosophers. Śākaṭāyana considered that nouns were derived from verbs or verbal roots, a principle whose universality was challenged by Gārgya on the basis that it often leads to forced etymology. According to Gārgya, if *aśva* (horse) was derived from *aś* (to travel) then other beings that travelled would also be called *aśva*, and states of being would be antecedent to objects. Since objects can be associated with variety of actions, Gārgya's objection was true. However, the significance of Śākatāyana's claim was to consider the object name to be derived from some (arbitrarily) chosen primary action associated with it.

Pāṇini, in his grammar, developed Śākatāyana's position with the difference that he considered some words to be ready-made stems, into whose formation he did not go. Pāṇini's successors continued this tradition.

A precise semantic analysis along these lines was developed by the school of New Grammarians started in early sixteenth century by Bhaṭṭoji Dīkṣita.[7]

Gārgya's position that considered nouns to be primary, together with ideas from logic (Nyāya), led eventually to the school of New Logic[8] (Navya Nyāya). The latter school was at its zenith in the sixteenth century during the times of Raghunātha (1475-1550). This school also developed a methodology for precise semantic analysis of language. The two schools influenced each other and it was recognized that, leaving aside the question of the focus being the noun or the verb, any system would have elements of both, a fact already assumed by Pāṇini.

The difference in paraphrase depending on the emphasis on the noun or the verb is shown by the following example:[9]

Harir vihagaṃ paśyati
Hari sees a bird

This is paraphrased by the grammarians as "the operation generating the activity of seeing which has a bird as object is qualified by Hari as its doer." The paraphrase by the logicians is: "Hari is qualified by effort which is qualified by the activity of seeing which has a bird as its object."

Dākṣīputra Pāṇini is believed to have lived during the 5th or 6th century BC. He was born in the town of Śālātura, modern Lahur, in Northwest India. Pāṇini's grammar Aṣṭādhyāyī (The Eight Chapters) deals ostensibly with the Sanskrit language; it, however, is really a model for a universal grammar, applicable to any language. His book consists of a little fewer than 4000 rules and aphorisms. Pāṇini's grammar attempts to completely describe Sanskrit as the spoken language of its time. Two important commentaries on his grammar, which are often studied along with it are those by Kātyāyana, and Patañjali (2nd century BC). Its philosophical underpinnings were discussed in an important work in the 5th century AD by Bhartṛhari.[10]

Pāṇini's grammar begins with metarules, or rules about rules. To facilitate his description, he establishes a special technical language (or metalanguage). This is followed by several sections on how to generate words and sentences starting from roots, as well as rules on transformations of structure. The last part of the grammar is a one-directional string of rules, where a given rule in the sequence ignores all rules that follow. This anticipates in form and spirit by more than 2500 years the idea of a computer program. The structure of this part of Pāṇini's grammar should rightly be termed the Pāṇini Machine).[11]

Note that in Pāṇini's system a finite set of rules is enough to generate infinity of sentences. The algebraic character of Pāṇini's rules was not appreciated in the West until very recently when search for similar generative structures was popularized by Chomsky and others. Before this, in the nineteenth century, Pāṇini's analysis of root and suffixes and his recognition of ablaut had led to the founding of the subjects of comparative and historical linguistics.

Despite similarities between Pāṇinian and modern generative grammars, there exist striking differences as well. Some of these differences are related to the nature of the languages under study: Sanskrit in the case of Pāṇini, and modern European languages in the other case. Furthermore, the contemporary evaluation of Pāṇini is still going on, a process that is slowed down by the fact that the original is inaccessible to most linguists and computer scientists. In any event, one may define an approach to language analysis as being Pāṇinian if it uses:

1) root and suffix analysis,
2) linear string of rules and analysis by rule sequence,
3) analysis by functional structure,
4) exhaustive description.

Let me enumerate some of the ambiguities that make machine translation such a difficult task. These ambiguities need to be resolved, if at all possible, in various steps to obtain a translation. Each kind of ambiguity is addressed separately in a sequence of steps, which constitutes the usual form of a computer based understanding system.

Lexical ambiguity. This arises from a single word having two or more different meanings, all of which are potentially valid. Consider 'Stay away from the range' which could be advice to a child to keep away from either the kitchen stove or the meadow. 'The court was packed' is a more complex example as the court may refer to a judicial court or a rectangular space and packed might mean a deceitful composition or a crowding by people.

Structural ambiguity. The source of this ambiguity is the many ways words in a sentence may be combined into phrases and then interpreted. Thus in 'He saw the crane fly outside' one might be referring to the crane fly, a long-legged two-winged fly. Other examples of this ambiguity are: 'My friend came home late last night' and 'Flying kites can be tricky.' Another kind of structural ambiguity is where the sentence has a unique grammatical structure but it still allows different meanings owing to different underlying 'deep structure.' For example, 'The policeman's arrest was illegal' does not tell us who was arrested. Another example is 'That leopard was spotted.'

Pragmatic ambiguity. This is related to the context of the sentence. Thus in 'She put the brick in the dryer and spoilt it' the meaning would be different depending on whether the brick was made of metal or wax. Likewise the meaning of 'John loves his wife and so does Bill' would be unambiguous only if it were known that Bill was a bachelor.

These difficulties are inherent in English but are not fundamental to all natural languages. Śāstric (scientific) Sanskrit is one natural language that appears to be particularly precise.

A language may be described at several hierarchically organized levels. At the lowest level a spoken language is characterized in terms of elementary sounds, the study of which constitutes phonology. A group of similar speech sounds that function in the same way, and which may be substituted for each other without changing the meaning of an utterance, is a phoneme. Natural languages are characterized by 30 to 80 phonemes. English is usually described in terms of about 40 phonemes. Sanskrit is described by 48 phonemes each of which is represented by a unique symbol in its alphabet (13 vowels and 35 consonants).

The study of the next level of linguistic analysis is morphology. Simple words, as well as inflectional sounds like the plural endings, prefixes and suffixes that convey meanings, are morphemes. Written words must be analyzed for their morphemic components in a natural language processing system. Thus a system might process 'unknowing' by finding its root form 'know,' and then determining the change in meaning affected by each of the additional morphemes 'un-' and '-ing.' Syntax deals with the manner in which the meaningful constituents are put together to form an utterance or sentence.

Some sentences can be parsed in many different ways, leading to different meanings. As example 'Traffic jams were caused by slow trucks and buses carrying heavy loads' may be parsed in at least four different ways. In these different parse trees 'slow' may qualify trucks only, or trucks and buses, and similarly 'heavy loads' may qualify buses only, or both trucks and buses.

A parse tree is generated by rules of the kind

S → NP + VP
NP → ADJ + N
NP → DET + N + PP
PP → PREP + NP and so on

A collection of such rules generates a grammar. Most traditional English grammars have this form.

The grammatical tradition that grew out of Pāṇini's work did not analyze sentences in the above noun-phrase/verb-phrase form. Rather, the description was a generative one where the structure of the sentence was derived from a number of primitive syntactic categories centered on some action. The Sanskrit language has seven case endings, not counting the vocative. These are nominative, accusative, instrumental, dative, ablative, genitive, and locative. Roughly, these correspond to

agent
object

instrument
recipient
point of departure
belonging to
location in time or space

The semantic interpretation of these categories can sometimes overlap. Thus point of departure could also stand for motive as in 'on account of.' Likewise instrument could also represent the sense 'by reason of,' 'in conformity with,' 'by the lapse of' and so on. Semantic networks are also used to represent the case structure of a sentence. Thus consider

I kicked the ball in my garden

Graphically this may be shown as the node representing the action kick connected to other nodes such as agent, object (ball), time (past) and location (garden). The node representing the location could be further qualified by means of another link representing ownership. Complex sentences have very intricate graphs, which can be interpreted by computer. However, if the sentence itself is ambiguous, it is associated with more than one graph. The number of case categories has been reorganized by artificial intelligence researchers into:

action
agent
conditional (logical condition between two events)
instrument
location
object
purpose
quality
recipient
time
truth (used for false statements)

Another representation defines eleven classes of actions where each action is associated with four cases: actor, object, direction and instrument. The classification of action is as:

transfer (a) (of abstract relationship)
transfer (p) (of physical location)
propel
move
grasp
ingest
expel
transfer (m) (of mental information)
build (m) (of mental information)

speak
attend

This representation is centered on human actors and it would not be useful in general situations.

A computer based system of speech or text understanding must perform several operations in sequence. For speech, the first operation is that of phonological analysis that transcribes sound waves into a series of phonemes. These may then be expressed as written words. The first analysis performed for written language is morphological, where each word is decomposed into its root and inflections. This is followed by lexical analysis where the words are assigned to different lexical categories such as noun, verb, adjective, etc. The next operation is that of syntactic analysis or parsing where the rules of grammar are used to ascertain the structure of the sentence. The next step is that of semantic analysis where the sentence is converted into a form so that inferences can be drawn. The last step is that of pragmatic analysis which makes the context of the sentence explicit. At the end of the sequence, the computer can announce its inferences and respond to questions. For such a sequence of operations to proceed effectively, it is necessary that the meaning underlying the sentences be represented in a convenient form. Different knowledge representation systems have been devised for this purpose. The sequence of operations in the understanding system is then a means of first generating information about the knowledge representation system which is followed by analysis.

A grammar may be coded in terms of a network where transitions between the constituents of a sentence are coded as transitions across the nodes. The arcs in the network contain additional information that instruct the parser as to what action it should take to generate a specific meaning structure. Such networks are called augmented transition networks (ATNs).

The ATN grammar is a standardized set of tests and operations that are performed on each sentence. Graphically, this is represented by a directed graph, where arcs represent test-operation pairs and nodes indicate common points joining arcs. The tests are generally conditions on an input word and the network represents the several ways a sentence can be analyzed. All operations are carried out in order and a complete analysis is produced by a path through the network on which all the tests are satisfied by the input words. Another useful grammar is the 'lexical function grammar' (LFG) in which grammatical functions are expressed in a form so that categories such as head, number, person, tense subject, object are tied to the words and phrases that serve these functions. Such categorization is a part of the Sanskrit grammar of Pāṇini where modifiers identify subject and object and word order is free and dictated mainly by style and convention. The LFG approach allows a sentence to be represented in a nested form if a part of it plays a role in another part.

For semantic analysis one needs to represent the sentence in a form so that the reasoning procedures can be applied on it. One may use the semantic network approach to classify objects through their relationships, which information can then be used with predicate calculus for further processing for the computer to draw its inferences.

In contrast to these methods, the analysis in Pāṇini's grammar is done by analyzing the forms of the various words in the sentence. The transformations define agents, recipients as well as time and space relationships. A recent development is the use of logic as the framework for a computer language to analyze linguistic expressions.

An algorithm can be expressed in terms of two components: the logic and the control, where the logic expresses the problem and its solution and the control expresses the method to be followed to solve the problem. One would like logic programming to be based only on the logic component of an algorithm, with the control being exercised by the machine. But for reasons of efficiency it is necessary to provide additional control information.

A serious problem afflicting logic programming schemes is the 'negation' problem. This refers to the difficulty of obtaining negative information about a database where the information is represented in a positive sense. Thus consider the database:

Devadatta was born in India

There is no way to show that Devadatta was not born in, say, Rome unless the database is enhanced by explicitly stating that Devadatta was not born in any country other than India. The other alternative is to use negation by failure, where any deduction not following from the database is taken to be false. The procedure of negation by failure works satisfactorily only in databases that have been organized in a particular way. Such an organization is not always feasible.

Another problem is related to the monotonicity property of logic: If certain consequences follow a set of statements, addition of new statements cannot alter the earlier consequences. How does one then deal with changing or incomplete knowledge? How can exceptions to definitions be incorporated? This has led some to criticize the use of logic in the representation of knowledge. Furthermore, inference obtained solely by deduction has its limitations.

That the problem of knowledge representation is extremely complex and difficult, and is summed up by the being-becoming dichotomy related to the motion picture. There are several perspectives from which one can view knowledge representation in a film. One of these is the succession of frames defining change; the other is that of close-up, which shows detail organized in a hierarchical sense; still another is a sequential representation of a phenomenon that is spread across time and space.

A motion picture represents knowledge in two layers: one of which is the frame sequence, and the other is the overlaying sound track. The sound track itself can either be commentary, or sounds of things, or utterances of persons. This defines a rich complex that represents knowledge through many interacting levels. If we leave out the sound track, temporal relationships between frames can be marked by the relative shape and sizes of objects (if the nature of their evolution were known) or other background cues.

In the most general case, one can see that representation of knowledge may be done at different levels, each representing a different understanding of the reality. This is, in fact, similar to the manner the human mind organizes knowledge.

Whereas knowledge representation by means of graphs and other devices will become more refined and thus useful in artificial intelligence applications, languages in representing physical reality will always be ambiguous, incomplete, and inconsistent. As we have seen a language is a highly structured representation of a reality that has infinitely many, mutually interacting facets. Such a representation is, therefore, bound to be incomplete in several ways.

Meaning of physical theories

Implicit in our review of the foundations of physics is the premise that a theory captures the essence of the physical phenomenon it describes. Our theories deal with isolated systems in controlled conditions found only in laboratories. Quite often, by means of reasonable assumptions, we are able to explain processes in the real world in terms of our theories. By creating desired conditions in laboratories and factories, we are also able to generate many phenomena at will. Because new behavior emerges as system complexity is increased, the scientific method is essentially one of analysis. Its predictive value is limited only to repeated experiments. This means that given the behavior of a system it is generally impossible, without experimentation, to predict the behavior of a more complex system built out of several primitive ones. Thus the chemical behavior of matter seems a far cry from the properties of nucleons and electrons. Similarly, in relation to the properties of simple molecules, the replicating behavior of DNA is fantastic.

A great part of our knowledge about the physical universe is speculative which is especially true of non-terrestrial processes. On the other hand, we cannot even speculate on what rich possibilities exist as far as biological structures are concerned. If the human mind with its ability to comprehend evolved out of inert matter, the evolution of new wonderful faculties should be possible.

To consider the meaning of the mathematical structure of a theory, note that the problem of divisibility is taken care of mathematically by the fact that the sum of its infinite series is finite. Apparently, without resolving the question of whether time and space are discrete or continuous, we resolve the paradox mathematically. Likewise, renormalization in quantum mechanics is a mathematical procedure that is not well understood -- it involves cancellation of infinities -- that works.

The uncanny effectiveness of mathematics has filled the hearts of high school students as well as accomplished scientists with wonder. Eugene Wigner terms it the unreasonable effectiveness of mathematics in the natural sciences. According to Einstein, "Here arises a puzzle that has disturbed scientists of all periods. How is it possible that mathematics, a product of human thought that is independent of experience, fits so excellently the objects of physical reality? Can human reason without experience discover by pure thinking properties of real things?"

Neuroscience may reveal why mathematics works so well. It is possible that patterns of thought and reasoning reflect the organization of the brain which in turn relates to the nature of physical reality. The plausibility of this notion is strengthened by the fact that the large and the small and seemingly diverse phenomena have deep connections. Certain characteristics of the elementary particles relate to the large scale structure of the universe; and the evolution of the universe in the big bang scenario is determined by the behavior of the most elementary particles. It may be that the uncertainty in quantum mechanics is a result of the interaction of the rest of the universe with the particle under study.[12] It is fitting, then, that there should exist connections between the way we think as represented by mathematics and the nature of our understanding of the universe.

Causality implies that a definite sequential connection exists between events. In other situations we can make probabilistic statements. When a fair coin is tossed a large number of times, heads and tails show up with equal frequency, even though no assertion can be made about the outcome of any particular toss. This is due to the fact that conditions at each toss are somewhat different and in the long run the differences influence each outcome equally. Many probabilistic statements imply a lack of knowledge.

Data obtained in experimental situations is affected by random background noise. This means that theoretical models, which invariably use coefficients derived by experiment, are probabilistic in nature. Sometimes measurements concern variables that are defined in statistical terms, as is true for temperature and pressure, and the model itself is intrinsically probabilistic. In quantum theory, probabilistic structure is posited for variables that appear to be intrinsically non-statistical, such as position and mass. Whether the basic uncertainty of quantum mechanics is a result of the influence of the rest of the universe on the object under study is a tantalizing question.

We know a great deal about our universe, but many questions that were raised by sages over two thousand years ago are still with us. Does an elementary atom, which combines to form other matter, exist? Are space and time discrete or continuous? Is the universe of our experience structured by the nature of the human mind? What is the size and age of the universe? How does self-awareness arise, and what are its limitations?

Current evidence suggests that in agreement with the conclusions of the Ṛgveda, it will be impossible to ever fully answer these questions.

IX EPILOGUE: HIDDEN ORDER AND CONSCIOUSNESS

Being and becoming

There are two essential parts to understanding the universe: its representation in terms of material objects, and the manner in which this representation changes with time. In philosophy, these are the positions of two different schools, one believing that reality is *being*, and the other that it is *becoming*.

The conception of the cosmos, consisting of the material universe and observers, has been shaped by ideas that belong to these two opposite schools. The idea of the world as *being* is associated with materialism, while that of *becoming* is associated with idealism. In the materialist view, mental experience is emergent on the material ground and contents of the mind are secondary to the physical world. In the idealist position, consciousness has primacy.

The question of consciousness hinges on the relationship between brain and mind. Reductionism considers them to be identical -- with mind as the sum total of the activity in the brain -- at a suitable higher level of representation. Opposed to this is the view that although mind requires a physical structure, it ends up transcending that structure. There exist other views of mind, shaped by culture and life-experience, which resonate with the tension among opposite beliefs applied to different aspects of life by the same individual.

Quantum mechanics is relevant to a discussion of the cosmos for it is the deepest theory of physics and it is a theory of observables in which information is the fundamental quantity. John Archibald Wheeler used the slogan '*It from bit*' to stress that our constructions of reality are based on readings on our instruments in response to yes-no questions. He declared "that all things physical are information-theoretic in origin and this is a *participatory universe,*"[1] where the term 'participatory' implies that observations effect the evolution of the universe. But there is nothing in quantum mechanics that describes the nature of the observers.

Just as there exists the outer cosmos – the physical universe –, there also exists the corresponding inner cosmos of the mind. The mind processes signals coming into the brain to obtain its understandings in the domains of seeing, hearing, touching, and tasting using its store of memories. The cognitive act is an active process where the selectivity of the sensors and the accompanying processing in the brain is organized based on the expectation of the cognitive task and on effort, will and intention.

The structure of the inner cosmos belongs to the domain of psychology, and it is fair to assume that at some level it mirrors the outer cosmos. In the schematic of the figure below we suggest that if quantum theory describes processes for the outer cosmos, consciousness does so for the inner cosmos. If quantum theory underlies the processes in the inner cosmos, consciousness must influence the outer cosmos.

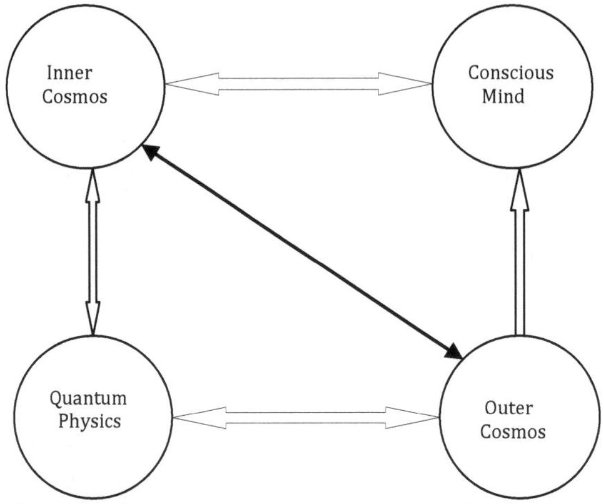

Inner and outer cosmoses, the law, and consciousness

If consciousness is complementary to space, time and matter, it needs material support to be embodied as 'awareness.' Also, we cannot speak of a universe if it is without observers. If we accept that we have discovered the basic laws of nature and that classical machines cannot be conscious, one may assume that quantum processing in the brain, given appropriate brain structures, leads to awareness. Different states of consciousness such as wakefulness, sleep, dream-sleep, coma have distinct neurochemical signatures, and these different states are modifications caused by the neural circuitry on a basic state of consciousness.

Although consciousness cannot be studied directly, it is accessible to further understanding indirectly. I suggest that improbable coincidences corroborated in literature support the existence of a universal consciousness principle, but, of course, they cannot be taken to be proof for it.

The observer paradox

The inner cosmos is physically located in the brain, but we cannot speak of where in the brain the perceiving self resides, because that would amount to a homunculus argument. The perceiving self cannot be in a unique neuron in the brain, because that would require such a neuron to have the capacity to process all the information that the individual possesses, which is clearly impossible for a cellular structure that can only do simple processing. Conversely, if the perceiving self was distributed over an area, then we need to postulate another homunculus within this area to process the information reaching the self.

Thus the conscious self can neither be localized to a single cell, nor assumed to be distributed over the entire brain or a part of it. We cannot speak of where the self is, but only of how the self obtains knowledge. Since the self is associated with the brain, it uses the brain as the lens through which to perceive the world. Our knowledge of the word is, therefore, contingent on the neurophysiologic nature of the brain. If we make sense of the world it is because we are biologically programmed to do so and we have innate capacity for it. Our conception of the cosmos is based on the relationship between our brain and mind that is expressed in the idea that the outer is mirrored in the inner. Patterns seen in the outer world must have corresponding traces in the inner world.

Sacred architecture in many cultures replicates conceptions of the universe. The cathedral is a representation of the heavens of the Christian cosmos. In ancient India, it was concluded, using elementary measurements, that the relative distance to the sun and the moon from the earth is approximately 108 times their respective diameters. The diameter of the sun is likewise approximately 108 times the diameter of the earth, and this fact could have been established from the relative durations of the solar and lunar eclipses.

The number 108, taken as a fundamental measure of the universe, was used in ritual and sacred geometry. Prominent gods and goddesses were given 108 names; the number of dance poses in the Nāṭya Śāstra, an ancient text on theater, dance, and music, was taken to be 108, as was the number of beads in the japa-mālā.[2] The Hindu temple had the circumference to the measure of 180 (half of the number of days in the year) and its axis had the measure of 54 (half the number 108),[3] and we find these dimensions in the sacred ground for fire altars of the second millennium BC to the thousand-year old Viṣṇu temple at Angkor Wat. The body, breath, and consciousness were taken to be equivalent to the earth, the space, and the sun, respectively. The counting of the prayer beads was to make a symbolic journey from the earth to the sun, from the body to the inner light of consciousness.

One kind of connection between the outer and the inner is provided by biological clocks in the cells which work according to the rhythms of the sun, the moon, the tides, and other astronomical phenomena.[4] Other biological processes are adjustments to sensory inputs and the observer may also be viewed as an ecological system seeking its balance in a complex environment and evolving to attractor states. In a dynamical system the observer has no direct role, excepting to alter probabilities associated with the evolution.

Quantum physics, observers, and the cosmos

The astonishing success of modern science rests on the discovery that the representation and its rate of change are proportionate. For example, in quantum physics, the evolution of a system or an object, represented by $|\varphi\rangle$ is given by the Schrödinger equation:

$$i\hbar \frac{d|\varphi\rangle}{dt} = H|\varphi\rangle$$

Likewise, in classical systems the unknown function and its various derivatives are related making it possible to compute future values. In discrete time systems found in plant and animals that are characterized by Fibonacci series, the time difference of the generative function equals the function itself.

Quantum physics is different from classical physics in so much that the quantum system is a superposition of many possibilities and while the evolution of the quantum state is deterministic (given by the Schrödinger equation) its observation results in a collapse of the state to one of its components in a probabilistic manner. Both classical physics and quantum physics present a machine-view of the universe. In social sciences and philosophy, freedom and agency for the observer is postulated, but these disciplines do not derive from physics. Either freedom is illusory or the machine paradigm is incomplete in describing the world.

Material physics can only be concerned with objective associations, and it can do no better than see each system as a mechanism of some kind. The brain is a machine, yet the brain-machine has awareness while the computer does not.

Quantum physics is associated with its own paradoxes related to observers such as those implying propagation of effects instantaneously across space (for entangled particles) and time (as in the Wheeler's delayed choice experiment) if one uses ordinary language to describe phenomena.[5] Clearly, reality has aspects that are not captured by consistent linguistic narratives.

Physics deals with space, time and matter. As observers we are more than matter at a specific location in space and time; we also have consciousness. Although it is logical to see consciousness as emergent on matter it is also tempting to see it having a more fundamental existence. To claim that consciousness is emergent and therefore inherent in the scientific law and yet deny it ontological reality is not reasonable.

The anthropic principle is invoked to explain the nature of laws. In one formulation of the principle, the physical laws are restricted by the requirement that they should lead to intelligent life at some stage in the evolution of the universe. Since life on earth would cease when the sun exhausts its fuel, and as evolution of consciousness could not have been in vain, it is argued that man will create silicon-based 'conscious machines' that will seed the universe and the entire universe will become a conscious machine.[6]

In the archaic view, the universe is conscious. In more sophisticated versions of this archaic view, consciousness itself is the ground stuff of reality and on this ground the complex of space, time and matter is seeded.

Evolution in quantum mechanics is deterministic except for the state collapse that takes places as the system interacts with another system. But this can only happen if there exist separated systems, in which one of them is being observed by the other. Given that the state of the entire universe is defined at the initial point, its evolution must be completely deterministic. Any seeming randomness should merely be an amplification of the randomness in the initial state and the entropy at the origin should not change as the universe evolves. In other words, the physical universe governed by quantum laws has no place for the emergence of life.

Our currently accepted conceptions of the beginning of the universe postulate much more uniformity than exists now. One way entropy could increase in the universe is by the process of reduction of its state function by some other system. Since the universe, by definition, is unity, it becomes essential to postulate a mechanism other than that of physical laws, which permits the state function to reduce. This other mechanism may be the working of the 'consciousness principle' which can just by the process of 'observation' increase entropy.[7]

But the 'consciousness principle' cannot be a new physical law, because if it were so then it would only replace the currently accepted dynamics of the universe by a different one. Such a physical law would not alter the conception of the universe as a deterministic or stochastic machine without any possibility of life. Consciousness or awareness implies binding to events and entities, abstract or real, that are separated in time and space, and the perceptible influence of the 'consciousness principle' may be seen in improbable correlations as a result of drift of probabilities in the equations of dynamics.

A 'consciousness principle,' rather than the improbable creation of complex molecules by chance that has been refuted,[8] must be the explanation for the rise of life all over the universe. Consciousness interpenetrates the universe, but it needs appropriate physical structures to be embodied. Molecules of life at the general level, and the brains of animals under appropriate biochemical conditions at a higher level, represent such physical structures.

Information in the cosmos

One cannot speak of information in a universe without observers. Information arises out of a communication game played between a sender of signals and the recipient. For physical systems, the game may be seen as being played between Nature and the scientist. The average information obtained from a quantum system is given by the von Neumann measure, which is a generalization of thermodynamic entropy and perfectly in accord with commonsense when we consider a mixed quantum state. But this entropy for an unknown pure state is zero even though testing many copies of such a state can reveal information about the choice that was made by the sender.

The idea of zero entropy for an unknown pure state is reasonable from the perspective that once the state has been identified; there is no further information to be gained from examining its copies. But it is not reasonable if the game is being played between sentient beings. Assume the sender chooses one out of a certain number of polarization states (say, for a photon) and supplies several copies of it to the receiver. Measurements made by the receiver on the copies will reveal information regarding the choice made by the sender. If the set of choices is infinite, then the "information" generated by the source is unbounded. The information in the pure state is limited by the "relationship" between the source and the receiver, and by the precision of the receiver's measurement apparatus. If the sender chose a polarization state that the receiver's measurement apparatus was already synchronized with, the receiver could recognize the state quite readily.

In my view, entropy has two components: one informational (related to the pure components of the quantum state, which can vary from receiver to receiver), and the other that is thermodynamic (which is receiver independent). The increase of information with time is a consequence of the interplay between unitary (related to pure states) and non-unitary (related to mixed states) evolution, which makes it possible to transform one type of information into another.[9] This complementarity indicates that a fundamental duality is essential for information.

The receiver can make his estimate by adjusting the basis vectors so that he gets *closer* to the unknown pure state. The information that can be obtained from such a state in repeated experiments is potentially infinite in the most general case. But if the observer is told what the pure state is, the information associated with the states vanishes, suggesting that a fundamental divide exists between objective and subjective information.

This approach is consistent with the view that one cannot speak of information associated with a system excepting in relation to an experimental arrangement together with the protocol for measurement. The experimental arrangement is thus integral to the amount of information that can be obtained.

The information measure outlined here resolves the puzzle of entropy increase. We can suppose that the universe had immensely large informational entropy associated with a pure state in the beginning, a portion of which has, during the evolution of the universe, transformed into thermodynamic entropy.

The problem of consciousness

The reason why consciousness is not accessible to science is that it is not objective. It is the light that the observer shines on objects but this light cannot be turned upon itself. Rational science is related to associations and it must, therefore, be material and reductionist and consciousness cannot be fitted in the framework of rational science. But there are indirect ways to study consciousness. Neurophysiological experiments have shown that the mind orders events in order to provide consistent picture and that there is a small time lag between initiation of neurological function and its conscious awareness. Mind is an active participant in the creation of models of the world, seen most clearly when subjects who have impairments resulting from strokes or trauma are studied.[10]

Some say that once machines become sufficiently complex they would be conscious. But machines only follow instructions and it is not credible that they should suddenly, just on account of the increase in the number of connections between computing units, become endowed with self-awareness. To speak of consciousness in the machine paradigm is a contradiction in terms. If a machine could make true choices (that are not governed by a random picking between different alternatives), then it has transcended the paradigm because its behavior cannot be described by any mathematical function.

Some ascribe awareness of the brain to the fact that the brain is a self-organizing system which responds to the nature and quality of its interaction with the environment, whereas computers can't do that. But other ecological systems, which are biological communities that have complex interrelationship amongst their parts, are self-organizing, without being self-aware. This suggests that while self-organization is a necessary pre-requisite for consciousness, it is not sufficient.

Cognitive scientists and biologists have considered evolutionary aspects related to cognitive capacity, where consciousness is viewed as emerging out of language. Linguistic research on chimpanzees and bonobos has revealed that although they can be taught basic vocabulary of several hundred words, this ability does not extend to syntax. By contrast, small children acquire much larger vocabularies -- and use the words far more creatively -- with no overt training, indicating that language is an innate capacity.

It is theorized that human language capacities arose out of biological natural selection because they fulfill two clear criteria: an extremely complex and rich design and the absence of alternative processes capable of explaining such complexity. Other theories look at music and language arising out of sexual selection. But, howsoever imaginative and suggestive these models might be, they do not address the question of how the capacity to visualize models of world that are essential to language and consciousness first arose.

According to the nativist view, language ability is rooted in the biology of the brain, and our ability to use grammar and syntax is an instinct, dependent on specific modules of the brain. Therefore, we learn language as a consequence of a unique biological adaptation, and not because it is an emergent response to the problem of communication confronted by ourselves and our ancestors. This is seen most tellingly amongst deaf children who are not taught a sign language. Such children spontaneously create their personal signs, slowly adding grammatical rules, complete with inflection, case marking, and other forms of syntax.[11]

Creativity and discovery

Some individuals, who have serious developmental disability or major mental illness, perform spectacularly at tasks in the areas of mathematical and calendar calculations, music, art, memory, and unusual sensory discrimination and perception.[12] Such cognitive ability cannot be viewed simply as processing of sensory information by a central intelligence extraction system.

There also exist accounts in the literature speaking of spontaneous discovery in a variety of creative fields. But as unique events that happened in the past, they cannot be verified. In the scientific field, Jacques Hadamard surveyed 100 leading mathematicians of his time, concluding many of them appeared to have obtained entire solutions spontaneously. This list included the claim by the French mathematician Henri Poincaré that he arrived at the solution to a subtle mathematical problem as he was boarding a bus, and the discovery of the structure of benzene by Kekulé in a dream.[13] More recently, the physicist Roger Penrose claims to have found the solution to a mathematical problem while crossing a street.[14]

Intuitive discovery must be common, and the reason why we don't hear of more such stories is because some people are unprepared to appreciate their intuition or translate it into a meaningful narrative, and others feel uncomfortable speaking of their personal experience. The preparation of the scientist comes in the amplification of his intuition. It is also true that the creative intuition is not always correct, and the scientist's judgment is essential in separating the false solution from the true one.

Anomalous abilities and first person accounts of discovery that appear to be spontaneous could either indicate that consciousness is more than a phenomenon based solely on matter or that these accounts are just coincidences. Conversely, there is no way to prove the veracity of the scientist's account of discovery. It is possible that the account is one that the scientist has come to believe over time and it does not correspond to fact.

Coincidences

The standard scientific view on coincidences is that correlated spatially or temporally separated events must be entirely by chance. Scientific cosmology cannot suppose otherwise, because doing so would imply that it is not complete. Furthermore, many claims of coincidence cannot be accepted at face value. They may be a result of poor observation or recall, self-deception, or deception by others.

In some coincidence events a person may claim to obtain information from another person without the use of the currently known senses or inference, and in precognition one may claim to have knowledge of a future event. In parapsychology experiments, volunteers guess random choices that are made at a remote location to determine if these guesses deviate from chance. The sender attempts to mentally communicate a randomly chosen 'target' to the receiver. The sender and receiver are in separate acoustically shielded rooms. A computer is used to choose a target from a large selection of possible targets that may be video clips, and plays that clip repeatedly to the sender. At the same time, the receiver reports out loud any thoughts or images that come to mind, and these verbal reports are recorded. Neither the experimenter nor the receiver has any idea of what target the sender is viewing. At the end of the sending period, the sender remains in his room while the computer plays four video clips to the receiver - the target plus three decoys. The receiver's task is to compare each clip to the mentation, and to select which of the clips most closely matches it.

If no information transfer is taking place, then we would expect the receiver to correctly identify the clip that was viewed by the sender 25 per cent of the time by chance alone. Extrasensory or telepathic perception is inferred to have taken place if the target is correctly identified more often than chance expectation.

The results of such experiments are not quite supportive of the idea of extrasensory communication. According to researchers in the field, deviation from chance is limited to participants tested by believer experimenters; participants tested by skeptical experimenters obtain chance results!

If it is taken that the experiments are negative, they only rule out the idea of communication of images by some as-yet unknown process. There is also a basic weakness in the conception of the experiment. Unlike images stored in a computer, those presented to human subjects carry varying value and they are remembered in association with prior memories, which are unique for each individual.

A well-known coincidence concerns the fictional account of cannibalism in the novel The Narrative of Arthur Gordon Pym of Nantucket by the American author Edgar Allan Poe (1809-1849) published in 1838. In a complicated story of sailing adventure involving shipwreck, the cabin boy Richard Parker is chosen and killed for food.

In 1884, in a real-life event that became a sensation in Britain, a 17 year old named Richard Parker, a runaway who becomes a cabin boy, is shipwrecked together with the crew. After several days of starvation, the crew kills Parker for food. The crew is eventually rescued, brought to

London, and tried for murder. Although this coincidence is striking, it may be attributed to the popularity of the name Richard Parker in that period.

Another coincidence is that of the novel, Futility (1898), by Morgan Robertson about the unsinkable ship Titan that is shipwrecked with much loss of life when it strikes an iceberg on its maiden voyage. In 1912, the Titanic struck an iceberg at midnight on her maiden voyage and sank on 15 April with great loss of life. There are several correspondences between the two boats but these may be due to the fact that both the novel and the design of the actual ship were based on proposals that were being written about in the 1890s. The coincidence may not be as remarkable as appears on first sight.

Scientific coincidences

Speed of Light. A striking coincidence concerns an early value of the speed of light in the well-known commentary on the Ṛgveda by the medieval scholar Sāyaṇa (1315-1387), prime minister in the court of the Vijayanagara Empire. It associates the speed of 2,202 yojanas in half a nimeṣa with the sun (or sunlight).[15] The distance and time measures of yojana and nimeṣa are well attested in Indian astronomical and encyclopedic texts and this number corresponds closely to the correct value of the speed.

The division of time according to the medieval Viṣṇu Purāṇa 1.3.3 is:

1 day = 30 muhūrtas
1 muhūrta = 30 kalās
1 kalā = 30 kāṣṭhās
1 kāṣṭhā = 15 nimeṣa

One day = 86,400 seconds = 405,000 nimeṣa

Thus, 1 nimeṣa = 16/75 seconds and half a nimeṣa would be 8/75 seconds. It is clear that half a nimeṣa was used in the text because that is the thirtieth part of a kalā in the regular sequence where the larger units are greater by a factor of 30.

One yojana is defined in the Arthaśāstra (of Kauṭilya who was advisor to the Mauryan emperor Candragupta who reigned 322 - 298 BC) as being equal to 8,000 dhanus or bows. The Arthaśāstra further takes a dhanus to equal 108 aṅgulas (finger widths).

Independent confirmation of the dhanus unit is made possible by examining ancient monuments and seeing the largest unit that maps the main dimensions of the monument in meaningful integer multiples of the unit. This has been done both for the third millennium BC city of Dholavira from West India as well as from monuments of medieval India, and it is found that there exists continuity across ages in the use of this unit. The unit of dhanus in use in Dholavira and later India is 1.904 meters. The unit of aṅgulas has been validated from scales obtained in Harappa and is 1.763 cm long.

Therefore, the speed of 2,202 yojana in half a nimeṣa is:

$$\frac{2202 \times 8000 \times 1.904 \times 75}{8} = 314{,}445.6 \text{ kilometers per second}$$

Other scholars take dhanus to be equal to six feet or 1.83 meters and with this Sāyaṇa's number is 3.02×10^8 meters per second which corresponds closely to the correct value of the speed of light.

Since there was no way this speed could have been measured in medieval India, it is a very improbable coincidence. Note further that until just over 200 years ago it was not even known in the Western tradition that light had finite speed. In 1676, Rømer calculated this speed in terms of the speed of earth's rotation around the sun, and this value, we now know, was about 26% less than the modern value. Sāyaṇa could not have obtained this figure from the West or anywhere else.

Distance to the sun: Until modern times, the solar system was taken to be much smaller than its currently accepted value. Pappus of Alexandria writing in the fourth century took the distance to the sun to be about 490 earth radii. At the beginning of modern Western astronomy, Tycho Brahe took the distance between the earth and the sun to be 8 × 106 kms and Kepler took it to be about 24 × 106 kms.

In the Indian Purāṇas, the earliest of which predates fifth century, the sun is associated with two 'axles': the first one is 15.7×10^6 yojanas long and the second one is 45,500 yojanas long (section 2.8 of the Viṣṇu Purāṇa). One can presume that the longer axle represents the distance to the earth and the shorter axle represents the deviation from the circular path. Speaking of this astronomical reference, we cannot prove that it is from the earliest layer of the text, but there is general scholarly consensus that the text is at least 1,500 years old.

One of the variant definitions of yojana, which was prevalent in Kashmir (a region where many Purāṇas were written), is given by Stein[16] (footnote to verse 393) where he takes it to be about 6 miles (Stein: "The direct distance by road from Srinagar to Vijebror is about thirty miles. This corresponds exactly to five yojanas."). If this yojana was meant (6 miles or 9.6 km), then the distance to the sun is about 150.72×10^6 kms. Given that the distance between the two cities is an approximate value, the distance to the sun can be taken to be identical to the modern value of 149.598×10^6 kms.

One might complain that we are picking a value of yojana that was only used regionally. This criticism is valid, but we are not trying to find a scientific basis to the choice of the distance to the sun. Rather, we are showing that the choices presented by intuition, without any firm basis in physical theory, can be surprisingly accurate. Accepting the validity of such a way of knowledge is against the mainstream program of science and current schoolbook theories of mind.

It is indeed possible that even before modern telescopic astronomy, which did not exist in India, a reasonable estimate of the distance to the sun could be made based on durations of lunar and solar eclipses. But there is no evidence that such calculations were made by astronomers.

Perhaps the value of the speed of light should not surprise us since there are other numbers the precision of whose value in the ancient texts cannot be explained. These include the size of the earth which is described to within one percent accuracy in the accounts of Eratosthenes, Āryabhaṭa, and al-Bīrūnī. The apocryphal account of Eratosthenes's measurement of the size indirectly by measuring the shift in the shadow of the sun at noon between Syene and Alexandria is not credible since the distance between the two cities was not known accurately and the shift in the angle of the shadow could not have been measured with the accuracy that the calculation of the earth's diameter demands.

The philosopher David Hume argued that scientific understanding is a consequence of inductive inference, which involves a leap of imagination from the world of the observed to that of the unobserved, which is "beyond the present testimony of the senses, and the records of our memory." He argued that it was instinct, rather than reason, that explained our ability to make inductive inferences.

In the traditional explanation of the workings of mind, habits picked up in childhood and in school are the impediments that prevent one from being connected to one's intuition (Hume's instinct). Real creativity requires challenging dogma as well as one's own certitudes. One sees unexpected connections, which is an element of creativity, in extraordinary states of mind. Looking within can reveal unexpected knowledge about the universe for we are a part of the universe.

Hidden order

It is well known that formal systems are incomplete and inconsistent, meaning that our knowledge of the physical reality as a formal system can never be complete, even in principle. The problem of incompleteness can be seen from a different perspective, where it is a consequence of a deeper order. This order is opposite to that of explicit order of classical scientific theory in which an isolated system is localized and separate from the rest of the world. Hidden order implies strong correlations across space and time as are true for quantum theory. Similar correlations appear to exist in the domain of human affairs. We propose that such correlations are also present across structure and, therefore, the origins of design lie in this hidden order.

If we step back and consider what we mean by a system, we realize that its mathematical conception creates interesting problems. At the philosophical level, objects of study may either be seen to be *real* or only *phenomenal* contents of our mind. At a more practical level, when it is posited that agreement on the phenomenal contents of many minds implies real existence, the question of the nature of the qualities of the objects arises. Do these attributes and concepts have a real existence or do they arise from the intuition of the observers? This question cannot be resolved using logic.

The scientist's intuition is central to a personal understanding of reality. Certain concepts must be left undefined in any theoretical framework because otherwise the framework would involve circular reasoning. Undefined concepts are understood intuitively. Time and space are left undefined in physical theory and our intuitions about these arise from our personal experience of change and extension. Objects that go directly into physical theory are defined in operational terms and related by well-defined protocols of measurement.

The standard scientific view of the evolution of the universe by the flow of spacetime and matter may be seen to emerge through the prism of laws. To the extent these laws are linear, it is possible to study local regions. Although this picture has served science well in determining the large scale structure of the universe, it doesn't work as well in the investigation of teleological systems.

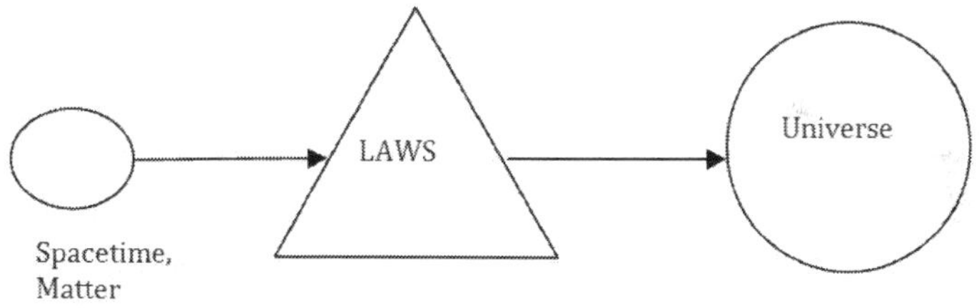

Universe unfolding out of the prism of laws

Philosophers are aware of the limitations of 'scientific explanations.' The Skeptics in Greece spoke of the impossibility of 'complete explanations' when they said that demonstration depends either on things that demonstrate themselves, or on principles which are indemonstrable.

In the Vedic view, reality is unitary at the deepest level for otherwise there would be chaos. This reality engenders and, paradoxically, transcends the mind/matter split. It may be seen as consciousness at the cosmic scale that informs individual minds. Turning focus to the very nature of the mind provides insight about consciousness. Since it is linear, whereas the unfolding of the universe takes place in a multitude of dimensions, language is limited in its ability to describe reality. Because of this limitation, reality can only be experienced and never described fully. All descriptions of the universe lead to logical paradox.

Higher knowledge, which is intuitive, concerns the perceiving subject (consciousness), whereas lower knowledge concerns objects. Higher knowledge can be arrived at indirectly without effort or by contemplation on the paradoxes of the outer world. Lower knowledge is empirical and analytical and it represents standard science with its many branches. There is complementarity between the higher and the lower, each being necessary to define the other. This complementarity mirrors the one between mind and matter. According to the Vedic view, it is impossible to develop a language-based 'theory of consciousness.' It views individual consciousness as reflection of the universal consciousness on the neurophysiological apparatus of the brain.

Those aspects of reality that are well described by theories of physics are mathematical. But currently there is no single overarching theory of reality, and the theories that we have are valid only over specified domains, leaving other conditions where the outcome of experiments is far from certain. Even if one were to assert that reality at the deepest level is mathematical, the question of the relationship between paradoxes of mathematics and physics arises.

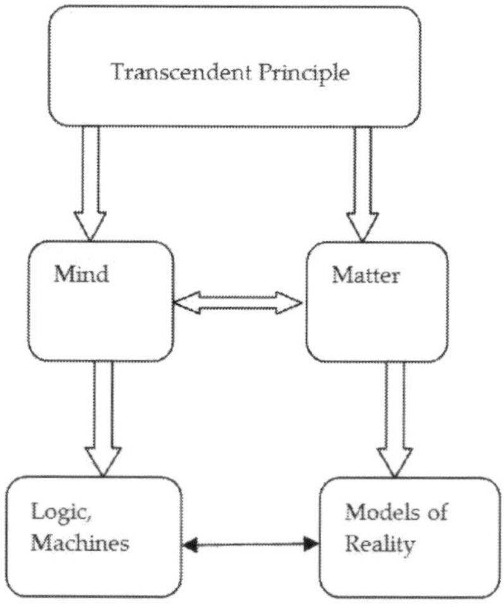

Universe as projection of transcendent principle (broad arrow is projection; narrow arrow is full representation)

A scientific theory expresses relationships between concepts that are abstractions of observational processes. Equivalently, a theory is a linguistic description of natural processes that highlights causal relationship between variables. Logic and mathematics are the languages of science and as the capacity of instruments to observe phenomena increases, it becomes possible to examine relationships between new objects or concepts and thus new theories are born. Linguistic descriptions of reality are, by definition, rational.

A scientific theory is a formal or logical system; therefore, there is a connection between limits of formal systems and limits of science. But it is well known that given *any* consistent set of axioms, there are true mathematical statements that cannot be derived from the set.

Since a scientific theory is a formal system, it follows that such a theory must be incomplete and it must have paradoxical aspects. Conversely, one can think of simple formal systems (such as those that are applied to the social world), which are consistent, but which do not have any predictive power. Furthermore, going from theory to physical systems, one may assert that a physical system will show paradoxical behavior, and if a system's behavior is consistent, that is only because it has not been explored for the entire range of possibilities.

Quantum mechanics may be viewed as an information theory related to observations associated with measurements. In the standard Copenhagen interpretation, it is assumed that one cannot speak of a reality outside of one's observations and, therefore, there is a deeper order underlying the observations.

Hidden order not only characterizes quantum systems but also classical systems in the many correlations across time, space, and structure. These correlations explain why complex organic structures, which should be improbable based on frequency considerations, are commonly encountered in asteroids and meteors. Although panspermia provides a resolution to the origin of life by assuming that it exists all over the universe, it doesn't address the problem of the origin of consciousness.

Contradictions and paradoxes are a consequence of conflation of different intuitions or self-referral. M*athematical objects must have proper predicative definition* in which their properties are fully defined, but it is not always that we can find mathematical objects that correspond completely to physical objects.

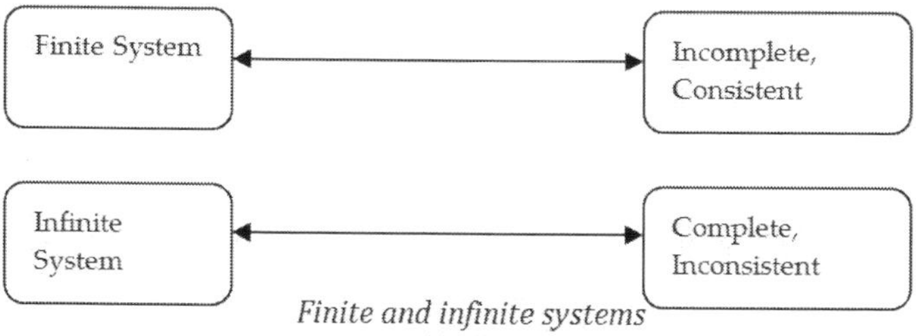

Finite and infinite systems

A finite mathematical system can be completely defined, at least in principle, in terms of all the possible relationships that are associated with its elements. But a finite system is fundamentally incomplete since more elements can be added to it where finiteness is being seen with respect to the number of elements as well as rules that govern the relationships amongst the elements.

Complete enumeration cannot be done for an infinite system. Furthermore, if the infinity is uncountable, as is true for our conceptions of time and space, then its mathematical and logical representations are not complete.

There exists the paradox of deriving the complex from the simple. Since the inconsistent complex cannot be directly derived from the simple and consistent basis, we possess limited capacity to understand the origins. For example, the theory of cosmological inflation in the early universe is a device that is used to explain away correlations in the cosmos. The other option is to discount a specific origin of the universe and assume that it has always been infinite.

Genetics and evolution

New evidence challenges the orthodox version of evolution according to which adaptation occurs only through natural selection of chance DNA variations. It is known that organisms have evolved mechanisms to influence the timing or genomic location of heritable variability and, therefore, selection and variability are not independent.

Epigenetic inheritance is brought about by chemicals that change the way enzymes and proteins have access to DNA. One of the best understood mechanisms of epigenetic change is nucleotide methylation that can alter gene expression. DNA methylation is a crucial step in memory formation.[17]

Rando and Verstrepen provide the following summary of the influence of epigenetic inheritance:[18]

> Many of the most convincing examples that demonstrate a correlation between selective pressure and heritable variability come from the microbial world. This is partially due to the fact that laboratory studies are relatively easy in these organisms, so our knowledge of variability is simply greater for microbes. But there may be additional reasons. First, microbes tend to have much larger effective population sizes than do multicellular organisms, whose evolution is therefore more likely to be influenced by genetic drift. More interestingly, when compared to cells in multicellular organisms where homeostatic mechanisms maintain relatively constant conditions for most cells, microbial cells are under severe and extremely variable selection. Microbes often find themselves subject to rapid environmental change (and thus variable selection) without any measure of escape. They experience rapid changes in nutrient levels, osmolarity, concentration of (toxic) chemicals, and, in the case of pathogens, the continuous dynamic battle against host immune defense. Hence, it is perhaps not surprising to find that at least some microorganisms have developed mechanisms to maximize variability when and where it is most needed. Most of the described variability is in the cell surface, which is the cell's most direct interface with the

environment. Notably, the best known example of regulated variability in higher eukaryotes is that of increased variability in the immune system (which interacts with highly variable pathogens).

The extreme environmental change experienced by microbes mentioned above is paralleled by the extreme changes in the inner environment experienced by humans.

Jablonka and Lamb speak[19] of four inheritance systems that play a role in evolution: genetic, epigenetic, behavioral, and symbolic, which interact amongst each other. The system of the interactions between them may be viewed as the hidden order underlying evolution.

A sentient being is a biological singularity in the sense that he possesses freedom of action. This is especially true of humans since they have greater autonomy and independence than other animals. The autonomy and selfhood of humans leads to its own paradoxes. Some of these are:

1. Humans reject the idea that they are mere machines, yet they often equate their 'self' with the machinery of the body.
2. The human's self-image is that of the body, together with transient thoughts, but it is overseen with the observing 'I' within.

A distinction is made between the 'autobiographical self,' which is the normal self-conception based on the recounted life, and the 'core self,' which is rooted in the momentary present. The 'autobiographical self' is *nāmarūpa* (Sanskrit for name and form) that is partly a result of one's imagination since it is an interpretation of the past and it includes hopes for the future. The 'core self' is elusive; it seems to be the light that shines on things around and forms association with them in time and space.

Explicit and hidden orders

In classical physics, the time evolution of a system is completely given by initial conditions and differential equations that characterize the system. Such characterization is valid only for the defined range of applicability. The characterization considers ideal behavior and departures from it are due to the limits of precision in modeling the system and its conditions and also the random perturbations affecting the system. At a broader level, such characterization is circumscribed by the limitations of formal systems.

Photons or electrons sent one at a time through a double-slit experiment strike the screen at random locations individually but collectively they form dark and light bands. Although this is viewed as individual particles going through both slits and interacting with themselves, this is impossible in a discrete conception of the photon or electron. The alternative explanations are in terms of hidden order in collectives or the dual complementarity view.

The reductionist conception of simultaneous passage through two slits shows the inadequacy of logic to explain the phenomenon. Quantum theory uses the language of superposition of mutually exclusive properties and collapse upon observation. This is a dual description: the system is deterministic as long as it is left alone to evolve by itself, but upon interaction with the environment (which could be the observer) it reduces into one of its components. In other words, a web of interactions, which is not just local, determines the unfolding of the system. Particles that are far removed from each other can be strongly correlated, as is true for entangled particles, due to hidden order.

If one insisted on the use of particle concepts for understanding how two entangled particles far apart from each other can share the same information, one must postulate the existence of zero-mass information-carrying particles that travel at infinite speed between them. Are these particles the missing dark matter of the universe?

It is common to speak of chemistry arising out of physics and biology out of chemistry, and consciousness out of biology. Just as the physical laws do not completely describe the universe and since chemistry, biology, and consciousness are latent in physics, so it must be accepted that order and structure is latent.

In addition to matter one must also consider potentiality and virtual states. Potentiality states are quantum states that are described in terms of probabilities and virtual states are empty states that are a part of the system. The evolution of the system is predicated on an order that is not apparent from the filled matter states alone. Likewise evolution cannot be viewed as a consequence of random events and flourishing of the forms that are best able to survive in the environment.

The hidden order may be mapped into the geometry of the attraction basins of the complex dynamics of the system. Stable structures are attraction basins that are latent in the framework of laws together with the environmental conditions.

Improbable coincidences corroborated in literature support the view that nonmaterial entities have independent existence. The most compelling of these is the speed of light in medieval literature that could not have been obtained from measurement because the science and technology to do so did not exist at that time. It is fascinating that this number was justified by fitting it into an archaic conception of the universe. But such evidence, just like first person accounts of spontaneous scientific discovery, cannot be conclusive in establishing that the world of ideas has independent existence.

Evolution in quantum physics is deterministic, together with a mechanism for the collapse of the state function. Absent such collapse, the framework of quantum physics -- like that of classical physics -- has no place for observers. A quantum mechanical universe will evolve by a global unitary operator in a purely deterministic manner. Quantum mechanics is not a local theory in the sense that parts far apart cease to be causally connected to each other; entanglement between particles persists no matter how apart they are. It came about in a non-unitary manner, leading to creation of information.

Since information in the universe is increasing, it can only come about by a principle that lies outside of quantum theory. Entropy increase in the universe requires reduction of its state function by some other physical system but the universe, by definition, does not have any other matter in it. We are compelled, therefore, to postulate a state function reducing mechanism other than that of physical laws. We believe that this mechanism evolves out of the consciousness principle and it has, by means of probability enhancement of events (which is non-unitary), generated conditions that favor life.

The working of the consciousness principle may be seen in the quantum Zeno effect in which the process of observation increases entropy. This principle, rather than the creation of complex molecules by chance, can explain the rise of life in the universe.

The idea that observed laws are a consequence of the large-scale structure of the universe means that the conception of the localized early universe will be characterized by further paradoxes. For example, we have the paradox that if entropy was a maximum at big bang, how can it still increase?

One way to circumvent these paradoxes is to acknowledge a veil over the earliest period so that one need not worry about the system being consistent as required for a complete description. Consistency is problematic, because if the universe is completely predictable and consistent in the early phase, it should be so at later phases, which is contradicted by the Incompleteness Theorem.

Conversely, one must postulate new mechanisms, such as inflation in cosmology, or live with big gaps in the descriptive framework as is done by assuming dark matter and dark energy, and continue to ignore the problem of the origins of consciousness.

The use of logic in physical reality is restored by seeking and invoking order which is otherwise hidden owing to the principle of veiled nonlocality.[20] It is the hidden order that makes the probability of complex structures to be much higher than what would be the case from chance. The concept of hidden order is not a matter of change of terminology since it should be possible to design experiments to confirm or refute it at the macroscopic level.

NOTES

INTRODUCTION

1. The Ṛgveda hymns have been dated at 3000-1500 BC based on linguistic evidence. As they do not mention any region outside of Northwest India, nor of any wars with any non-Aryans, it may be safely assumed that they were originally composed earlier rather than later. Various aspects of the Vedic world are described in Majumdar (1951). "The vernal sun rose in Taurus (the Bull) between 4000 BC and 2000 BC... but it shifted to Aries (the Ram) before the Ṛgveda was completed. Indra, leader of the gods, is the 'Bull of Heaven' in many poems and the 'Ram' in others," McClain (1978). For reviews of the archaeological evidence, see Possehl (1982), Feuerstein et al (1995), Lal (1997), Kak (2008), Kak (2009b), Kak (2010b).

   Kramer (1963) identified the Harappan India to be Tilmun (or Dilmun) -- the fabled land of the Sumerian gods. Recent excavations have shown farming settlements in the Indus Valley going all the way back to 6000 BC; see Jarrige and Meadow (1980) for a review of this work.

   Genetic evidence indicates that populating of India took place thousands of years before Europe and significant outward migration from South Asia to Europe began about 40,000 years ago (Oppenheimer, 2003).

2. Kak (2000a), (2008); see also Johnson (1980). The Ṛgveda can be understood through the philosophy of the Upaniṣads (1000 BC onwards). Its insights are presented in a coded form in the myths of the encyclopedic Purāṇas.
3. See Raju (1971, p. 145).
4. Philip Frank in Neurath, Carnap, and Morris (1938, 1955).

I: PARADOX AND REALITY

1. There are differences between computer programs and the DNA instructions, particularly in the manner of their execution. For a discussion of this and a general review of the life science see Luria, Gould and Singer (1981). It is possible that more than one code for life exists.
2. These and other related paradoxes have been discussed in Kline (1980); see also Davis (1965). See Laërtius (1853) for discussion of the Zeno paradox.
3. We do not deal with cognition, perception and psychological aspects of knowledge here. For these topics, see Kak (2004).
4. A great deal of literature exists on the mind-body problem, but no real advance has occurred since the question was first formulated. Anderson (1981) reviews several issues related to the problem. Also see Comfort (1979), Josephson and Ramachandran (1980), Bunge (1980), Fox (1984).
5. Quoted in Springer and Deutsch (1985).
6. For introductions to Indian philosophy see Dasgupta (1955), Radhakrishnan (1931), and Raju (1971).
7. Sarkar (1918), Seal (1916).
8. Sedlar (1980) reviews parallels with Greek science.

9. An interesting interpretation of the kalpa and the yuga is discussed by Brennand (1896). According to this view the kalpa concept was very useful in astronomical computations. See also Kak (2000b).
10. See Sarkar (1918), Seal (1916), Cajori (1919), Datta and Singh (1962), Kak (1986), Sarasvati Amma (1979), Srinivasiengar (1967), Kak (1995), Kak (2000a), Kak (2010b).
11. Scharfe (1977).
12. Claims have been made that Parmenides, Pythagoras, and Plato were influenced by Indian philosophy. These arguments are reviewed by Sedlar (1980), Majumdar (1958), Singhal (1969), and Lomperis (1984). Neugebauer (1969) describes the Babylonian antecedents of Greek science.
13. Two examples of this are Capra (1975) and Zukav (1979).
14. Hume's argument is similar to that of the Charvakas. See Raju (1971, page 87).
15. Sambursky (1956).
16. See the following for physics and the scientific method: Bernal (1965), Blanpied (1969), Bohr (1961) Carnap (1966), Eddington (1958), Frank (1969), Jeffreys (1973), Nagel (1961), Ziman (1978).
17. Wigner (1967), d'Espagnat (1983), and Mehra (1973).

II: SPACE AND TIME

1. Seidenberg (1978); for Chinese mathematics see Needham (1959).
2. It should be noted that the name Egypt was often used indiscriminately by many Greek writers to include Babylon, Iran, and India. Neugebauer (1975) remarks, "The traditional stories of discoveries made by Thales and Pythagoras must be discarded as totally unhistorical."
3. See, e.g., Kak (2000a) and Kak (2010b).
4. Bisht (1997) from where the map of the city has been taken.
5. See Gray (1979), Weyl (1969), Whitrow (1980).
6. Shukla and Sarma (1976).
7. For a historical development and references, see Pauli (1958).
8. Prokhovnik (1967) presents an unusual interpretation of the special theory of relativity.
9. Kaivola *et al.* (1985).
10. See, for example, Terletskii (1968).
11. Kak (2007b).

III: MATTER AND MOTION

1. Brennand (1896) and McClain (1978) review evidence suggesting that ancient civilizations were aware of the precession of the equinoxes and the epicyclic model of planet motion; for a more recent review see Kak (2000a). Neugebauer (1975) is a comprehensive treatment of Babylonian and Greek contributions. Brecher and Feirtag (1979) present some of the little known contributions of the ancients.
2. Quoted in Gray (1979).
3. This matter includes mass resulting from energy. For overviews of theory of gravitation see Cohen (1981), Hawking and Ellis (1973), Hoyle and Narlikar (1980), Misner *et al.* (1973), and Will (1974).

4. This phenomenon is equivalent to electromagnetic waves having lower speed in the presence of gravity. Implications of this alternative interpretation have not been determined.
5. The big bang picture leads to several puzzles of its own: How did causally separated regions of the universe come to have the same temperature and expansion rates today to within at least one part in 1000? Why is the universe anisotropic in the small scale, but more and more regular in its large scale structure?
6. For a distant observer the object inside the event horizon becomes unobservable. We can thus visualize small local regions - in which special relativity is valid - being dragged, in the large scale, into the black hole at a speed without limit.
7. See Harrison (1981) for a summary of different proposals.

IV: WAVES AND FIELDS

1. See Sexl and Sexl (1979). The LIGO Scientific Collaboration announced that they detected gravitational waves on 14 September 2015 from a merger of two black holes about 400 megaparsecs (1.3 billion light years) from Earth.
2. A perspective is provided in Diner *et al.* (1984).

V: THE WORLD OF QUANTA

1. See, for example, Raju (1971).
2. Dirac (1958). For a collection of original papers see van der Waerden (1967).
3. This new state is the eigenfunction of the measurement operator, the value of the measurement being the corresponding eigenvalue. The simultaneous measurement of two canonically conjugate variables is subject to uncertainty limitations. See Dirac (1958), for technical details.
4. Everett's dissertation is reprinted in DeWitt and Graham (1973). This as well as other interpretations are critically reviewed in Jammer (1974).
5. For further discussion see d'Espagnat (1983) and also Schrödinger (1959).

VI: THE BUILDING BLOCKS

1. For general references see Bars *et al.* (1984), Weldon *et al.* (1983).
2. See Georgi (1981).
3. See Harari, Composite quarks and leptons, in Breitenlohner and Durr (1982).
4. Further implications of this idea are explored in Kak (1984).

VII: ORDER AND CHAOS

1. For general discussions of arrow of time see Davies (1977), Narlikar (1977), and Narlikar (1982).
2. See Narlikar (1977).
3. Prigogine and Stengers (1984), Colodny (1977).
4. Venkatesananda (1993); for the Sanskrit text, see *Yoga Vāsiṣṭha (*1981), Munshiram Manoharlal, New Delhi.
5. An early and influential discussion of this question is in Schrödinger (1965) and Wigner (1967).
6. Recent research indicates that more than one genetic code may exist.

VIII: THE LOGIC OF PHYSICS

1. For a discussion of Dirac's hypothesis see Mehra (1973).
2. See Jordan in Mehra (1973).
3. Benancerraf and Putnam (1983), Meschkowski (1965), and Weyl (1969).
4. Greenspan (1973) is an example of the use of discrete models to solve problems for which continuous models have been used conventionally.
5. Kline (1980).
6. Bloomfield (1933).
7. Briggs (1985), gave an overview of the techniques of unambiguous knowledge representation developed by Sanskrit grammarians and compared it to the results obtained in recent years by researchers working in artificial intelligence. According to Briggs, the results of the Sanskrit grammarians cast "doubt on the humanistic distinction between natural and artificial intelligence, and may throw light on how research in Al may finally solve the natural language understanding and machine translation problems." This optimistic assessment of the future of artificial intelligence cannot be accepted; see also Kak (2010a).
8. Ingalls (1951) and Matilal (1968) summarize some of the main achievements of the New Logic School.
9. Staal (1976).
10. Coward (1976) discusses Bhartṛhari's contributions to the philosophy of language in a modern setting. For other Sanskrit grammarians see Staal (1972).
11. Kak (1986).
12. Patrascioiu's paper In Guth *et al.* (1983) makes the case "that in a closed universe charged particles and electromagnetic fields obeying classical dynamics create the stochastic process responsible for the experimentally observed quantum behavior of particles and fields."

IX: EPILOGUE: HIDDEN ORDER AND CONSCIOUSNESS

1. Wheeler (1990).
2. Kak (2008).
3. Kak (2009b).
4. Winfree (1987).
5. Kak (2004).
6. Barrow and Tipler (1986).
7. Kak (2007a).
8. Hoyle and Wickramasinghe (1984), Wickramasinghe (2009).
9. Kak (2007a)
10. Gazzaniga (1995).
11. Goldin-Meadow and Mylander (1998).
12. Sacks (1985).
13. Hadamard (1954).
14. Penrose (1989).
15. Kak, S. (1999) and Kak, S. (2009a).
16. Stein (1900); see also Sachau (1964).
17. Miller and Sweatt (2007).
18. Rando and Verstrepen (2007).
19. Jablonka and Lamb (2005).
20. Kak (2014), Kak (2015)

BIBLIOGRAPHY

Anderson, A.R. (1964) (editor). Minds and Machines. Englewood-Cliffs, N.J.

Benacerraf, P. and H. Putnam (1983). Philosophy of Mathematics: Selected Readings. Cambridge.

Barrow, J.D. and Tipler, F.J. (1986). The Anthropic Cosmological Principle. Oxford .

Bars, I., A. Chodos and C.H. Tze (1984) (editors). Symmetries in Particle Physics. New York.

Bernal, J.D. (1965). Science in History. New York.

Bisht, R.S. (1997). Dholavira Excavations: 1990-94. In Facets of Indian Civilization Essays in Honour of Prof. B. B. Lal, ed. J. P. Joshi. New Delhi.

Blanpied, W.A. (1969). Physics: Its Structure and Evolution. Waltham.

Bloomfield, L. (1933). Language. New York.

Bohm, D. (1982). Wholeness and Implicate Order. . London.

Bohr, N. (1961). Atomic Physics and Human Knowledge. New York.

Brecher, K. and Feirtag, H. (1979) (editors). Astronomy of the Ancients. Cambridge, MA.

Breitenlohner, P. and Durr, H.P. (1982) (editors). Unified Theories of Elementary Particles. Berlin.

Brennand, W. (1896). Hindu Astronomy. London.

Briggs, R. (1985). Knowledge representation In Sanskrit and Artificial Intelligence. The Al Magazine , Spring.

Bunge, M. (1980). The Mind-Body Problem. Oxford.

Cajori, F. (1919). A History of Mathematics. New York.

Capra, F. (1975). The Tao of Physics. Boulder.

Carnap, R. (1966). Philosophical Foundations of Physics. New York.

Cohen, I.B. (1981). Newton's discovery of gravity. Scientific American 244.

Colodny, R.G. (1977) (editor). Logic, Laws, and Life. Pittsburgh.

Comfort, A. (1979). I and That. New York.

Coward, H.G. (1976). Bhartrhari. Boston.

Dasgupta, S. (1955). A History of Indian Philosophy. Cambridge.

Datta, B. and Singh, A.N. (1962). History of Hindu Mathematics Parts I and II. Bombay.

Davies, P.C.W. (1977). The Physics of Time Asymmetry. Berkeley.

Davis, M. (1965). The Undecidable: Basic papers on undecidable propositions, unsolvable problems and computable functions. New York.

Diner, S., Fargue, D., Lochak, G. and Selleri, F. (1984) (editors). The Wave-Particle Dualism. Dordrecht.

Dirac, P.A.M. (1958). The Principles of Quantum Mechanics. Oxford.

DeWitt, B. and Graham, N. (1973) (editors). The Many-Worlds Interpretation of Quantum Mechanics. Princeton.

d'Espagnat, B. (1983). In Search of Reality. New York.

Eddington, A. (1958). The Philosophy of Physical Science. Ann Arbor.

Feuerstein, G., Kak, S., Frawley, D. (1995). In Search of the Cradle of Civilization. Wheaton.

Fox, S. W. (1984) (editor). Individuality and Determinism. New York.

Frank, P. (1969). Modern Science and its Philosophy. Cambridge.

Gazzaniga, M.S. (1995). The Cognitive Neurosciences. Cambridge.

Georgi, H. (1981). A unified theory of elementary particles and forces. Scientific American 244, April.

Goldin-Meadow, S., Mylander, C. (1998). Spontaneous sign systems created by deaf children in two cultures. Nature 391: 279-281.

Gray, J. (1979). Ideas of Space. Oxford.

Greenspan, D. (1973). Discrete Models. Reading, MA.

Guth, A.H., Huang, K. and Jaffe, R.L. (1983) (editors). Asymptotic Realms of Physics. Cambridge, MA.

Hadamard, J. (1954). The Psychology of Invention in the Mathematical Field. New York.

Harrison, E.R. (1981). Cosmology. London.

Hawking, S.W. and Ellis, G.F.R. (1973). The Large Scale Structure of Space-Time. London.

Hoyle, F. and Narlikar, J.V. (1980). The Physics-Astronomy Frontier. San Francisco.

Hoyle, F. and Wickramasinghe, C. (1984). Evolution from Space. New York.

Ingalls, D.H.H. (19151). Materials for the Study of Navya-Nyāya Logic. Cambridge, MA.

Jablonka, E. and Lamb, M.J. (2005). Evolution in Four Dimensions. MIT Press.

Jammer, M. (1974). The Philosophy of Quantum Mechanics. New York.

Jarrige, J.-F. and Meadow, R.H. (1980). The antecedents of civilization in the Indus Valley. Scientific American 243.

Jeffreys, H. (1973). Scientific Inference. London.

Johnson, W. (1980). Poetry and Speculation of the Rg Veda. Berkeley.

Josephson, B.D. and Ramachandran, V.S. (1980). Consciousness and the Physical World. Oxford.

Kaivola, M., Poulsen, O., Rils, E. and Lee, S.A. (1985). Measurement of the relativistic Doppler shift in neon. Physical Review Letters 54.

Kak, S. (1984). On information associated with an object. Proceedings of Indian National Science Academy 50.

Kak, S. (1986). The roots of science In India. India International Centre Quarterly 13: 181-196.

Kak, S. (1995). The astronomy of the age of geometric altars. Quarterly Journal of the Royal Astronomical Society 36: 385-396.

Kak, S. (1999). The speed of light and Puranic cosmology. Annals Bhandarkar Oriental Research Institute 80: 113-123.

Kak, S. (2000a). The Astronomical Code of the Rgveda. New Delhi.

Kak, S. (2000b). Birth and early development of Indian astronomy. In Astronomy Across Cultures: The History of Non-Western Astronomy, Helaine Selin (ed). Kluwer, 303-340.

Kak, S. (2004). The Architecture of Knowledge. Delhi.

Kak, S. (2007a). Quantum information and entropy. International J. of Theoretical Physics 46: 860-876.

Kak, S. (2007b). Moving observers in an isotropic universe. International J. of Theoretical Physics 46: 1424-1430.

Kak, S. (2008). The Wishing Tree. New York.

Kak, S. (2009a). The universe, quantum physics, and consciousness. Journal of Cosmology 3: 500-510.

Kak, S. (2009b). Time, space and structure in ancient India. Presented at the Conference on Sindhu-Sarasvati Valley Civilization: A Reappraisal, Loyola Marymount University, Los Angeles, February 21 & 22.

Kak, S. (2010a). Machines and consciousness. In P.K. Sengupta (ed.), History of Science and Philosophy of Science. Delhi.

Kak, S. (2010b). Visions of the cosmos. Journal of Cosmology 9: 2063-2077.

Kak, S. (2014). From the no-signaling theorem to veiled non-locality. NeuroQuantology 12: 12-20.

Kak, S. (2015). Veiled nonlocality and quantum Darwinism. NeuroQuantology 13: 10-19.

Kline, M. (1980). Mathematics: The Loss of Certainty. Oxford.

Kramer, S.N. (1963). The Sumerians. Chicago.

Laërtius, D. (1853). The Lives and Opinions of Eminent Philosophers. C.D. Yonge (tr.). London.

Lal, B.B. (1997). The Earliest Civilization of South Asia. New Delhi.

Lomperis, T.J. (1984). Hindu Influence on Greek Philosophy. Calcutta.

Luria, S.E., Gould, S.J. and Singer, S. (1981). A View of Life. Menlo Park.

Majumdar, R.C. (1951) (editor). The Vedic Age. London.

Majumdar, R.C. (1968) (editor). The Age of Imperial Unity. Bombay.

Matilal, B.K. (1968). The Navya-Nyāya Doctrine of Negation. Cambridge, MA.

McClain, E.G. (1978). The Myth of Invariance. Boulder.

Mehra, J. (1973) (editor). The Physicist's Conception of Nature. Dordrecht/Boston.

Meschkowski, H. (1965). Evolution of Mathematical Thought. San Francisco.

Miller, C.A. And Sweatt, J.D. (2007). Covalent modification of DNA regulates memory formation. Neuron 53: 857-869.

Misner, C.W. Thorne, K.S. and Wheeler, J.A. (1973). Gravitation. San Francisco.

Nagel, E. (1961). The Structure of Science. New York.

Narlikar, J. (1977). The Structure of the Universe. London.

Narlikar, J. (1982). Violent Phenomena in the Universe. London.

Needham, J. (1959). Science and Civilization in China. London.

Neugebauer, O. (1969). The Exact Sciences in Antiquity. Providence.

Neugebauer, O. (1975). A History of Ancient Mathematical Astronomy (In Three Parts). Berlin.

Neurath, O., Carnap, R. and Morris, C. (1938, 1955) (editors). International Encyclopedia of Unified Science. Chicago.

Oppenheimer, S. (2003). The Real Eve: Modern Man's Journey out of Africa. New York, 2003.

Pauli, W. (1958). Theory of Relativity. New York.

Penrose, R. (1989). The Emperor's New Mind. Oxford.

Possehl, G.L. (1982) (editor). Harappan Civilization: A Contemporary Perspective. Warminster, England.

Prigogine, I. and Stenger, I. (1984). Order out of Chaos. Toronto.

Prokhovnik, S.J. (1967). The Logic of Special Relativity. London.

Radhakrishnan, S. (1940). Indian Philosophy, Vols. I, II. London.

Raju, P.T. (1971). The Philosophical Traditions of India. London.

Rando, O.J. and Verstrepen, K.J. (2007). Timescales of genetic and epigenetic inheritance. Cell 128: 655-668.

Sachau, E.C. (1964). Alberuni's India. Delhi.

Sacks, O. (1985). The Man Who Mistook His Wife for a Hat. New York.

Sambursky, S. (1956). The Physical World of the Greeks. London.

Sarasvatl Amma, T.A. (1979). Geometry in Ancient and Medieval India. Delhi.

Sarkar, B.K. (1918). Hindu Achievements in Exact Science. New York.

Scharfe, H. (1977). Grammatical Literature. Wiesbaden.

Schrödinger, E. (1959). Mind and Matter. Cambridge.

Schrödinger, E. (1965). What is Life? New York.

Seal, B. (1916). The Positive Sciences of the Ancient Hindus. London (Reprinted Delhi, 1985).

Sedlar, J.W. (1980). India and the Greek World. Totowa, N.J.

Seidenberg, A. (1978). The origin of mathematics. Archive for History of Exact Sciences 18: 301-342.

Sexl, R. and H. Sexi (1979), White Dwarfs-Black Holes. New York.

Shukla, K.S. and Sarma, K.V. (1976). The Āryabhaṭīya of Āryabhaṭa. New Delhi.

Singhal, D.P. (1969). India and World Civilization. East Lansing.

Springer, S.P. and Deutsch, G. (1985), Left Brain, Right Brain. New York.

Srinivasiengar, C.N. (1967).The History of Ancient Indian Mathematics. Calcutta.

Staal, J.F. (1972) (editor). A Reader on the Sanskrit Grammarians. Cambridge, MA.

Staal, J.F. (1976). Sanskrit philosophy of language. In History of Linguistic Thought and Contemporary Linguistics, Edited by H. Parret. Berlin.

Stein, M.A. (tr.) (1900). Kalhana's Rajatarangini. A Chronicle of the Kings of Kasmir, Vol. 1. Delhi (1961).

Terletskii, Y.P. (1968). Paradoxes in the Theory of Relativity. New York.

van der Waerden, B.L. (1967) (editor). Sources of Quantum Mechanics . New York.

Venkatesananda, S. (1993) (editor). Vāsiṣṭha's Yoga. Albany.

Weldon, H.A., P. Langacker, P., and Steinhardt, P.J. (1983) (editors). Fourth Workshop on Grand Unification. Boston.

Weyl, H. (1969). Philosophy of Mathematics and Natural Science. Princeton.

Wheeler, J.A. (1990). Information, physics, quantum: the search for links. In Complexity, Entropy, and the Physics of Information, W.H. Zurek (Ed.). Reading.

Whitrow, G.J. (1980). The Natural Philosophy of Time. Oxford.

Wickaramasinghe, C. (2009). Astrobiology, Comets and the Origin of Life. Singapore.

Wigner, E.P. (1967). Symmetries and Reflections. Bloomington.

Winfree, A.T. (1987). The Timing of Biological Clocks. New York.

Will, C. (1974). Gravitation theory. Scientific American 231.

Ziman, J. (1978). Reliable Knowledge. London.

Zukav, G. (1979). The Dancing Wu Li Masters. Toronto.

INDEX